FUTURE OF THE INDIAN EDUCATION SYSTEM

Also by The Same Author

New-Age Technology and Industrial Revolution 4.0
Global Public Policy Issues in Economy, Democracy, National Security and World Peace

Bharat Ratna Dr Babasaheb Ambedkar
An Intellectual Colossus, Great National Leader and Universal Champion of Human Rights (Photo-Biography in English and Marathi)

Ambedkar *An Economist Extraordinaire*

Ambedkar *Awakening India's Social Conscience* (An Intellectual Biography) (English and Marathi)

Ambedkar Writes
Completed Writings of Dr Ambedkar (Edited) (English, Marathi and Hindi)
Vol. I: Political Writings, Vol. II: Scholarly Writings

Ambedkar Speaks
Seminal Speeches Edited: Vol. I, II and III (English 300, Marathi 500)

Trilogy on Ravindranath Tagore (Marathi)
Ravindranath Tagore: Yuga Nirmata Vishvamanav
Ravindranath Tagore: Samagra Sahitya Darshan
Bhaya Shoonya Chitta Jeth: 151 Pratinidhik Kavita

Untouchables
My Family's Triumphant Journey Out of the Caste System in Modern India (International Bestseller – in 15 languages)

Monetary Policy, Financial Stability and Central Banking in India

Re-emerging India – A Global Perspective

Challenges to Indian Banking: Competition, Globalization and Financial Markets (Edited)

Monetary Economics for India

Aamcha Baap Aan Amhi (Marathi, Family Autobiography)
The largest selling book in the history of Marathi literature (201st edition to be released shortly)

FUTURE OF THE INDIAN EDUCATION SYSTEM

How Relevant is the National Education Policy, 2020?

Narendra Jadhav

COUNCIL
FOR SOCIAL
DEVELOPMENT

in association with

KONARK

Konark Publishers Pvt Ltd
New Delhi • Seattle

Konark Publishers Pvt Ltd
206, First Floor,
Peacock Lane, Shahpur Jat,
New Delhi - 110 049
Tel : +91-11-4105 5065
Mob : +91-93552 93900, +91-93552 94900
e-mail : india@konarkpublishers.com
website : www.konarkpublishers.com

Konark Publishers International
8615, 13th Ave SW,
Seattle, WA 98106
Phone : (415) 409-9988
e-mail : us@konarkpublishers.com

ISBN No.: 978-81-942018-5-4

Editors: Preeta Priyamvada and Padma Alva
Cover jacket: Idesign
Cover image: *Augmented Humanity* by Tanmoy Jadhav
Printed and bound at Saurabh Printers Pvt Ltd

To

Three Great Friends

Prof. Muchkund Dubey,

Dr Vinod Shah,

and

Shri K.P.R. Nair

for enriching my life

in their own distinct ways.

Contents

Part Two

Part Three

Part Four

List of Tables

List of Charts

List of Boxes

Foreword

Professor Narendra Jadhav has the distinction of writing 41 books during a working life span of nearly 50 years. Considering the mastery he has acquired in the domains of his expertise and the ease with which he can move from one subject to the other, more and the best are yet to come. This volume on India's New Education Policy is both timely and significant – timely because the new National Education Policy (NEP 2020) has been announced recently and significant because education shapes the destiny of a nation as no other variable does. The book compels attention also because of the clarity, lucidity and forcefulness of its style. That is how Dr Jadhav has breathed in a new life, vigour and power of agency into a staid Government of India report. Because of these traits, this book should be of interest to general readers as well as educationists, policymakers, researchers, teachers and students. I felt honoured and privileged when Dr Jadhav invited me to write a Foreword for the book. I promptly accepted the invitation as this is an area where our interests converge.

There are two points on which there is a little divergence in our approach. Firstly, whereas Dr Jadhav has based his summarization, exposition and analysis primarily on the Draft New Education Policy 2019, I have taken the last draft of the year 2020 of the NEP as the reference for writing this Foreword. Dr Jadhav is justified in taking the NEP 2019 as the basis for writing his volume because this version is the most thorough and well-researched, both technically and policy-wise, among the drafts circulated so far. Secondly, while Dr Jadhav's book deals with education as a whole, as does the NEP the Foreword is confined to school education. I sincerely hope that my small contribution would be an important value addition to the book.

There is no doubt that we need a New Education Policy (NEP) for India. The last National Education Policy was adopted in 1986, and revised in 1992. Since then, changes of momentous significance have taken place, both nationally and internationally. The most important among them are the advances made in the areas of technology, particularly information and communication technology, which have a bearing on the kind of education that is most relevant today and the modality of providing it. Therefore, when the task of formulating a NEP was initiated in 2015, it was acclaimed by all concerned with education. But the meandering course that the process has taken since then has deprived it of much of its urgency and significance.

The process was initiated by holding a series of consultations in 2015. This was followed by establishing a committee headed by Mr T.S.R. Subramanian, former Cabinet Secretary to the Government of India. He submitted his report in 2016. Based on this report and on other inputs, the Government issued a 40-page document under the title: 'Some Inputs for the Draft National Education Policy'. After this, the task was entrusted to a committee headed by Dr K. Kasturirangan, former Head of ISRO and member of the NITI Aayog. This Committee submitted its report in June 2019. This was a rather lengthy report written after a good deal of in-depth research and studies. But this report was also sidetracked and the Government came out with a draft National Education Policy of its own towards the end of 2019. This was followed by two other versions of the Draft circulated in the first quarter of 2020.

By far the most important change since 1986 that NEP should take into account, is the adoption of the Right of Children to Free and Compulsory Education (RTE) Act, 2009. The RTE Act is the highest stage reached in the evolution of education policy in India. The most important feature of this Act is that it has, for the first time, conferred upon the children of the country fundamental right to elementary education. The Act also significantly sets a time limit of five years, for the universalisation of quality elementary education in India. Yet another distinguishing feature of the Act is that it is based on a holistic approach whereby the state is obliged to act simultaneously on all variables in order to reach the objective of universalising quality school education within the stipulated five years. The Act also stands apart from all previous policies on education because it establishes a set of norms which were to be applied to all schools in the Indian school education system.

The period of five years for the universalisation of quality elementary education provided for in the Act expired at the end of March 2010. But several of the most important provisions of the Act have remained unimplemented. One of the important tasks before the nation is to adopt a revised timeframe for the achievement of the principal objective of the Act and to ensure that necessary funds are made available for this purpose.

NEP and RTE Act

A policy document cannot dilute, drastically alter, or supersede the provisions of a legislation enacted by the Parliament. In a policy document there is generally enunciation of policies of a recommendatory nature, a reflection of the intentions of the Government for future actions and an appeal to all concerned to act on the ground. Such a document has to be subordinated to an Act of Parliament.

Lofty objectives

There are several laudable elements in the objectives and visions of education projected in the NEP. For example, the document very rightly states that there will be emphasis on conceptual understanding rather than on rote learning. Creativity and critical thinking will be encouraged. There will be emphasis on ethics and human and Constitutional values such as empathy, respect for others, elementary courtesy, democratic spirit, spirit of service, scientific temper, liberty, responsibility, pluralism, equality and justice. The objective of promoting multilingualism will be pursued in teaching and learning. There will be focus on regular formative assessment for learning rather than on the summative assessment that encourages today's 'coaching culture'. There will also be emphasis on respect for diversity and for the local context in all curriculum, pedagogy and policy. An attempt will be made to ensure full equality and inclusion as the cornerstone of all educational decisions. The document seeks prime position for teachers in society. It states that teachers and faculty will be 'the heart of the learning process'. Another encouraging feature of the document is that it calls for a substantive investment in a strong vibrant public education system. An important recommendation included in the document is a promise of a renewed effort to bring to school, all out-of-school children. [Finally, a recommendation of considerable significance made in this document is that all substandard stand-alone Teacher Education Institutions (TEIs) running in the country will be shut down. These are mainly private teacher training colleges which are at the root of the miserably low quality of education in India.][1] P.S.

If these objectives are applied to the education system in India, they can bring about a drastic change in the system. But it is easier to enunciate such principles than to implement them. Such objectives have been declared several times in the past and yet the Indian education system finds itself in its present poor plight. Moreover, suggestions made elsewhere in the Draft go to undermine these objectives and have the effect of taking the education system in the opposite direction. One example in this context should suffice.

Undermining Teachers' Position

The Draft assigns to the teacher the central position in the system. To quote from the Draft, 'the teacher and the teacher's conditions must and will be at the centre of these changes. The New Education Policy must help reinstate teachers, at all levels, as the most respected and essential members of our society'. In spite of this, the Draft suggests that 'teaching requirements of schools should be met by peer tutoring, educated members of the community and volunteers'. This suggestion goes against one of the basic provisions of the RTE Act, i.e. exclusive reliance on fully qualified and well-trained teachers for providing free and compulsory quality education. The implementation of this suggestion will seriously undermine the position of teachers in the system. It will also reverse the recent progress made in eliminating informalisation of school education, which was introduced officially for the first time in the 1986 National Education Policy and which assumed ominous proportions after the onset of the current process of liberalisation and globalization. Economists Jean Dreze and Amartya Sen characterised this informalisation of school education 'as neither effective nor equitable nor sustainable'. One of the very disturbing forms of informalisation was the expanding army of para teachers.

The RTE Act provided for the elimination of these forms of informalisation by placing wholesale reliance on fully trained and qualified school teachers. The recommendation made in the NEP for peer tutoring and the involvement of members from the community and

1. P.S. (Postscript). This has been considerably diluted in (NEP 2020).

volunteers drafted on in a gratis basis for teaching, is a huge retrograde step in this context. The task involved in teaching, across the schools in the country is so vast that the informal arrangement of the kind suggested in the Draft can touch only the fringe of the problem.

ECCE

One of the positive features of the document is its section dealing with the problems of health, nutrition, safety, development and education of children in the age group below 6 years. It may be recalled that this cohort of children was not covered by the RTE Act which turned out to be one of its biggest deficiencies. The Government, therefore, deserves to be commended for bringing the problems of the children in this age group in a fairly extensive manner in the Draft.

It is pointed out in the Draft that over 85 per cent of child brain development occurs prior to the age of 6, indicating the critical importance of appropriate care and stimulus of the brain in a child's early years. It has also been brought home that, currently quality Early Childhood Care and Education (ECCE) is not available to crores of young children, particularly those from socio-economically disadvantaged background. The document, therefore, recommends that universal provisioning of quality early childhood development, care and education should be achieved as soon as possible and no later than the year 2030, in order to ensure that all students entering Grade I are school ready. The document provides that an excellent curricular and pedagogical framework for early childhood education will be developed by the National Council for Educational Research and Training (NCERT). For universal coverage of ECCE, *Anganwadi* centres will be strengthened with high-quality infrastructure, equipment and well-trained *Anganwadi* workers.

In the earlier drafts of the Policy, it was indicated that ECCE will become a part of RTE through an amendment of the Act. As it happens, this provision was dropped in the subsequent drafts.

The deadline of 2030 for universalising ECCE is too long. The RTE Act provided for the universalisation of elementary school education within a period of five years. If we have to set a new deadline, it should not be too much longer than five years—a time frame which is both desirable and feasible.

Language Policy

It is indeed commendable that in the NEP the Government, after a long delay, returns to the crucial question of a language policy for school education. A separate section on this subject is devoted in the NEP. It is very rightly recognized in the Draft that children can grasp ideas and notions principally through their mother tongue. The Draft, therefore, suggests that medium of instruction up to Class V, and if possible, further on, should be the mother tongue. But, as in the RTE Act, in the NEP also, this provision is qualified by the words 'whenever possible'. This gives a carte blanche to school management, particularly in the private sector, to continue to use English as a medium of instruction.

The Draft very rightly points out that switching over to the mother tongue or a regional language, as a medium of instruction will require high quality translations of textbooks and other reference material, from other languages on a very large scale. It will also require training of teachers in these languages. These have been the principal constraints to making mother tongue a medium of instruction and implementing the Three-Language Formula. The country never came to investing for this purpose on the scale required. The result is that we are one of the few countries having a very rich tradition of local languages and culture but sticking mainly to a foreign language as a medium of instruction. This has been a major cause for the perpetuation of inequality in the education system and in society and the very poor quality of education in the country.

On the question of languages, the Draft expectedly takes up the issue of the Three-Language Formula. At the early stage of the preparation of the Draft, the Government tried to introduce some clarity on implementation of the Three- Language Formula, but the very mention of the words Three-Language Formula was taken by the people in the southern states of India as imposition of Hindi upon them. This led to a fairly large-scale agitation and other forms of protests in the country. A process of placating the opponents followed to manage the situation by the Government. The retreat was so complete that all attempts to implement the formula were given up. A large number of qualifications were introduced with regard to the scope and implementation procedure of the formula. As a result, the mention of the Three-Language Formula in the Draft is only a formality.

Futile Input-Output controversy

In recent instructions issued by the Government and literature publicised by it, a false dichotomy has been drawn between inputs and outputs of education. The Draft NEP repeatedly underlines that there will be a shift from input to output. This idea suffers from two basic fallacies. Firstly, it assumes that enough has been done so far as the provision of inputs is concerned. However, the facts on the ground are that a vast number of schools in India do not have even the basic infrastructure. Three years ago, only 12.7 per cent of the schools were compliant with all the norms prescribed in the RTE Act. The second major fallacy implicit in the artificially created controversy relating to input versus output is that it is forgotten these two are embilically linked. The creation of a child-friendly environment in a school, which depends a great deal on the provision of inputs, has a critical bearing on learning.

Norms

Norms define the kind of education that is being made available to students. They are also a critical determinant of the quality of education. One of the most effective means of ensuring quality is to lay down norms of high standard and apply them rigorously.

Norms also ensure equality in the education system. There is no better way of ensuring equality than applying a set of norms uniformly to all schools in the system. Most developed countries have laid down extensive norms for their schools and have been legally enforcing them. This is one of the principal reasons of their becoming developed and finding themselves in the forefront of economic and social progress.

One of the distinctive features of the RTE Act is that it provides, for the first time, a set of legally enforceable norms. In the interest of national unity and in order to make Indian school education system equitable and inclusive, it is necessary to retain and expand the scope of the RTE norms and ensure that they are applied in all schools.

Instead of doing this, the Draft belittles the importance of norms, particularly those included in the RTE Act, and makes suggestions for whittling them down. It does this principally in two ways. Firstly, it declares its intention to modify the RTE norms. It is stated in the Draft that the RTE norms will be made substantially less restrictive. The fact is that the norms under the RTE Act are highly limited and they are hardly being applied. Therefore, the question of making them liberal and flexible does not arise. Moreover, the RTE norms are the legal rights of the children of India and they cannot be taken away from them without an amendment of the RTE Act which is the prerogative of the Indian Parliament. The second way in which the RTE norms are intended to be undermined is the suggestion in the document that each school will have its own norms 'based on local needs and constraints' (page 37). Permitting each school to have its own norms will create chaos in the system in which it will move towards the lowest common denominator. There are certain norms the observance of which is essential for fostering national unity, protecting sovereignty, ensuring equality, meeting the basic needs of the people and upholding the essential values cherished in the Constitution. These norms will have to be applied to the school education system if we are to survive as a nation.

Resources

Theodore Schultz who propounded the human capital theory, is said to have advised somewhat to this effect: 'If you have money to invest and you do not know where to do so, then invest in education'. The authors of the Draft NEP are making the same point when they say: '...There is no better investment towards a society's future than the high quality education of our young people'.

There is no doubt that India has grossly under-invested in education and is continuing to do so. As the Draft states, 'it is far smaller than most developed and developing countries'.

The Tapas Majumdar Committee (1999) was the first to calculate, by assuming a set of norms, the additional expenditure required for universalising elementary education within a period of 10 years. The estimate came to Rs 1,37,000 crore of additional expenditure for a period of 10 years from 1998–1999 to 2007–08. On an annual basis, an amount of Rs 13,700 crore of additional resources were considered necessary. The investment of this modest amount at that time would have decisively reshaped the nation's destiny. But we failed to display the wisdom or political will to do so. Consequently, the cost of achieving the same objective has multiplied. In 2004-05, a Sub Committee of the CABE Committee was requested to estimate, as a part of the process of preparing the RTE Bill, the resources required for implementing the bill. The estimate came to Rs 72,743 crore per annum under the best scenario and Rs 53,532 crore under the worst scenario, for a period of five years.

When the RTE Act was legislated and went into effect, the Government did not accept the demand of the HRD Ministry, endorsed by the then Planning Commission, to make a sum of nearly Rs 43,000 crore per annum available for the purpose. The sum really made available was around Rs 30,000 crore. This sum was reduced, from time to time, to meet budgetary exigencies. In 2014-15, the amount allotted was Rs 24,376 crore. In 2015-16, it was brought down to Rs 22,000 crore.

On the basis of the recommendation made by the Kothari Commission in the early 1960s, the Government envisaged in the 1968 National Education Policy a level of public expenditure for education amounting to 6 per cent of GDP. This recommendation was reiterated in the 1986 Education Policy and further reaffirmed in the 1992 review of this Policy. In spite of this, the current public expenditure on education in India has hovered around 4.43 per cent of GDP. As a percentage of total Government expenditure of both the Central and State Governments, it has been around 10 per cent of the total Government spending.

The NEP 'endorses and envisions an increase in public investment in education to reach the 6 per cent target at the earliest and reach 20 per cent of all public expenditure over a 10-year period. This is considered extremely central for achieving the high quality and equitable public education system that is truly needed for India's future economic, social, cultural, intellectual and technological progress and growth' (P. 69 of the Draft).

The Committee also calls for the rejuvenation, active promotion and support for private philanthropic activities in the education sector. Let us dispose of this exhortation first. We do not share the Government's enthusiasm for the private sector or philanthropy providing finances for education on any substantial scale. There is no empirical evidence to support it.

Regarding public provisioning, the real problem is the manner in which the additional resources required for financing education is calculated. In our view, the best way to estimate the total amount of resources to be provided for school education would be first to define the objective to be realised, i.e., universalisation of elementary education, then establish a set of norms which will be applied to the reconstruction of the Indian school education system to realise the objective, and then to fix a price tag on all major items of expenditure based on the norms. This will make it possible to estimate the financial expenditure required for achieving the defined objective within a specified time period, say five years as in the case of the RTE Act. In the NEP instead of calculating the total resources required in a scientific fashion, the chimera of a target, i.e. 6 per cent of GDP and 20 per cent of public spending, has been pursued. Such targets have not been a reality so far, and are unlikely to be realised in the near future.

[However, one should welcome every suggestion which has the effect of making additional resources available for education in India. From this point of view, the recommendation that 'all States allocate 20 per cent of their overall spends to education' and the 'Central Government expenditure has to double' is most welcome. But there are several problems besetting this recommendation. Firstly, a 10-year period to reach the target of 20 per cent is too long, particularly when the RTE Act provided a decade ago for the universalisation of elementary education in five years. Secondly, the document does not spell out how the states will be persuaded or obliged to accept and implement this target. Will there be a national legislation to this effect? Will it be possible to arrive at a consensus for such a legislation? Thirdly, as the Draft points out, some of the Indian States might already be devoting 20 per cent of their budget to education. The problem in such a situation will be to persuade the States which are devoting much lesser proportion of their budget, to raise their allotment for education to 20 per cent. Most of these States happen to have fragile financial conditions. It is very likely that these States would demand that the Central Government should make available the resources which are expected from them.] P.S.

In the ultimate analysis, there is no escape from the State providing all the resources needed for universalising school education. For this purpose, there should be a reprioritisation of education in the economic and budgetary schemes of the country.[2] P.S.

RTE Act, the Pending Agenda for School Education

The Government has recognized that 'a major development since the last Policy of 1986/92 has been the Right of Children to Free and Compulsory

2. P.S. This has been excluded from the NEP 2020.

Education Act, 2009 which lays down the legal underpinning for achieving universal elementary education'. It is a pity, if not a great irony, that the only place where the RTE Act finds a mention in this document is this sentence. It is not mentioned anywhere thereafter in the Draft. There are several very important aspects of the RTE Act which constitute the pending agenda of school education in India. These should have been dealt with in the Draft as matters of high priority and in sufficient detail to bring out their importance and mobilise the support of the people for any significant changes to be made in the Act. The following are some of the matters of high priority in school education in India:

i. The first priority indeed is the implementation of the Act, as most of the important provisions of the Act remain unimplemented. The implementation of the Act is not possible without investing a substantial amount of additional resources.
ii. To universalise ECCE, the most appropriate way to proceed is to amend the RTE Act in order to confer upon the children upto six years old, the same rights as are available under the Act to elementary school children.
iii. A very important pending item on the education agenda is the universalisation of quality secondary education. For this purpose also, extending the RTE Act in order to bring in children in the age group 15-18 in its ambit would be the most appropriate thing to do. But it pre-supposes the mobilisation of a substantial amount of resources.
iv. Enough resources should be invested for the effective functioning of Cluster Resources Centres, Block Resources Centres, DIETS and State Council for Educational Research and Training (SCERT).

Making the system Equitable and Inclusive – The role of Common School System

Several measures have been suggested in the Draft NEP to make education equitable and inclusive. They are, basically, identifying categories which are economically backward or suffer from inherent social and economic backwardness and provide special measures for them. These measures include creating funds, providing facilities like hostels, transport and scholarships which are dedicated to meet the needs of the identified categories, selecting backward regions and districts and making them the focus of attention for applying special measures.

Most of these measures have been tried before in the country in the wider context of the development of the economy and alleviation of poverty, but they have all failed. One of the reasons for failure is that the funds allotted for them were never adequate. Besides, the upper strata of the population managed to pre-empt a good chunk of the resources.

All these measures are based on the assumption, not publicly declared, that enough resources will never be available to universalise services in social sectors within an agreed timeframe. This is indeed a very grim prognosis for our society.

These measures have worked to perpetuate inequality and exclusion by evading or postponing changes of a structural nature and somehow managing the situation politically by placating the poor and the backward. Even if the RTE Act is extended to pre-primary and secondary education, as demanded by civil society organisations in the country, and the revised Act is implemented within a new timeframe to be agreed upon, school education in India is likely to remain a den of discrimination and a source of perpetuating and accentuating economic and social inequality in society. This is principally because of the continued existence of a multi-layered school education system in India which has discrimination built into it. The only way to remove this built-in discrimination is to introduce a common school system in the country, which ensures the availability to all the school students in India more or less the same quality of education. The adoption and implementation of a common school system was the main instrument adopted by what is now known as the category of developed countries, for mitigating social inequality. An important policy document like the New Education Policy has to have an overall vision for the future of education and, for that matter for the future of the country. The most ennobling vision it can have is to embrace the goal of building a Common School System for India. The NEP should, therefore, provide for introducing such a system of education at the very early stage in the implementation of the new Policy.

New Delhi

Prof. Muchkund Dubey,
President,
Council for Social Development

Preface

As compared to all the 40 books that I have written or edited so far, this book has taken the longest time—over five years.

It started out in 2014 as a project for the Council for Social Development (CSD), New Delhi. Professor Muchkund Dubey, President of CSD, had first invited me to join the Institution as a Distinguished Professor and later as a Chaired Professor (Dr Durgabai Deshmukh Chair in Social Development, Equity and Human Development). The title of my project was: 'Harnessing and Leveraging the Demographic Dividend through Inclusive and Equitable Education and Skill Development'.

My draft Report on the subject was presented and discussed in CSD in 2015. Several insightful comments were received, especially from Prof. Muchkund Dubey, Prof. Manoranjan Mohanty, Prof. Imrana Qadeer, Prof. K.B. Saxena, Prof. T. Haque and Prof. Ashok Pankaj, among others. Finalisation of my Report, however, slowed down somewhat when in April 2016, the President of India nominated me as a Member of Parliament (MP) in the Upper House (i.e., Rajya Sabha).

Before I could complete the Report, I was hit by cancer (of sigmoid colon) in March 2017. Following four surgeries, chemotherapy and radiation therapy, when recovery began, my topmost priority was to finish the Report and submit it, which I finally did in mid-2018.

The next task was to convert the Report into a book. This posed yet another challenge. It so happened that in the interregnum, two important official documents were released:

i. Some Inputs for Draft National Education Policy 2016 and,
ii. Draft National Education Policy 2019.

Both of these important documents, released by the Ministry of Human Resource Development (MHRD) of the Government of India, transformed the entire focus of the earlier project. Importantly, it called for three additional chapters, including a comprehensive summary of the Draft National Education Policy (NEP) 2019, its detailed critique and way forward. This took some more time.

On 29 July 2020, the Union Government rolled out the National Education Policy, 2020 (NEP 2020), paving way for transformational reforms in the education sector to make India a 'Global Knowledge Superpower'. Accordingly, I have written a Postscript which compares the recommendations in the new Policy with that of NEP 2019.

I am truly delighted that this book could finally see the light of the day. I am also glad that a Hindi translation of the book is also being released at the same time.

I hope that this book—the first one on the subject after the announcement of the National Education Policy, 2020—would be welcomed by scholars, researchers, practitioners, civil society activists and lay readers alike.

Narendra Jadhav

Acknowledgements

Feedback

Prof. Muchkund Dubey, Prof. Manoranjan Mohanty,
Prof. Imrana Qadeer, Prof. K.B. Saxena
Prof. T. Haque, Prof. Ashok Pankaj
All colleagues from Council for Social Development, New Delhi
Cathal Leslie (Australian Intern)

Research Support

Dr C. Chandramohan, backed up by
Suman Shukla, Arnaaz Ameer, Pratima Garg and Torsha Dasgupta

Editorial Assistance and Plagiarism Check

Preeta Priyamvada, Padma Alva, Jiza Joy and Lekshmi Parameswaran

Technical Assistance

Sudha Rajagopalan, Prabhakar Gaikwad and Kanakpriya

Other Assistance

Deepak Negi, Rajesh Kumar, Bhura Ahirwar and Samir Arora

Family Support

Vasundhara Jadhav (Wife)
Tanmoy (Son) and Dr Apoorva (Daughter)
Kejal (Daughter-in-law), Dr Ekim Muyan (Son-in-law)
Agastya, Eymir, Kimaya and Keyan (Grandchildren)

Acronyms

ACS	Academic Staff Colleges
AECs	Adult Education Centres
AICTE	All India Council of Technical Education
AIE	Alternative and Innovative Education
AISHE	All India Survey on Higher Education
BITE	Block Institute of Teacher Education
BRC	Block Resource Centre
CABE	Central Advisory Board of Education
CABE	Central Advisory Board of Education
CBSE	Central Board of Secondary Education
CCE	Continuous and Comprehensive Evaluation
CCES	Continuous and Comprehensive Evaluation System
CFTIs	Centrally-Funded Technical Institutions
CIAE	Central Institute of Adult Education
CPD	Continuous Professional Development
CRC	Cluster Resource Centre
CUs	Central Universities
CWSN	Children with Special Needs
DIET	District Institutes of Education and Training
DISE	District Information System for Education
DNTs	Denotified and Nomadic Tribes
DPEP	District Primary Education Programme

DSE	Directorate of School Education
DWS	Drinking Water Supply
EBBs	Educationally Backward Blocks
ECCE	Early Childhood Care and Education
EFA	Education for All
EGS	Education Guarantee Scheme
ESD	Education for Sustainable Development
EWS	Economically Weaker Sections
FM Lit	Female literacy
FREEEDN	Free Education
GEC	General Education Council
GER	Gross Enrolment Ratio
GNP	Gross National Product
GoMs	Group of Ministers
GPI	Gender Parity Index
HCR	Head Count Ratio
HEGC	Higher Education Grants Commission
HEIs	Higher Education Institutions
HRD	Human Resource Development
IAs	Instructional Assistants
ICDS	Integrated Child Development Services
ICSE	Indian Certificate of Secondary Education
ICT	Information and Communications Technology
IDMI	Infrastructure Development in Minority Institutions
INIs	Institutions of National Importance
IRAHE	Independent Regulatory Authority for Higher Education
ISL	Indian Sign Language
JNVs	Jawahar Navodaya Vidyalayas

KGBV	Kasturba Gandhi Balika Vidyalaya
KVs	Kendriya Vidyalayas
LSS	Licence to Start a School
MCBs	Minority Concentrated Blocks
MCDs	Minority Concentrated Districts
MDG	Millennium Development Goal
MDMS	Mid-Day Meal Scheme
MERUs	Multidisciplinary Education and Research Universities
MGNREGA	Mahatma Gandhi National Rural Employment Guarantee Act
MHRD	Ministry of Human Resource Development
MN	Mission Nalanda
MoE	Ministry of Education
MPCE	Monthly Per Capita Consumption Expenditure
MsDP	Multi-sectoral Development Programme
MT	Mission Takshashila
MWCD	Ministry of Women and Child Development
MYS	Mean Years of Schooling
NAAC	National Assessment and Accreditation Council
NAG	National Agenda for Governance
NAS	National Achievement Survey
NCERT	National Council for Educational Research and Training
NCF	National Curricular Framework
NCFAE	National Curriculum Framework for Adult Education
NCIVE	National Committee for the Integration of Vocational Education
NCTE	National Council for Teacher Education
NCVET	National Council for Vocational Education and Training

NEC	National Education Commission
NETF	National Educational Technology Forum
NHEQF	National Higher Education Qualifications Framework
NHERA	National Higher Education Regulatory Authority
NIEPA	National Institute of Educational Planning and Administration
NIOS	National Institute of Open Schooling
NKC	National Knowledge Commission
NLCP	National Child Labour Projects
NPE	National Policy on Education
NPEGEL	National Programme for Education of Girls to Elementary Level
NP-NSPE	National Programme of Nutritional Support to Primary Education
NRED	National Repository of Educational Data
NRF	National Research Foundation
NSDA	National Skills Development Agency
NSQF	National Skills Qualifications Framework
NSS	National Sample Survey
NTA	National Testing Agency
NTP	National Tutors Programme
NUEPA	National University of Educational Planning and Administration
NVs	Navodaya Vidyalayas
NVS	Navodaya Vidyalaya Samiti
ODL	Open and Distance Learning
OECD-PISA	Organisation for Economic Co-operation and Development's Programme for International Student Assessment

OLS	Ordinary Least Squares
OoSC	Out-of-School Children
PCEE	The per capita expenditure on education
PCIEE	Per Child Investment in Elementary Education
PHCs	Primary Health Centres
PoA	Programme of Action
PSSBs	Professional Standard Setting Bodies
PTR	Pupil-Teacher Ratio
PUIs	Private Unaided Institutions
PwDs	Persons with Disabilities
R&I	Research and Innovation
RIAP	Remedial Instructional Aides Programme
RIs	Research Institutions
RjSA	Rajya Shiksha Aayog
RMSA	Rashtriya Madhyamik Shiksha Abhiyan
RPL	Recognition of Prior Learning
RSA	Rashtriya Shiksha Aayog
RTE Act	Right to Education Act
RUSA	Rashtriya Uchchatar Shiksha Abhiyan
SAS	State Assessment Survey
SCERT	State Council for Education and Training
SDGs	Sustainable Development Goals
SEC	State Education Commission
SECC	Socio-Economic and Caste Census
SEdZs	Special Education Zones
SES	Selected Education Statistics
SFDs	Special Focus Districts
SHGs	Self-Help Groups

SIEMAT	State Institute of Educational Management and Training
SIOS	State Institutes of Open Schooling
SMC	School Management Committee
SPQEM	Scheme for Providing Quality Education in Madrasas
SQAAF	School Quality Assessment and Accreditation Framework
SSA	Sarva Shiksha Abhiyan
SSDM	State Skill Development Mission
SSRA	State School Regulatory Authority
TET	Teacher Eligibility Test
TSP	Total Sanitation Programme
UDHR	Universal Declaration of Human Rights
U-DISE	Unified District Information on School Education
UGC	University Grants Commission
UNGA	United Nations General Assembly
URGs	Underrepresented Groups
USE	Universalisation of Secondary Education
VE	Vocational Education

1

Introduction

Education plays a vital role in the growth and development of any nation. It is increasingly being recognised the world over that countries with greater capacity to absorb and generate new knowledge and skilled human power are likely to have a comparative edge in attaining and sustaining higher economic growth than those countries that do not. The underlying logic is straightforward. What education does essentially is to improve functional and analytical abilities of individuals. This opens up numerous possibilities for individuals and social groups to achieve greater access to employment opportunities as well as professional fulfilment.

Education is not only an instrument for enhancing efficiency but also has been widely accepted as the basis of socio-economic transformation, for widening and augmenting democratic participation and upgrading the overall quality of individual and societal life. Education is probably the most important lever for social, economic and political transformation. A well-educated population, equipped with relevant knowledge, aptitudes and skills is essential for both economic and social development. Education is the most powerful tool for achieving socio-economic mobility besides being a key instrument for building an equitable and just society. In addition to providing skills and competencies for economic well-being, education strengthens democracy by imparting values that foster social cohesion and national identity.[1]

Evidently, education is likely to be more meaningful only if it is capable of equipping and creating a knowledge society that is well prepared to face the challenges of sustainable development. Across the world, there is a surge of interest and genuine concern over sustainability issues in governments, communities and organisations as well as in business and industry. Thanks to the UN Conference on Environment and Development (1992), there is now a widespread understanding that 'the creation of a sustainable world that includes humanity depends on fundamental changes in our socio-economic systems as a whole, supported by a critical re-orientation of our principles, values, behaviours and lifestyles'. Education for Sustainable Development (ESD) is seen as 'the total sum of diverse ways to arrive at a "learning society" in which people learn from and with one another and collectively become more capable of withstanding setbacks and dealing with sustainability-induced insecurity, complexity and risks'.

Major Goals Set by the United Nations

The following major goals set by the UN for education and training are most relevant[2]:

1. **Promote and improve the quality of education:**
   The aim is to refocus lifelong education on the acquisition of knowledge, skills and values needed by citizens to improve their quality of life.
2. **Reorient the curricula:**
   From pre-school to university, education must be rethought and reformed to be a vehicle of knowledge, thought patterns and values needed to build a sustainable world.

---

1. This broad view of education has been emphasised by various UN Reports, especially UNESCO (2006) and United Nations Conference on Environment and Development, 1992. Also see Planning Commission, 'Twelfth Five Year Plan (2012–17)', Social Sectors, vol. III, p. 47.

2. UN Decade of Education for Sustainable Development (DESD 2005–2014), 'Review of Contexts and Structures for Education for Sustainable Development for a Sustainable World 2009', (Paris: UNESCO, 2009), p. 7, https://unesdoc.unesco.org/ark:/48223/pf0000184944

3. **Raise public awareness of the concept of sustainable development:**
   This will make it possible to develop enlightened, active and responsible citizenship locally, nationally and internationally.
4. **Train the workforce:**
   Continuing Technical and Vocational Education of directors and workers, particularly those in trade and industry, will be enriched to enable them to adopt sustainable modes of production and consumption.

These goals are interdependent and essentially inclusive in realigning the educational system that promotes not only country-specific but also global solutions for sustainable development.

The right to education has been well recognised by the United Nations General Assembly (UNGA) under Article 26 of Universal Declaration of Human Rights (UDHR) as:

- Everyone has the right to education. Education shall be free, at least in elementary and fundamental stages …
- Education shall be directed to the full development of human personality and to the strengthening of respect of human rights and fundamental freedoms.
- Parents have a right to choose the kind of education that shall be given to their children.

Recognizing the importance of education in national development, India has placed, especially in the recent years, an unprecedented emphasis on the expansion of education, on significantly improving its quality and on ensuring that educational opportunities are available to all segments of the society.

Against this backdrop, the present introductory chapter has been organised as follows:

Section I traces the evolution of National Policy on Education in India. Landmark developments from the Independence in 1947 to date have been reviewed in broad terms. Section II dilates briefly on the contemporary opportunities and challenges facing the education sector in India. The final section, i.e., Section III then lays out the organisational structure of the book.

I. Evolution of National Policy on Education

When India became Independent, the need for improving the education structure in conformity with national aspirations was duly recognised. In fact, while inaugurating an education conference in January 1948, the then Prime Minister Jawaharlal Nehru had said:

> Whenever conferences were called (earlier) to form a plan for education in India, the tendency, as a rule, was to maintain the existing system with slight modification. This must not happen now. Great changes have taken place in our country and the Education System must also be in keeping with them. The entire basis of education must be revolutionised.[3]

To begin with, the Government of India appointed University Education Commission in 1948 under the Chairmanship of S. Radhakrishnan. The Commission made wide-ranging recommendations about university education in India, including the establishment of a Central University Grants Commission (UGC) for country-wide expansion of University Education. Importantly, the Commission recommended a reorganisation of Secondary Education (10+2 structure) as a prerequisite for University Education. In the meantime, when India became a Republic on 26th January 1950, the Constitution of India made education a State subject and divided the responsibility of developing the education sector between the Central Government and the States. Interestingly, the Directive Principles of the State Policy incorporated in the Constitution included 'providing free and compulsory education for all children up to 14 years of age'.[4]

In 1952, the Secondary Education Commission was appointed under the Chairmanship of Dr A.L. Mudaliar. This Commission submitted its report in 1953, which recommended, inter alia, the schooling duration to be reduced from 12 years to 11 years and transferring the conduct of Secondary School Certificate examination from the universities to the specially constituted Boards of Secondary Education.

---

3. Suresh Chandra Ghosh, *The History of Education in Modern India: 1757–2012,* 4th edition, (New Delhi: Oriental Blackswan, 2013), p. 178.

4. Durga Das Basu, *The Constitution of India,* 11th edition, 1985, pp. 137–46.

While these reforms were significant, the emphasis on mass education, especially the programmes of adult education and elimination of illiteracy, continued to be neglected. Indeed, 'the vision of a national system of education seen in 1947 ... got blurred within two decades'.[5]

The first National Policy on Education emerged finally in July 1968, based on a path-breaking comprehensive Report of Education Commission under the Chairmanship of D.S. Kothari.[6] The Kothari Commission recommended a drastic reconstruction and complete transformation of the Indian Education System.

Although education was then a State subject, on public demand, the Government of India referred the report to a Committee of Members of Parliament for consideration. Kothari Commission's recommendations along with the Report of the Parliamentary Committee were subsequently discussed in both Houses of Parliament and later in the Union Cabinet. The first-ever National Policy on Education in Independent India, thus, emerged in the form of a Union Cabinet Resolution in 1968.

While the recommendations of the Kothari Commission were progressively diluted during successive discussions, it is noteworthy that the National Policy on Education that came out therefrom remained the basic framework for all government interventions in the education sector till the emergence of 'New Education Policy' nearly two decades later.

Unlike the earlier National Education Policy of 1968, the new policy did not emanate from any Education Commission preceding it. Apparently, the policy proposals were formulated by the bureaucracy and were then presented to academicians and politicians for national debate and discussion. The Parliament approved the 'New National Education Policy' in May 1986.

The New National Education Policy (1986) stressed the imperative of inclusiveness in the Indian Education System. The policy emphasised the need for equal access to educational opportunities, eliminating the disparities based on class, caste, creed, sex or region. With a common educational structure of 10+2+3, the New Education Policy paved the way for attending to specific needs of the historically underprivileged, i.e., Scheduled Castes (SCs), Scheduled Tribes (STs) and women, besides the

5. Ghosh, *History of Education in Modern India* (2013), p. 182.

6. Secretary of this Commission, J.P. Naik played a highly significant role in the preparation of the Report.

physically challenged as well as the social groups which are educationally deprived or backward including the people belonging to remote and inaccessible areas.

Launching of the New National Education Policy (NEP) 1986 meant operationalising several innovative programmes. Especially noteworthy were the following:

- *Operation Blackboard* (1987): This aimed at providing the bare minimum critical facilities to all Primary Schools in the country.
- *Navodaya Vidyalaya System:* This was set up to harness the best of rural talent by providing them with quality education in a residential school network.
- *District Institutes of Education and Training (DIETs):* DIETs were established to function as the resource centre at the district level for systematic planning and implementation of programmes for education and training of teachers in Elementary Schools.
- *Shiksha Karmi Project* (1987): With the help of Swedish International Development Cooperation Agency, this project aimed at addressing the problem of teacher absenteeism by substituting teachers in dysfunctional schools with local youth, known as *Shiksha Karmis*.

In the arena of higher education, several important institutions were created at the national level. These included, inter alia, All India Council of Technical Education (AICTE), National Council for Teacher Education (NCTE) and National Assessment and Accreditation Council (NAAC). Moreover, Academic Staff Colleges (ACS) were set up at selected universities to refresh and reorient the knowledge of the university and college teachers.

There was a major setback to the implementation of the New National Education Policy of 1986 when in 1989, the Congress Government (led by Rajiv Gandhi) was replaced by the National Front Government (led by V.P. Singh). The National Front Government appointed a Review Committee (on the New National Education Policy) in May 1990 under the Chairmanship of Acharya Ramamurti. The Review Committee submitted its report in December 1990, but soon thereafter the National Front Government (then led by Chandrasekhar) fell, and in the general election that followed, Congress Government under the leadership of P.V. Narasimha Rao came to power in July 1991.

The Narasimha Rao Government restored the New National Education Policy of 1986, but issued the so-called 'Revised Programme of Action 1992'. The revised action programme included setting up of the District Primary Education Programme (DPEP) emphasising commitment to the Universalisation of Elementary Education (UEE). The Government of India also introduced, in 1995, a scheme then called the National Programme of Nutritional Support to Primary Education (NP-NSPE), which later in the year 2001 came to be called the Mid-Day Meal Scheme (MDMS).

In 1996, when United Front Government came to power under Deve Gowda (with Congress support from outside), a Committee of State Education Ministers was formed (in August 1996) under the Chairmanship of Muhi Ram Saikia (who was Union Minister of State for Education). The mandate of the Saikia Committee was to suggest a roadmap towards UEE by the year 2000. The Saikia Committee proposed, inter alia, to amend the Constitution to make Elementary Education up to 14 years of age a Fundamental Right. The United Front Government even prepared the relevant Bill and introduced it in the Parliament. However, before the passage of the Bill, the United Front Government lost power in April 1998 and the BJP-led Government under the leadership of Atal Bihari Vajpayee took over.

The BJP-led Government took the process further through what was referred to as the National Agenda for Governance (NAG) in Education. A landmark development was the merger of DPEP, launched in 1994, which was operating in educationally backward districts only, with universalised Sarva Shiksha Abhiyan launched in 2000-01 with the help of World Bank, Department for International Development (DFID) of the UK and UNICEF. The NAG stressed 'a sustained educational development in the country according to the 1992 Programme of Action revised in the light of three key principles of the Ramamurti Committee recommendations, i.e., universalisation, vocationalisation and decentralisation'.[7]

When the Congress-led UPA Government came to power in 2004 under the leadership of Manmohan Singh, the National Knowledge Commission (NKC) was appointed under the Chairmanship of Sam Pitroda in August 2005.

The NKC submitted its final report in January 2007. Its main recommendations included:

---

7. Ghosh, *History of Education in Modern India* (2013), p. 209.

- Massive expansion of Higher Education: The number of universities to be increased from 350 to 1,500 by the year 2015,
- Increase in private investment in Medical and Engineering courses in the universities,
- Reform in the existing universities and restructuring of the undergraduate colleges,
- Bringing the entire eco-system of Vocational Education under the Ministry of Human Resource Development (MHRD),
- Establishment of an Independent Regulatory Authority for Higher Education (IRAHE), which would divest UGC and AICTE of their regulatory powers, and
- Development of a deprivation index so as to provide weighted scores to students.

The NKC report was not fully accepted by the then HRD Minister Arjun Singh. The only recommendation of the NKC that was seemingly found acceptable by the HRD Ministry was expansion of Higher Education.

In the context of NKC's recommendation of setting up of an IRAHE, Arjun Singh appointed a Committee under the Chairmanship of Prof. Yashpal, with a mandate to examine the functioning of the UGC and the AICTE. The Committee submitted its report in 2009.

When the Congress-led UPA Government came to power for the second term in 2009, the new HRD Minister, Kapil Sibal began with passing of the much-delayed 'Right to Education Bill' into an Act on 26 August 2009 which became effective from 1 April 2010.

When Yashpal Committee submitted its report, it endorsed many of the NKC recommendations. Since the Cabinet Committee had endorsed the Yashpal Committee's comments favouring the NKC recommendations, the new HRD Minister focused his attention on implementing them.

The Right to Education (RTE) Act of 2009, undoubtedly, was a highly significant step in the right direction. The salient features of the RTE Act included the following:

- Prescription of some common standards aimed at addressing the long-standing issue of poor quality of infrastructure—drinking water, toilets, library, playing fields and 1:40 teacher-student ratio;
- Reservation of 25 per cent of seats at the entry level for students belonging to the Economically Weaker Sections (EWS) category

(including the physically challenged) in private institutions;

- Ban on charging fees, on screening and interviewing of parents and students before admission, on corporal punishment and on private tuition by teachers;
- Government reimbursement to private schools on the basis of what it spends on education (per student) in its own schools; and
- Inclusion of 50 per cent women in the school management committees.

The total financial commitment of the Central Government was placed at Rs 1.71 lakh crore for five years. The HRD Ministry also proposed a change in the funding pattern between the Centre and States for the ongoing Flagship Programme of Sarva Shiksha Abhiyan (SSA) from 55:45 to 65:35 for the first two years of the Eleventh Plan (2007–12), 60:40 for the third year, 55:45 for the fourth year and 50:50 thereafter.

In the arena of Higher Education, the HRD Ministry led by Kapil Sibal drafted five major bills, as under:

- Bill to ban unfair practices in Medical and Technical Institutes,
- Bill to set up Educational Tribunals at the Central and State levels for dispute settlement,
- National Accreditation Bill aimed at assessing and accrediting institutions in Higher Education,
- Bill to set up National Commission for Higher Education and Research (NCHER) as a regulatory body to supervise the Higher Education sector, and
- The Foreign Educational Institutions (Regulation, Entry and Operation) Bill for allowing foreign educational institutions to open campuses in India.

These bills were at various stages of finalisation when the BJP-led Government under Narendra Modi took over in May 2014.

The Modi Government has initiated the process of formulating a 'National Education Policy', which is currently under way. The National Policy on Education framed in 1986 and modified in 1992 called for a revision in view of the fact that several changes have taken place in the interregnum, including the RTE Act, setting of global standards in education and benchmarking excellence, as also rapid expansion in the use of information and communication technologies, especially the Internet.

Incorporating global standards in education requires forward-looking policy programme and promotion of cutting-edge research and development in science and technology. Accordingly, the Government of India envisaged to bring out a National Education Policy in order to 'meet the changing dynamics of the population's requirements with regard to quality education, innovation and research, aiming to make India a knowledge superpower by equipping its students with the necessary skills and knowledge and to eliminate the shortage of manpower in science, technology, academics and industry'.[8] The main emphasis of NEP was going to be on accessibility, equity, quality, affordability and accountability. For the first time, the Government of India embarked on a time-bound grass-root level consultative process so as to enable the HRD Ministry to reach out to individuals across the country through over 2.75 lakh direct consultations while also taking input from citizens online.

In order to facilitate further meaningful discussion at the State and sub-State levels and also lead a general debate facilitating online consultations and eliciting views or comments, the HRD Ministry had placed a document titled 'Some Inputs for Draft National Education Policy, 2016', on its official website.

These inputs were processed by a five-member Committee headed by former Cabinet Secretary T.S.R. Subramanian. The Subramanian Committee submitted its report in May 2016. The report suggested a range of reforms, including setting up an India Education Service (with cadre-controlling authority entrusted to the HRD Ministry), compulsory licensing of teachers at government and private schools, no detention till Class V, extension of the Mid-Day Meal Scheme to Secondary School level and allowing foreign universities to open campuses in India.

As per the draft, the NEP 2016 envisioned a credible and high-performing education system capable of ensuring inclusive quality education and lifelong learning opportunities for all and producing students or graduates equipped with the knowledge, skills, attitudes and values that are required to lead a productive life, participate in the country's development process, respond to the requirements of the fast-

8. HRD Minister, 'Formulating the New Education Policy', MyGov Blog, 29 November 2015.

changing, ever-globalising, knowledge-based economy and society. The overall goal was to 'foster quality and relevance of education and raise the credibility of India's Education System, improve employability of the products of School and Higher Education System, ensure equitable access to education, from early childhood education to Tertiary Education including Technical and Vocational Education and Training (TVET), as well as lifelong learning opportunities, and ensure that educational opportunities are available to all segments of the society'.[9]

The key elements of NEP 2016 included:

- Provision for pre-Primary Education, which remained hitherto neglected;
- Measuring learning outcomes and enhancing academic performance of students;
- Expansion of premier educational institutions like Kendriya Vidyalayas (KVs), Navodaya Vidyalayas (NVs) and Kasturba Gandhi Balika Vidyalayas (KGBVs);
- Curricular reforms by Central and State Boards of Education at school education and time-bound revisions at the university/college levels;
- Reforms in Teacher Education, including leadership development and setting up of a National Teacher Education University;
- Setting up of an Education Commission every five years to assist the Ministry of HRD on a regular basis;
- Integrating Undergraduate, Postgraduate and Doctoral studies to create vibrant research environment in Higher Education Institutions;
- Quality assurance mechanism in Higher, Technical and Professional Education; and
- Internationalisation of education, among others.

The NEP 2016 continued to reiterate much elusive educational investment goal of 6 per cent of GDP,[10] which is currently around 4 per cent.

In June 2017, the HRD Ministry appointed an eight-member Committee

9. MHRD, 'Some Inputs for Draft National Education Policy 2016', pp. 14–15, https://mhrd.gov.in/sites/upload_files/mhrd/files/nep/Inputs_Draft_NEP_2016.pdf

10. Ibid, pp. 1-43.

headed by K. Kasturirangan to draft a new National Education Policy. This Committee was expected to examine the Subramanian Committee report in detail and also consider inputs received from the Members of Parliament, teachers, students and educationists.

As Kasturirangan puts it:

> All this seemed very doable in six months. However, what followed was something entirely different...It became clear very soon that this Committee was going to be "out-of-the-box" in its thinking.[11]

The Committee ended up taking 'bold decisions towards attempting to craft a completely new and far-sighted Policy', with the understanding that New Education Policy (NEP) 'must be relevant and applicable for at least two decades, within the context of the dynamic and fast-changing nature of the education space in India and the world'.

The Kasturirangan Committee submitted a detailed (436 pages) 'Draft National Education Policy 2019' to the HRD Ministry on December 15, 2018 which was released for public on the website of the HRD Ministry apparently in July 2019.

And, finally on 29 July 2020, the Government of India rolled out the National Education Policy, 2020.

II. Contemporary Challenges and Opportunities in India's Education and Skill Development Sector

The importance of the education sector in India today is more than ever before, mainly because of the fortuitous occurrence of the so-called 'Demographic Dividend'. As pointed out by Ross (2004), for any economy, Demographic Dividend occurs when a falling birth rate changes the age distribution in such a way that fewer investments are needed to meet the needs of the youngest age groups and resources are released for investment in economic growth, development and family welfare. That is, a falling birth rate makes for a proportionately smaller population at young, dependent ages and for relatively more people in the adult age groups who comprise the productive labour force. In other words, the

11. MHRD, Draft National Education Policy 2019, Preamble, July 2019, pp. 23–24.

Demographic Dividend improves the ratio of productive workers to child dependents in the population. That paves the way for faster economic growth and fewer burdens on families.[12]

In India, a persistent decline in the dependency ratio (i.e., ratio of dependent to working age population) from 0.8 in 1991 to 0.73 in 2001 and further down to 0.59 in 2011 has meant India having the world's youngest labour force. Median age for India in 2020 has been projected to be only 29 compared with 37 in China and the US, 45 in Western Europe, and as much as 48 in Japan. While elsewhere in the world — in China and Industrial countries, dependency ratios are rising and youth population shrinking, India is blessed with the population of which about 70 per cent are below the age of 35 years. In fact, in India the population in the age group of 10-19 years has been placed at 253 million,[13] which happens to be the largest ever cohort of young people making a transition to adulthood in the history of mankind.

This would potentially offer India a comparative cost advantage over others for another 15-20 years. In other words, India has a unique opportunity to potentially complement what the ageing rest of the world needs most. It is important to note, however, that the Demographic Dividend is a transitory phase that offers a limited window of opportunity. The Demographic Dividend does not last forever, and it is not automatic either. Needless to say, this tremendous human resource potential would have to be harnessed and, in this process, it is the Education and Skill Development sectors that hold the key.

The enormous physical and spatial expansion of the Higher Education sector in India over the years had, until recently, prompted many to boast about the country having the third largest trained person power in the world. Not anymore. Increasingly, it is being recognised that adequacy and relevance of the Indian Education System is questionable. Of late, more pertinent questions are being asked: Is the enlarged education sector consistent with national aspirations such as achieving and maintaining the high growth trajectory? In similar vein, it is being asked whether the enlarged education sector is capable of delivering outcomes that would facilitate transformation of India as a major knowledge economy.

These questions can be addressed only through a comprehensive

---

12. John Ross, 'Understanding the Demographic Dividends', *POLICY Project,* 2004.
13. Census 2011.

analysis of access, equity, quality and employability of the Indian Education System today. While a more detailed analysis of these issues is presented in Chapter 2, salient features may be summarised as under:

(A) School Education

Sarva Shiksha Abhiyan (SSA) has brought India close to the target of Universalisation of Primary Education (UPE). The Right to Education Act (RTE) 2009 makes eight years of Elementary Education a Fundamental Right for all children. The Mid-Day Meal Scheme (MDMS) has ensured that retention in schools improve greatly. However, the learning outcomes for a majority of children continue to be disappointing, particularly in the publicly funded schools.[14] Providing good quality foundational education is critical for the effective development of human capabilities and for achieving the objective of equality of opportunities. The quality of teachers in the schools and, even more important, their motivation and accountability will have to be improved. Many of the school children in India are first-generation learners and they need supplementary instruction. This is not an easy task, given the shortage of qualified teachers in many schools across the country. New and innovative approaches, therefore, would have to be adopted to ensure equitable education.

The success of SSA in terms of near universal access, universal enrolment, retention and vastly improved transition rates has put pressure on expanding the capacity of Secondary Schools, particularly in the rural areas. Accordingly, a comprehensive Rashtriya Madhyamik Shiksha Abhiyan (RMSA) was launched in 2009-10 to holistically address the issues relating not only to expanding access but also to the quality and equity of Secondary Education. While there is a sharper focus on providing secondary school access, the dropout rates at Elementary Education continue to be unacceptably high in several States. In Secondary/Higher Secondary Education, which is the gateway to Higher and Technical Education, the dropout rates are even higher. This is particularly a serious problem for girls, who often have to travel long distances to attend Secondary School.

One of the serious fallouts of national and State entrance examinations

14. As documented by a series of reports titled 'Annual State of Education Reports (ASER)'.

for various Medical, Engineering and Management courses is the mushroom growth of tuition centres or teaching shops in the State capitals and other cities. Some private agencies have successfully converted tuition centres as residential tuition schools with due recognition with State and Central Educational Boards where tutors often address over 100 pupils through public address system gearing them for entrance examination. A small town of Kota in Rajasthan has become India's most successful haat for all sorts of entrance examinations. They market their services through reputed newspapers and other mass media. What is surprising is that instead of coming up with innovative ways to save the sanctity of the institution, some schools have now joined hands with their competitors, and the classes are often conducted under one roof.[15] Classrooms are rented out for tuitions.

Students from rural areas need a level-playing field to aspire and be successful in entrance examination. Therefore, extra coaching will have to be necessarily school-based as the bulk of students in government schools are poor and cannot afford exorbitant fees charged by the tuition centres. The credibility of educational institutions and the vital role and responsibility of teachers in shaping the country's future needs to be restored.

Curricular and examination reforms in Secondary Schooling also need to receive special attention especially aimed at fostering critical thinking and analytical skills, and preparing students for further education.

(B) Higher Education

The last decade has also seen a significant increase in the demand for Higher Education and this is expected to increase further as more children complete school and as high-quality jobs are mostly seen to require higher level qualifications. There are acute regional imbalances in access to Higher and Technical Education. Besides, Higher Education Institutions in India also suffer from problems of quality. Too many Indian universities are producing graduates in subjects that are not required or suited to the changing job market, and the quality also leaves much to be desired. The

15. Patricia Mascarenhas, 'The Great Indian Tuition and Coaching Industry', *Daily News & Analysis (DNA)*, Mumbai, 1 April 2014, https://www.dnaindia.com/academy/report-the-great-indian-tuition-and-coaching-industry-1973985

mismatch between the demand and supply is one of the reasons for a high rate of educated unemployment and underemployment in the country.

Policy on Higher Education would have to be driven by four 'E's—Expansion, Equity, Excellence and Employability. Of these, the third E 'Excellence' is the most difficult one to achieve. However, as Schreuder (2013) has emphasised:

> Taking advantage of the ICT explosion, new pedagogies and new modes of delivery are transforming the student experience as well as underpinning e-learning plus the shift to lifelong learning among age mature citizens. New vistas of knowledge and professional skills are opening up for individuals who previously could never have contemplated a university experience or graduate training. Forms of knowledge generation and knowledge transfer have been massively advanced. Exceptional basic research is currently being undertaken right across the spectrum of natural and human science—quite often in the new accelerator of research centers—while new ways have been created to connect laboratory research with commercial production through systems of innovation. Top-class universities are invariably research-intensive, nurture talents and have maintained high quality and outcomes without entirely losing their academic souls.[16]

Not even one Indian university figures in the latest list of the top 200 universities in the world (Times and Shanghai Ratings). This is symptomatic of a deeper malaise in India's Higher Education System whose quality and standards have been deteriorating. India cannot hope to be competitive in an increasingly knowledge-driven world unless Indian Higher Education Institutions achieve the global standards of excellence.

(C) Skill Development

A complete overhaul of the Vocational and Technical Education System is imperative. An ambitious Skill Development Mission was launched to skill at least 50 million individuals by the end of the Twelfth Plan

16. Deryck M. Schreuder (Ed.), *Universities for a New World,* The Association of Commonwealth Universities (New Delhi: Sage Publication, 2013).

(2017). Skill development programmes in the past were run mainly by the Government, with insufficient connection with market demand. To ensure that the skills match demand, special efforts are needed to ensure that employers and enterprises play an integral role in the conception and implementation of Vocational Training programmes, including managing Industrial Training Institutes (ITIs) and in the development of faculty. An enabling framework is needed that would attract private investment in Vocational Training through public-private partnership (PPP). Mobilising the required investment, setting up first-rate ITIs, ensuring efficiency in operations and management and enabling post-training employment should ideally be the primary responsibilities of private sector entities while the Government should provide the enabling framework and the requisite financial support especially in respect of SCs, STs, Minorities and Differently Abled Persons (Divyang) and other deprived sections of the society.

(D) Education, Skill Development and Demographic Dividend

The so-called 'Demographic Dividend' can add to India's economic growth potential through its impact on the supply of labour and on the rate of domestic savings (boosted through the falling dependency ratio). Moreover, a young population brings with it the aspirations and impatience of youth, which in turn can become strong drivers for bringing about change and innovation. Clearly, therefore, in order to reap the Demographic Dividend, India must ensure that younger citizens come into the labour force with higher levels of education and skills needed to support rapid growth.

In other words, even if there is a resurgence of economic growth, sustainability of the high growth trajectory would critically depend upon India's ability to leverage the Demographic Dividend. This would, in turn, be contingent on making the Education and Skill Development sectors robust, vibrant and forward-looking. Indeed, if India fails to harness this Demographic Dividend, not only will the country be squandering an opportunity that comes into the life of a nation only once, but India would also be facing a non-trivial risk of the Demographic Dividend becoming a demographic nightmare!

III. Organisational Structure of the Book

The broad outline drawn above lends itself to the following building blocks for the book:

- A detailed analysis of India's educational attainments and skill development status (Chapter 2).
- Analytical examination of the Demographic Dividend fortuitously said to be available to India for the next 10-15 years, say, up to the year 2030. In addition to the overall extent (i.e., the quantum) of the Demographic Dividend, its specific dimensions such as social and regional distribution are also examined (Chapter 3).
- A critical assessment of the current state of preparedness of the Education and Skill Development sector in India for harnessing and leveraging the Demographic Dividend in an inclusive and equitable manner (Chapter 3).
- Identification of gaps in terms of key indicators (such as Mean Years of Schooling, access, equity, quality, employability, etc.) which must be filled so as to fully harness and leverage the Demographic Dividend, quantitatively and qualitatively (Chapter 4).

Having assessed in detail the prevailing state of the Indian Education System, the attention is now focused on the Draft National Education Policy 2019.

First, the main proposals put forth in the Draft National Education Policy 2019 are summarized (Chapter 5).

Secondly, a comprehensive critical appraisal is presented in a constructive spirit (Chapter 6).

Finally, a programme of action – i.e., the way forward is proposed for the Indian Education System in 2020 and beyond.

A Postscript has been added on the National Education Policy, 2020. It draws a comparison of the content between the Draft NEP 2019 and the NEP 2020, and offers a critical appraisal of the additions, deletions and modifications therein.

Part One

2

India's Educational Attainments and Skill Development Status

It is widely recognized that education brings enormous benefits to any country by unlocking the creative potential of its people. In the contemporary world, therefore, educational attainment of a nation is considered as a good proxy for adjudging the socio-economic development of its population.

This chapter is devoted to an assessment of educational attainments and skill development status in India. It has been organised as follows: Section I examines the overall educational attainment in India in terms of the Mean Years of Schooling (MYS) and the underlying aggregate literacy rates. Against that background, Sections II, III, IV and V examine, in detail, the specific stages of education—Primary (including Upper Primary), Secondary (including Higher Secondary), Vocational Education and Tertiary Education (including Technical Education) in that order. While the first five sections of the chapter present a comprehensive assessment of the Indian Education System upto the year 2013-14, the final Section VI offers a perspective on the latest developments and policy issues under consideration by the Modi Government, to date.

I. India's Mean Years of Schooling: Temporal and Spatial Dimensions

There are several indicators to assess the educational attainments of any population such as literacy rates, Gross Enrolment Ratio (GER), Net Enrolment Ratio (NER), school attendance rates, pass percentages, the proportion of graduate population, etc. These are often meaningfully applied at various stages or levels of education to assess the educational status of a country. However, the MYS is regarded as the most comprehensive indicator of educational attainments as it covers all the three major stages of education, viz., Primary, Secondary and Tertiary Education. Not surprisingly, therefore, it has been appropriately inducted in the UNDP Human Development Index (HDI) replacing the earlier indicators such as adult literacy rates.

Mean Years of Schooling (MYS)

The pioneering work on Mean Years of Schooling (MYS) done by Barro and Lee[1] is well recognized globally. In simple terms, the average years of schooling of adults is defined as the years of formal schooling received or completed, on an average, by adults. The MYS is often related to the population in the '25 and over' age group as most people would have completed their educational pursuits by 25 years of age to enter the world of work.

The comprehensiveness of MYS has been so overwhelming that some institutions (e.g., Sachar Committee, National Family Health Survey [NFHS], National Human Development Report [HDR] 2013) have attempted to provide MYS estimates for '7+' age group where not even Primary Education could be expected to be completed at the lower end.

Barro–Lee found it appropriate to provide more realistic global estimates in their National Bureau of Economic Research (NBER) data

1. Robert J. Barro and Jong-Wha Lee, 'A New Data Set of Educational Attainment in the World, 1950-2010', *The National Bureau of Economic Research (NBER)*, Working Paper No. 15902, April 2010. Subsequently published in the *Journal of Development Economics*, vol. 104.

set for '15+' age group along with '25+' age group. Barro–Lee study has used Census data for their estimation. Since they provide historical data set, it is also comparable over time. UNDP utilised Barro–Lee estimates in Human Development Index (HDI) calculations. This book has adopted Barro–Lee's realistic approach and focused on estimating MYS for the '15+' age group.

The basic data sources for estimating MYS in India at the national and State levels are (a) Census, (b) National Sample Survey (NSS), (c) National Family Health Survey (NFHS) and (d) Socio-Economic and Castes Census (to the extent data are released). Although at the national level, the estimates of NSS and NHFS are robust, the same cannot be said about the State/UT level estimates which often suffer due to small sample errors, particularly in the Northeast region and smaller States/UTs. On the other hand, since Census is based on complete enumeration, national and State level estimates are apparently more reliable and the exercise could be extended to sub-State levels as well. The Census provides raw data on population by age structure as well as by the level of education with rural-urban, male-female criteria as per the standard nine-fold classification from which one could estimate MYS for the desired age groups. Similar data are available for various social and religious groups as well.

The NSS provides basic information of population by age structure and by the level of education with rural-urban, male-female classification in distributional form and sample estimates. Normally population estimates by Registrar General (RG) office or Expert Committee are applied adjusting for actual survey period (July–June). A common practice is to use NSS proportions on estimated Census population as NSS population estimates often tend to be lower than the estimates based on Census. In fact, NSSO urges data users to utilise Census population projections.

One could estimate MYS for the desired age groups (15+ or 25+) and also for labour force age groups (15 to 59 or 15 to 64). World Bank India has calculated MYS for '15+' age group (NSS 2007-08) and UNDP-India has done it for '25+' age groups for HDI (NSS 2004-05). We have also calculated MYS for 2007-08 for '15+' population and also for labour force (NSS 2007-08).

Analysing the impact of institutional reforms on educational attainments in 24 European countries, Michela Braga et al (2011)[2] show that reforms expanding the access to pre-Primary Education; the length of compulsory education; expansion of schools, colleges and universities; widening admission rules; and/or support through grant policies for constrained students had a positive impact on raising the MYS. Such inclusive policies were also associated with inequity reduction. These reforms impacted on the mean achievement by raising the bottom tail of the distribution.

The Indian Constitution (in Part IV on Directive Principles of State Policy) has provided for Elementary Education for all children in the age group of 6 to 14 years. However, the goal remained elusive for long and educational attainments suffered, partly due to the dominance of selective policy reforms that appeared to have more impact on the Higher Education sector. There was neither a firm commitment nor the will to implement inclusive policies adequately backed with resources. Moreover, resource constraints coupled with selective policies, which focussed on the upper tail of distribution apparently, created and sustained iniquitous educational attainments for the country.

Added to the woes, education remained a State subject for quite some time and the Central Government played only a marginal role in some key interventions promoting educational attainments for the masses till mid 1990s; the Government of India's contribution to Elementary Education was practically non-existent. As a matter of fact, the National Education Policy (1968) had detailed a comprehensive support system for those with low educational attainments, and these were mostly rural-based. A pragmatic scholarship regime was also suggested by Kothari Commission right from Upper Primary level to University levels. These policies were not pursued rigorously. Not surprisingly, this is reflected in India's MYS.

Table 2.1 provides data on the evolution of MYS (age group 15+) for India in the global context. Given the sizeable early entry to the workforce, age group '15+' is more relevant for developing countries.

As is evident from Table 2.1, India's MYS remained at abysmally low levels, less than three years before 1990, and with a significant male-female gender gap in educational attainments. The MYS improved gradually thereafter, while the gender gap continued to be at the same level.

2. Michela Braga, Daniele Checchi, and Elena Meschi , 'Institutional Reforms and Educational Attainment in Europe: A Long Run Perspective'. IZA Discussion Paper No. 6190, December 2011.

Table 2.1: MYS for Total Population and Female Population (age groups 15+) (No. of years)

Region/ Country	Educational Attainment of Total Population (aged 15 and over)					Educational Attainment of Female Population (aged 15 and over)				
Period	1970	1980	1990	2000	2010	1970	1980	1990	2000	2010
World (146)	4.45	5.29	6.09	6.98	7.76	3.86	4.70	5.58	6.47	7.28
Advanced Countries (24)	7.74	8.82	9.56	10.65	11.03	7.38	8.42	9.29	10.39	10.90
Developing Countries (122)	3.39	4.28	5.22	6.15	7.09	2.73	3.63	4.65	5.59	6.54
South Asia (7)	1.59	2.10	3.41	4.22	5.24	0.87	1.41	2.26	3.40	4.25
India	**1.57**	**2.34**	**3.45**	**4.20**	**5.12**	**0.83**	**1.37**	**2.25**	**3.03**	**4.07**
China	3.43	4.75	5.62	7.11	8.17	2.78	4.04	5.34	6.42	7.61
Indonesia	2.85	3.98	4.25	5.23	6.24	2.10	2.91	3.47	4.62	5.64
Thailand	3.63	4.40	5.41	6.11	7.50	3.14	4.00	5.18	5.84	7.34
Malaysia	4.17	5.69	6.97	9.09	10.14	2.96	4.80	6.55	8.72	9.92
Brazil	2.81	2.77	4.46	6.41	7.54	2.66	2.73	4.65	6.55	7.69

Source: R. Barro and J.W. Lee (2010) NBER, MA; India's MYS for 2000 and 2010 are based on the projected population of Census 1991.

The long-term trends in India's MYS together with international comparison given in Table 2.1 clearly shows India's poor performance not only in comparison with the advanced economies, but also with respect to developing countries as a group and individually vis-à-vis China, Indonesia, Thailand, Malaysia and Brazil.

Our estimates based on a subsequent Census, i.e., Census 2001, placed India's MYS at 4.44 for 15+ age group which was higher than Barro-Lee estimates of 4.20 for the year 2000. The Barro–Lee team had to project 1991 Census data, as Census 2001 data were not available to them. The World Bank (India) had carried out exercises of MYS based on NSS 2004-05 and placed India's MYS at 5.07 in 2004-05. The Planning Commission's estimate based on subsequent NSS Rounds of 2007-08 and 2009-10 placed India's MYS at 5.55 and 5.98 years, respectively.

Our own estimate of MYS, as per Census 2011, works out to 5.51, as shown in Table 2.2. Table 2.2 also provides our estimates of male-female and rural-urban breakdown of MYS based on Census 2011 (Cultural Tables released so far).

Table 2.2: All-India MYS, Census 2011

Classification	Persons	Male	Female
Rural	4.47	5.50	3.40
Urban	7.59	8.30	6.84
Rural + Urban	5.51	6.43	4.53

Source: Derived from Cultural Tables, Census 2011.

As is evident from Table 2.2, the rural-urban gap in MYS is over three years and that between male and female is around two years. The gender gap in MYS is higher in rural areas as compared to urban areas.

The MYS estimates for States and Union Territories estimated from Cultural Tables, Census 2011, for this book, are presented in Table 2.3. These estimates show that seven States/UTs have already achieved the Twelfth Plan target and eight other States/UTs have nearly achieved the targeted MYS of seven years. The lagging States which include Bihar, Jharkhand, Rajasthan and others are at the bottom where educational attainment has been painfully slow; a detailed analysis and explanations for this are provided elsewhere in the book.

The latest estimates based on NSS (2011-12) place India's MYS at 6.27 years. The Twelfth Five-Year Plan (2012-17) had envisaged achieving an MYS of eight years in the next 10 years, i.e., by 2021-22. This meant MYS should be close to seven years by the end of the Plan, i.e., 2016–17. Since the impact of Sarva Shiksha Abhiyan (SSA) was expected to fully reflect on '15+' age group only by 2015-16, in all probability the target of MYS of seven years by 2016-17 has been achieved.

In international comparisons, however, India's MYS has been low and it really does not augur well for a country trying to establish a knowledge society. There are several factors that affect educational attainments in India such as lack of access to education, widespread poverty and inequality in income and wealth, high dropouts, a large number of 'out-of-school children' (OoSC), high opportunity cost of education, low per capita public expenditure on education, social and gender discrimination and exceptionally large illiteracy, particularly among females, in a few States with large population.

As per NSS (2011-12), 46.6 per cent of Scheduled Castes (SC)

Table 2.3: MYS for 15+ Years Age Group, Census 2011

Sr. No.	States/ UTs	Rural			Urban			Rural + Urban		
		Persons	Male	Female	Persons	Male	Female	Persons	Male	Female
1	Andhra Pradesh	4.03	5.05	3.03	7.23	8.20	6.26	5.11	6.12	4.12
2	Arunachal Pradesh	4.17	5.00	3.28	7.51	8.31	6.57	4.99	5.84	4.05
3	Assam	4.38	4.96	3.77	7.92	8.47	7.34	4.94	5.52	4.34
4	Bihar	3.73	4.88	2.48	6.87	7.87	5.74	4.12	5.25	2.88
5	Chhattisgarh	3.94	5.02	2.88	7.41	8.33	6.46	4.80	5.85	3.75
6	Delhi	7.31	8.35	6.11	8.53	9.14	7.82	8.50	9.12	7.78
7	Goa	6.52	7.21	5.85	7.99	8.53	7.42	7.43	8.04	6.81
8	Gujarat	4.11	5.16	3.03	7.11	7.82	6.32	5.45	6.37	4.46
9	Haryana	5.57	6.79	4.23	8.26	8.98	7.46	6.54	7.58	5.38
10	HP	6.81	7.73	5.90	9.56	9.84	9.23	7.10	7.97	6.23
11	J&K	5.02	6.21	3.72	7.64	8.43	6.68	5.81	6.91	4.58
12	Jharkhand	3.63	4.83	2.38	7.63	8.64	6.51	4.68	5.86	3.44
13	Karnataka	4.48	5.43	3.53	7.98	8.71	7.23	5.86	6.73	4.97
14	Kerala	7.47	7.74	7.22	8.22	8.48	7.99	7.83	8.09	7.59
15	Madhya Pradesh	3.64	4.71	2.49	7.36	8.19	6.47	4.75	5.75	3.67
16	Maharashtra	5.02	6.07	3.94	8.04	8.66	7.36	6.42	7.29	5.50
17	Manipur	6.05	6.95	5.13	8.55	9.47	7.66	6.81	7.70	5.92
18	Meghalaya	3.44	3.61	3.27	7.96	8.26	7.66	4.49	4.68	4.30
19	Mizoram	4.50	5.01	3.96	7.76	8.11	7.42	6.29	6.69	5.89
20	Nagaland	5.07	5.57	4.55	7.76	8.08	7.41	5.89	6.35	5.40
21	Odisha	4.27	5.20	3.34	7.63	8.52	6.68	4.86	5.80	3.91
22	Punjab	5.61	6.15	5.03	8.12	8.47	7.73	6.56	7.04	6.04
23	Rajasthan	3.73	5.22	2.17	6.97	8.11	5.74	4.59	6.00	3.11
24	Sikkim	4.59	4.99	4.13	7.63	8.05	7.16	5.39	5.77	4.94
25	Tamil Nadu	5.48	6.40	4.57	7.89	8.61	7.18	6.66	7.48	5.85
26	Tripura	4.66	5.37	3.91	7.28	7.88	6.66	5.40	6.07	4.69
27	Uttarakhand	6.11	7.40	4.87	8.55	9.13	7.90	6.88	7.98	5.78
28	UP	4.67	5.92	3.32	6.97	7.62	6.24	5.22	6.33	4.01
29	West Bengal	4.02	4.69	3.31	6.99	7.57	6.38	5.02	5.66	4.35
30	Andaman and Nicobar	6.27	6.68	5.79	8.27	8.57	7.92	7.03	7.40	6.60
31	Chandigarh	7.18	7.74	6.29	8.96	9.36	8.46	8.91	9.32	8.41
32	Dadra and Nagar Haveli	3.64	4.79	2.23	7.88	8.45	6.98	5.74	6.71	4.39
33	Daman and Diu	5.82	6.74	4.73	7.29	7.65	6.56	6.96	7.47	6.02
34	Lakshadweep	6.25	6.78	5.67	6.79	7.57	5.96	6.68	7.40	5.90
35	Puducherry	6.94	7.95	5.98	8.53	9.37	7.74	8.03	8.92	7.19
	All India	4.47	5.50	3.40	7.59	8.30	6.84	5.51	6.43	4.53

Source: Computed from Cultural Tables, Census 2011.

households, 47.3 per cent of Scheduled Tribes (STs) households and 39.3 per cent of Other Backward Castes (OBCs) households in the rural areas did not have a single literate woman! The national average in this regard is 30.7 per cent. In other words, almost one-third of rural households did not have a single literate woman, which does not augur well for India's future.

Let us examine this exceptionally large illiteracy prevailing in India in some detail.

(A) Literacy Rates in India

Chart 2.1 depicts trends in literacy rates in the temporal context.

Census 2011 revealed that the number of literates has increased by 218 million as compared to that in 2001. During this decade, the number of illiterates has declined in absolute terms by 31 million. While female literacy increased at a faster rate (11.79 per cent) than that for males (6.88 per cent), there is still a big gender gap in literacy—about 17 percentage points.

The adult literacy rate in India has increased from 52.21 per cent in 1991 to 74.04 per cent in 2011 – nearly 22 percentage points increase in two decades. The increase in adult literacy rate for females (26.2

Chart 2.1: Trends in India's Literacy Rates and Gender Gaps, 1951–2011

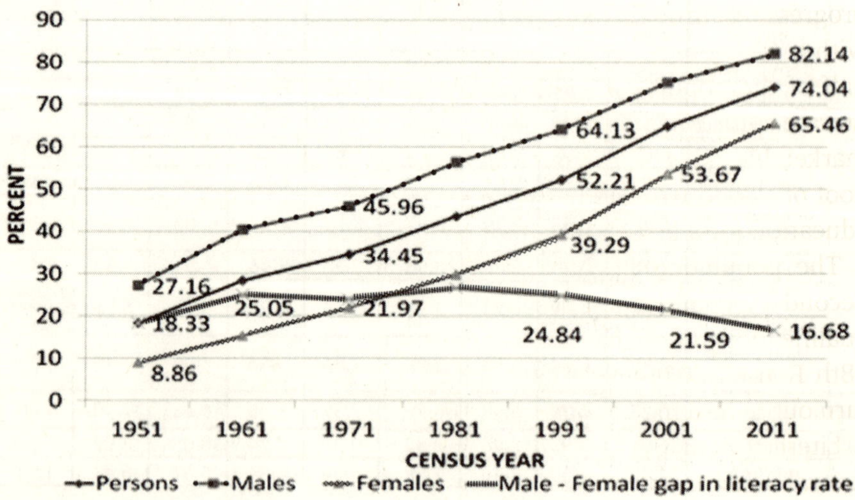

Chart 2.2: Distribution of Persons of Age Group 15+ Years, by the Level of Education

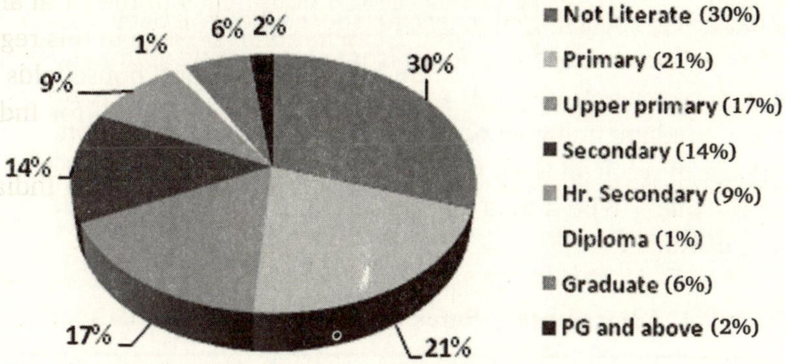

Source: National Sample Survey, 68th Round, 2011-12.

percentage points) has been significantly higher than that for males (18 percentage points) during the same period. Despite an impressive increase in overall adult literacy rate during the period 1991-2011, wide regional differentials persist.

Female literacy is a crucial determinant of school enrolments, retention and completion of basic education. Illiteracy combined with high Primary dropout rates and large OoSC seem to have resulted in high proportion (30 per cent) of 'no schooling' population as shown in Chart 2.2.

Although successive enrolment drives by the State Education Departments placed the children on school registers, they have not been progressing through the system satisfactorily. This has eroded the base with low school retention and transition rates. Consequently, more than half of the population in the country has remained illiterate and semi-literate with qualification up to Class V only, incapable of absorbing marketable skills other than traditional or family occupational skills. The pool of skilled workers has been seriously limited due to lack of general education for a large segment of population in the 15+ age group.

The population in the 15+ age group with Secondary and Higher Secondary qualification accounted for only 23 per cent and those with qualifications of degree and above was not more than 8 per cent (NSS, 68th Round, 2011-12). Thus, illiteracy and the lack of basic education turn out to be a major constraint for the Higher Education sector in India.

Literacy is at the heart of all human capabilities. As emphasised by several UN reports basic literacy is essential for eradicating poverty, reducing child mortality, curbing population growth, achieving gender equality and ensuring peace and sustainable development. Universal literacy has a very special significance for those who have been historically deprived of access to education. Apart from empowering youth and adults through a variety of educational programmes, achieving universal adult literacy is a fundamental goal of Adult and Continuing Education.

Estimates of adult literacy rates among Scheduled Castes (SCs) and Scheduled Tribes (STs) based on Census 2001 and Census 2011 are presented in Table 2.4.

Table 2.4: Adult Literacy Rates in Census 2001 and 2011 (%)

	2001		**2011**	
	SCs	**STs**	**SCs**	**STs**
Total	44.1	40.8	60.4	51.9
Male	59.3	54.8	71.6	63.7
Female	28.5	26.7	48.6	40.2

Source: Office of the Registrar General of India, Census 2001 and 2011

As can be seen from Table 2.4, the overall adult literacy rate for Scheduled Castes (SCs) improved from 44.1 per cent in 2001 to 60.4 per cent in 2011, remaining, however, much lower than the aggregate population. Notably, the gender gap among SCs narrowed from 30.8 percentage points in 2001 to 23 percentage points in 2011. Likewise, the overall adult literacy rate among Scheduled Tribes (STs) at 51.9 per cent in 2011 stood 11 percentage points higher than in 2001, but remained much lower than even Scheduled Castes (SCs). Here again, the gender gap narrowed from 28.1 per cent in 2001 to 23.5 per cent in 2011.

(B) Saakshar Bharat Scheme

Realising the importance of female literacy, the Government of India launched a Centrally Sponsored Scheme, Saakshar Bharat, in September 2009, with a prime focus on women and other disadvantaged groups in low literacy rural districts of various States/UTs. Through large-scale countrywide awareness building and mass mobilisation campaigns, voluntary teachers/*Preraks* have been motivated and trained in large numbers and community has been mobilised. The Twelfth Five-Year Plan (2012-17) aimed at raising the literacy rate to 80 per cent and reducing the gender gap to less than 10 percentage points.

It has been observed that at higher levels of literacy, the rate of growth of literacy tends to decelerate and greater efforts are required to reach the unattained. At the present stage of demographic transition, young adults, who are most vulnerable to the challenges of development with practically no marketable skills, obviously become the prime focus of the literacy programme. They are mostly in rural areas belonging to poor households with a high proportion of female illiteracy. Saakshar Bharat places a special emphasis on these young adults and 'out-of-school' adolescents with a paradigm shift from basic literacy to lifelong learning.

The National Literacy Mission under Saakshar Bharat envisages four broad objectives, viz.:

i. Imparting functional literacy and numeracy to non-literate and non-numerate adults;
ii. Enabling the neo-literate adults to continue their learning beyond basic literacy and acquire equivalency to formal educational system;
iii. Imparting relevant skills to non and neo-literates through Skill Development programmes to improve their earning and living conditions; and
iv. Promoting a learning society by providing opportunities to neo-literate adults for continuing education.

Accordingly, the programme has four principal components: (a) lifelong education, (b) basic education through equivalency to formal education system, (c) vocational skill development and (d) functional literacy. The programme targets about 410 districts which have low adult female literacy rate and includes districts affected by left wing extremism (LWE). In this regard, the Government of India had appropriately inducted the National Institute of Open Learning (NIOS) to undertake an assessment of basic competencies of neo-literates and to provide certification.

(C) MYS and Education System in India

India's low MYS is actually a pity. With over 14.5 lakh Elementary schools, 1.20 lakh Secondary and Higher Secondary schools, 700+ universities and 48,000+ colleges/institutions (2013-14 data), India's Education System is one of the largest in the world. The low MYS estimates reveal a very poor progression in various stages of educational system in the country despite impressive enrolments at the beginning of educational career of the pupils.

The Indian School Education System broadly comprises four stages: Primary, Upper Primary, Secondary and Higher Secondary. Five-Years of Primary Education and three years of Upper Primary Education constitute eight years of Elementary Education as stipulated in the Right to Education (RTE) Act 2009. Some States had four years of Primary Education and seven years of Elementary Education. The State Rules have been modified and all the 35 States/UTs have now aligned to the National Policy of eight years of Elementary Education. The national system of education envisages a 10+2 pattern of School Education. This pattern comprises two years of Secondary Education over eight years of Elementary Education and another two years of Higher Secondary Education. In some States, Higher Secondary Education continues with junior colleges linked with universities. Vocational Education has now become an integral part of Secondary Education removing the stigma attached to the former.

Tertiary Education covers the entire gamut of Higher, Technical and Professional Education. While the general education is governed by University Grants Commission (UGC) regulations, Technical, Medical, Nursing, Agriculture, Law etc. are governed by specific Councils. Moreover, there are some stand-alone institutions as well in the Higher Education sector that are not under the purview of UGC.

Table 2.5 depicts the vastness of the Indian Education System.

The new millennium ushered in an era of rapid development in the education sector and far-reaching changes have been affected in School as well as Higher, Technical and Professional Education in India. These included implementation of RTE Act; universalisation of Integrated Child Development Services (ICDS) and Early Childhood Care and Education (ECCE); secured funding for education through levying of 3 per cent cess; launching of pace-setting Model Schools in every block of the country; public-private partnerships in School as well as Higher and Technical Education; Aadhar-seeded direct benefit to students; expansion of Technical Education with new IITs, Indian Institutes of Information Technology (IIITs), Institutes for Scientific and Engineering Research (ISERs) and new School of Planning and Architecture (SPA) and IIMs. Other measures include setting up of Central Universities including

Table 2.5: Total Number of Educational Institutions and Enrolments (2013-14)

Stages	Sector	Institutions	Enrolments
SCHOOL EDUCATION		(Number)	(in million)
I. PRIMARY	a. Primary	8,58,916	132.40
	b. Upper Primary	5,89,796	66.50
	Total Elementary* (a +b)	14,48,712	198.90
II. SECONDARY	Secondary	1,31,287	37.30
	Higher Secondary	1,02,588	22.31
UNIVERSITY AND HIGHER EDUCATION			
III. TERTIARY	1. Universities	712	29.63
	2. Colleges	36,671	
	3. Others (Dip. in Tech Edu., PGDM, Nursing, etc.)	11,445	

Source: Educational Statistics at a Glance 2013-14 and Unified District Information on School Education (U-DISE) 2013-14 (Provisional).

Innovation Universities in the States; launching of 374 Model Colleges in low GER districts, now a part of the comprehensive Rashtriya Uchchatar Shiksha Abhiyan (RUSA); expansion of intake in medical colleges and setting up of new AIIMS in selected States; setting up of National Knowledge Commission (NKC) and tabling of several legislations in the Parliament to revamp the Tertiary Education. A large number of Education Bills are pending approval of the Parliament.

The current education and skill development status in the country, operational strategy and newer policies including reforms agenda for various stages of education—Primary (including Upper Primary), Secondary Education, Vocational Education and Higher as well as Technical Education are discussed in detail in the next four sections, in that order.

II. Elementary Education

Article 45 of the Indian Constitution in the Directive Principles of State Policy originally envisaged the State to endeavour to provide free and compulsory education to all children until they complete the age of

14 years within a period of 10 years from the commencement of the Constitution.

Some determined efforts were made since the Independence to achieve this goal and the National Policy on Education (1986) gave an unqualified priority to universalisation of Elementary Education. Yet, the goal remained unattained for decades for many reasons including resource constraints with the State governments. Education was in the State List and only a few States in the southern and western regions could take initiatives for universalisation of Elementary Education while the rest of the country made very little progress towards achieving the Constitutional Directive.

The Constitution was amended in 1976 to change education from a State subject to the Concurrent List, which implied that the responsibility for the development of education was now to be shared by both the Central and State Governments. The National Policy on Education (NPE) 1986 specifically highlighted some gross inadequacies in providing compulsory education to the children as envisaged in the Constitution and the Five Year Plans. The NPE 1986 identified unattractive school environment, unsatisfactory conditions of the buildings and insufficiency of instructional material as some of the major demotivating factors for children and their parents.

Accordingly, the Government of India, which was hitherto confined to running Central Schools to cater to the educational needs of wards of its employees and setting up premier institutions in Higher and Technical Education, launched several Centrally Sponsored Schemes such as Operation Blackboard, District Primary Education Programme (DPEP), Lok Jumbish Pariyojana, Shiksha Karmi, Teacher Education Programme, Mid-Day Meal Programme and National Literacy Mission. When DPEP (funded by World Bank) was coming to an end with the third phase, a comprehensive scheme, Sarva Shiksha Abhiyan (SSA), was launched (2001-02) in partnership with the States for universalisation of elementary education in the country. While the international development partners chipped in with some financial assistance, it was the Government of India that provided the lion's share for the implementation of SSA and continues to do so.

(A) Sarva Shiksha Abhiyan

The Constitution (Eighty-Sixth Amendment) Act, 2002 inserted Article 21-A in the Constitution of India to provide free and compulsory education for all children in the age group of 6 to 14 years as a Fundamental Right. A commitment to the provision of early childhood care and education to children below the age of six years was reiterated. The Act, 2002, also envisaged substitution of a new Article for Article 45. The substituted Article 45 stated: 'The State shall endeavour to provide early childhood care and education for all children until they complete the age of six years.' With the notification of 'Right of Children to Free and Compulsory Education Act 2009' (RTE) for implementation with effect from 1 April 2010, as per the 86th Amendment to the Constitution of India, SSA has been harmonised to meet the RTE Act mandate.

The SSA is Government of India's principal programme for universalising Elementary Education in the country. SSA covers about 200 million children in 1.45 million schools across 1.3 million habitations. The main features of RTE-harmonised SSA are summarised in Box 2.1. Some of the major activities of SSA include provision of educational infrastructure—new schools, construction of school buildings, appointment of teachers, teacher training and child entitlements such as the supply of textbooks, uniforms, etc.

SSA also provided for recruitment of additional teachers for the existing schools with inadequate teaching staff, strengthening of capacity of the existing teachers through extensive pre-service, and in-service teacher training, training grants for developing teaching learning materials (TLM) and strengthening of the academic support structure at cluster, block and district levels. SSA has sanctioned 19.84 lakh additional teachers and teacher training covered about 18.6 lakh teachers annually.

SSA seeks to provide good quality Elementary Education including life skills and has a special focus on girls' education and that of children with special needs. It has merged the components of National Programme for Education of Girls to Elementary Level (NPEGEL) and the residential school scheme for girls, Kasturba Gandhi Balika Vidyalaya (KGBV). About 3.6 lakh girls are studying in Classes VI to VIII in over 3600 KGBVs in the educationally backward blocks (EBBs). SSA promotes computer education to bridge the digital divide. SSA addresses access, equity and quality aspects of Elementary Education through a systems approach

Box 2.1: Sarva Shiksha Abhiyan (SSA) Goals

- All children in the 6 to 14 years age groups in school
- Bridging gender and social gaps
- All children retained in Elementary Education
- Elementary Education of satisfactory quality

Coverage: SSA is implemented in all schools except private unaided schools. Even private unaided schools have an obligation of admitting 25 per cent children belonging to disadvantaged groups and hence the coverage of SSA is universal.

Funding Pattern: SSA is implemented with the States/UTs with fund sharing arrangement of 65:35 between the Government of India and the normal States and 90:10 ratio for North Eastern States including Sikkim.

Allocation: The Central allocation for SSA in the Eleventh Five-Year Plan (2007–12) was Rs 710 billion. As against this, the Central Government release amounted to Rs 77,586 crore. The projected outlay for the Twelfth Plan (2012–17) was Rs 1,92,726 crore.

Activities:

- Provides for opening of new schools in habitations not having access to schooling facilities
- Residential schools for girls and strengthening existing school infrastructure with additional classrooms, toilets, drinking water, ramps, library, computers, etc.
- Providing various grants for school maintenance and development.

Source: MHRD and Planning Commission

with the perspective of rights regarding children's entitlements. SSA's Special Focus Districts (SFDs) targets 61 districts with high Scheduled Caste (SCs) population, 109 districts with high Scheduled Tribes (STs) population and 88 districts with high proportion of Muslim Minorities.

The number of Primary schools increased at an annual rate of 2.32 per cent and that for Upper Primary, at an accelerated rate of 9.59 per cent per annum between 2000-01 and 2013-14. There has been a significant improvement in the school infrastructure with the sanctioning of 2.1 lakh new Primary schools, 1.74 lakh new Upper Primary schools, 2.97 lakh new school buildings and 18 lakh additional classrooms, 7.44 lakh toilets and 2.24 drinking water supply works during this period. These have

Chart 2.3: Structure of SSA Expenditure

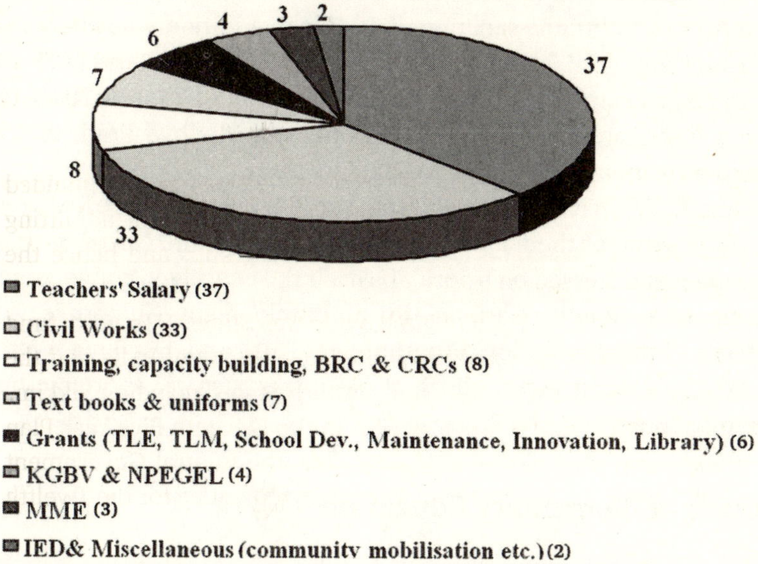

made a big dent in reducing the school infrastructure gap in the country.

The structure of SSA expenditure given in the pie chart, Chart 2.3, shows that a bulk of the expenditure is on school infrastructure and teachers.

The relaxation of ceiling for civil works from 33 per cent in respect of educationally fragile districts/States has accelerated the process of closing the infrastructure gap further. With it accessibility for Upper Primary schools has vastly improved contributing to accelerated enrolments, particularly for girls. However, there are still gaps in school infrastructure as about 3 per cent of the Primary schools and 2.4 per cent Upper Primary schools did not have all-weather buildings. About 15 per cent of schools lack girls' toilet and 5 per cent of schools lack drinking water facilities. About 18 per cent schools lacked ramps, 25 per cent kitchen sheds, 38 per cent boundary walls and 42 per cent playgrounds.[3]

SSA has posted credible performance in terms of access, enrolments and has greatly reduced gender and social gaps. Access to Primary Education (<1 km) increased from 87 per cent to 99 per cent and that for Upper

3. MHRD, Government of India, 'Fourth Year Right of Children to Free and Compulsory Education Act Report,' 2015.

Primary (<3 km), from 78 per cent to 95 per cent. About 93 per cent of the slum children had access to neighbourhood schools within 1 km from their homes.[4] With the sanction of 19.7 lakh additional teachers and actual recruitment of 12.5 lakh teachers, the Pupil-Teacher Ratio (PTR) at Primary stage has come down from 46:1 in 2004-05 to 31:1 in 2010-11. However, a few States like Bihar, Jharkhand and Madhya Pradesh still have a high PTR, much above the national average.

The residual gaps in RTE norms and standards of infrastructure facilities, particularly in some of the major States like Bihar, UP and North-Eastern States, are being addressed on priority basis. If the envisaged convergence of the Mahatma Gandhi National Rural Employment Guarantee Act (MGNREGA), Total Sanitation Programme (TSP) and Drinking Water Supply (DWS) Mission materialises, these infrastructural shortcomings would be overcome.[5]

(B) Growth of Elementary Education

The total number of Primary schools (schools with only Primary section) increased by 34.5 per cent from 6.39 lakh in 2000-01 to 8.59 lakh in 2013-14. During the same period, the total number of schools imparting Upper Primary Education increased by 185.9 per cent (from 2.06 lakh to 5.90 lakh). The total number of schools imparting Elementary Education (schools with Primary or Upper Primary sections, and Secondary/Higher Secondary schools with Primary and/or Upper Primary section) increased by 71.4 per cent from 8.45 lakh to 14.5 lakh schools for the corresponding period (Table 2.6). The total number of government and government-aided schools is estimated at 11.2 lakh accounting for four-fifth of the total Elementary schools in the country. The remaining 20 per cent schools with the private sector are mostly in urban areas. It may be noted, however, that since 2004-05 private schools are coming up in the rural areas at an accelerated pace.

Between 2000-01 and 2013-14, enrolment in Primary Education increased steadily up to 2010-11 and then showed a declining trend. The enrolment in Primary Education reached its highest level in 2011-

4. Planning Commission, Programme Evaluation Organisation (PEO), 'Study on SSA, 2010'.

5. Ibid.

Table 2.6: Growth of Elementary Educational Institutions, 2000-01 to 2013-14

Year	Primary Schools	Upper Primary Schools	Elementary Schools
2000-01	6,38,738	2,06,269	8,45,007
2005-06	7,72,568	2,88,493	10,61,061
2010-11	8,27,244	5,35,080	13,62,324
2011-12	8,42,481	5,69,697	14,12,178
2012-13	8,53,870	5,77,832	14,31,702
2013-14	8,58,916	5,89,796	14,48,712
CGR % pa	2.32	9.59	4.63

Source: MHRD.

CGR (Compound growth rate) per annum based on own calculations.

12 (137.1 million) and then declined to 134.8 million in 2012-13 and further down to 132.4 million in 2013-14. Between 2011-12 and 2013-14, the total enrolment in Primary Education came down by 4.7 million, wherein the enrolment of girls and boys declined by 2.5 million and 2.2 million, respectively.

While the child population for the relevant age groups showed a decline by about 5.5 million during the decade ending 2011, and the decline in enrolment to an extent is attributable to demographic changes, it is also a fact that the Integrated Child Development Services (ICDS) and Early Childhood Care and Education (ECCE) have been taking away a significant portion of underage enrolments in Primary schools. Private schools imparting Primary Education invariably have pre-Primary Education for two or three years of kindergarten prior to inducting in the Primary classes. A significant proportion of RTE children are reported to have been admitted in these schools who would have otherwise been enrolled in government or local body schools. This phenomenon is partly reflected in the decline in Primary enrolments but captured in improvements in age-specific Net Enrolment Ratios (NERs) and reduction in Gross Enrolment Ratios (GERs), as explained below.

Growth of enrolment in Elementary Education classified by gender and social categories, during the period 2000-01 through 2013-14, is presented in Table 2.7.

Considering the full period of implementation of SSA up to 2013–14, the performance in access and enrolment in Elementary Education has been remarkable. As can be seen from Table 2.7, the incremental enrolment in Elementary Education between 2000–01 and 2013–14 has been as much as 42.3 million, of which increment in girls' enrolment accounted for 28.8 million or as much as 68 per cent. This has virtually eliminated the gender gap in Primary and Upper Primary enrolment since 2011-12.

Table 2.7: Growth of Enrolment in Elementary Education by Social and Gender Classification (2000-01 to 2013-14) (in million)

	Scheduled Tribes			Scheduled Castes			Others			All Categories		
Year	Boys	Girls	Total	Boys	Girls	Total	Boys	Girls	Total	Boys	Girls	Total
2000-01	8.2	5.9	14.1	16.2	11.7	27.9	64.9	49.7	114.6	89.3	67.3	156.6
2001-02	8.8	6.3	15.1	16.9	12.2	29.1	64.0	50.5	114.5	89.7	69.0	158.7
2002-03	8.3	6.7	15.0	16.3	12.8	29.1	66.8	58.4	125.2	91.4	77.9	169.3
2003-04	8.9	7.2	16.1	17.5	13.6	31.1	69.3	60.6	129.9	95.7	81.4	177.1
2004-05	9.8	8.2	17.9	18.9	14.6	33.4	69.6	61.1	130.6	98.2	83.8	182.0
2005-06	10.0	8.6	18.7	19.3	15.1	34.4	70.1	61.2	131.2	99.4	84.9	184.3
2006-07	10.2	8.8	19.1	19.9	15.8	35.7	70.6	62.5	133.1	100.8	87.1	187.9
2007-08	10.3	9.2	19.5	19.0	17.2	36.2	72.9	64.4	137.3	102.2	90.8	193.0
2008-09	10.7	9.6	20.3	19.4	17.6	37.0	69.4	63.3	132.7	99.5	90.5	190.0
2009-10	10.6	9.6	20.3	19.6	17.8	37.4	72.5	65.0	137.5	102.7	92.4	195.1
2010-11	10.8	10.2	21.0	20.2	18.7	38.9	72.3	65.2	137.5	103.3	94.1	197.4
2011-12	11.2	10.6	21.7	20.3	19.1	39.4	71.2	66.8	137.9	102.6	96.4	199.0
2012-13	10.9	10.4	21.3	20.3	19.2	39.5	71.6	67.3	138.9	102.8	96.9	199.7
2013-14	10.8	10.2	21.0	20.1	18.9	39.0	71.9	67.0	138.9	102.8	96.1	198.9

Source: MHRD, Educational Statistics, various issues.

Table 2.8: GER in Primary, Upper Primary and Elementary Education (2000-01 to 2013-14)

Year	Primary (Classes I-V)			Up. Primary (Classes VI-VIII)			Elementary (Classes I-VIII)			Gender gap in GERs		
	Boys	Girls	Total	Boys	Girls	Total	Boys	Girls	Total	PS	UPS	EE
2000-01	104.9	85.9	95.7	66.7	49.9	58.6	90.3	72.4	81.6	19.0	16.8	17.9
2005-06	112.8	105.8	109.4	75.2	66.4	71.0	98.5	91.0	94.9	7.0	8.8	7.5
2010-11	115.4	116.7	116.0	87.7	83.1	85.5	104.9	103.7	104.3	-1.3	4.6	1.2
2011-12	106.8	109.3	108.0	72.9	76.3	74.5	93.3	96.3	94.7	-2.5	-3.4	-3.0
2012-13	104.8	107.2	106.0	80.6	84.6	82.5	95.6	98.6	97.0	-2.4	-4.0	-3.0
2013-14	100.2	102.7	101.4	86.3	92.8	89.3	95.1	99.1	97.0	-2.5	-6.5	-4.0

Source: Statistics of School Education, 2007-08, MHRD, Government of India; Educational Statistics at a Glance, 2011, MHRD, Government of India; Statistics of School Education, 2011-12, MHRD & U-DISE.

(i) Gross and Net Enrolment Ratios

Gross Enrolment Ratio[6] (GER) for Primary, Upper Primary and overall Elementary Education for the period 2000-01 through 2013-14 are provided in Table 2.8.

The GER for Primary Education which was 95.7 per cent in 2000-01 has been consistently more than 100 per cent, even for girls since 2005-06 and that for Elementary Education it increased from 81.6 per cent in 2000-01 to 104 per cent in 2010-11, but subsequently, declined to under 100 per cent. A GER more than 100 per cent reflected underage-overage enrolments, partly due to delayed access, lack of pre-Primary Education and on account of high repetitions.

The Net Enrolment Ratio[7] (NER) for Primary Education has increased from 84 per cent in 2005-06 to 88.08 per cent in 2013-14. The NER was higher for girls (89.26 per cent) than that for boys (87.2 per cent) in 2013-14. The age-specific enrolment ratio for children of age 6 to 10 years was 93.11 per cent for the year 2013-14. Annual Status of Education Report

6. Gross Enrolment Ratio (GER) is the total enrolment in a specific level of education, regardless of age, expressed as a percentage of the population in the official age group corresponding to that level of education.

7. Net Enrolment Ratio (NER) refers to the enrolment of the official age group for a given level of education expressed as a percentage of the corresponding population.

(ASER) also reported higher NER for girls (94.36 per cent) than that for boys (91.97 per cent).

As can be seen from Table 2.8, the gender gaps in GER at Primary and Upper Primary levels of education in 2000-01 were 19 and 16.8 percentage points, respectively. The gaps were eliminated over time and in the year 2013-14, the GER for girls were uniformly higher than that for boys. Another remarkable feature is the incremental enrolment in Elementary Education accounting for an overwhelming majority of children belonging to disadvantaged social groups, bridging social and gender gaps which is discussed elsewhere in this book (i.e., in Chapter 4).

It may be noted, however, that the progress on one of the prime goals of the SSA, i.e., to achieve universal retention by enabling children enrolled in Class I to complete eight years of Elementary Education has met with only a limited success despite substantial investment in infrastructure, enhanced teacher availability, massive Mid-Day Meal Scheme (MDMS) and increased community participation.

(ii) Dropout Rates

As can be seen from Table 2.9, the Primary dropout rates declined from 41 per cent in 2000-01 to 20 per cent in 2013-14 and that at Elementary level

Table 2.9: Dropout Rates in Primary and Elementary Education (%)

Year	Classes I–V			Classes I–VII		
	Boys	Girls	All	Boys	Girls	All
2000-01	39.7	41.9	40.7	50.3	57.7	53.7
2005-06	28.7	21.8	25.7	48.7	49	48.8
2006-07	24.6	26.8	25.6	46.4	45.2	45.9
2007-08	25.7	24.4	25.1	43.7	41.3	42.7
2008-09	29.6	25.8	27.8	41.1	36.9	39.3
2009-10	31.8	28.5	30.3	41.1	44.2	42.5
2010-11	29.0	25.4	27.4	40.6	41.2	40.8
2011-12	23.4	21.0	22.3	41.5	40.0	40.8
2012-13(P)	23.0	19.4	21.3	41.8	35.7	39.0
2013-14(P)	21.2	18.3	19.8	39.2	32.9	36.3

Source: Educational Statistics at a Glance, 2014, MHRD.

the corresponding rates were 54 per cent and 36 per cent respectively. The first half of the new Millennium decade showed a significant decline in Primary dropout rates. It declined by about 15 percentage points but in the second half it started rising. During the subsequent years, there has been a steady decline again. It may also be noted that although the Primary dropouts declined substantially during the first half of the last decade, the improvement was quite subdued at the Elementary level. The only redeeming feature was that the girls' dropout rates declined at much faster rate than that for boys. The dropout rates for both boys and girls continue to remain at unacceptably high levels.

(iii) Overall Impact of SSA

SSA has brought Primary Education to the doorsteps of villagers. India's progress in Primary Education has been universally hailed as a paradigm shift from hitherto piecemeal attempts through programmes like Operation Blackboard, Lok Jumbish, Shiksha Karmi and DPEP. Now, an overwhelming majority of children are attending schools.[8] The Millennium Development Goal (MDG) of universalisation of primary education by 2015 has already been achieved and the gender gap in Primary Education stands eliminated. The Joint Review Mission of international development partners on SSA has appreciated the efforts taken to increase the overall GER levels at Primary Education.[9]

Reaching the unreached against the odds of social and cultural discrimination has been yet another credible accomplishment of SSA. The rapid expansion in Primary schooling in India over the past decade has brought into the educational system many children from the marginalised strata of society. It has been noted that the share of socially disadvantaged groups in school enrolment was 32 per cent in rural and 30 per cent in urban areas, much higher than their share of population.[10] The number of out-of-school children (OoSC), placed at 32 million a decade ago, has come down to 8.1 million in 2009 and the States have reported further reduction to 2.94 million in 2011-12.

A subsequent Sample Survey—NSS of Estimation of Out-of-School

8. MHRD, Government of India, 'Sarva Shiksha Abhiyan (SSA): Seventeenth Joint Review Mission', Aide Memoire, 2013.

9. Ibid.

10. Planning Commission, Programme Evaluation Organisation (PEO), 'Study on SSA, 2010'.

Children 2014 (SRI-2014)—had brought out that at the national level, as against an estimated 20.41 crore children in the age group of 6-13 years, about 6.06 million children were out of school, accounting for 2.97 per cent of the child population. This proportion is considerably lower than that in 2005 (6.94 per cent) and 2009 (4.53 per cent). With RTE Act in force, the percentage of OoSC has declined across the States. It may be noted, however, that UP, Bihar and Rajasthan accounted for nearly 60 per cent of the total OoSC in the country calling for urgent action.

According to the same Sample Survey, the proportion of OoSC in the age group 11 to 13 years at 3.28 per cent was higher than that in 6 to 10 age group (2.77 per cent). Notably, the OoSC in the rural areas was higher at 3.13 per cent (4.7 million) as compared to that in the urban areas at 2.54 per cent (1.4 million). The Survey revealed that the number of OoSC has actually increased in urban areas from 1.13 million in 2009, which is a cause for concern. A gender composition of OoSC indicated 31.66 lakh boys and 28.98 lakh girls as out of school. In terms of proportions, out of school boys accounted for 2.77 per cent and out of school girls, 3.23 per cent. Thus, despite elimination of gender gaps in GER, a higher proportion of girls is still out of school in the 6 to 13 years age group. Both push and pull factors adversely affect the enrolment of school girls. Lack of girls' toilet in schools hinders their enrolment in Upper Primary schools. In certain regions, access is also a problem.

The percentage of OoSC was highest among Muslim children (4.43 per cent) indicating cultural factors also need to be overcome. Opportunity costs and sibling care were found to be the principal reasons for children not attending schools (NSS, 2009-10). Notably, as against an estimated 21.4 lakh Children with Special Needs (CWSN) (1.05 per cent) in the age group of 6 to 13 years, 5.9 lakh children or 28.23 per cent were out of school.

Sarva Shiksha Abhiyan through its successive enrolment drives and campaigns has brought about a tremendous awareness, particularly in the rural areas, about the importance and utility of basic school education. This in turn has also induced private investments in education even in the rural areas. The number of private unaided schools has increased and accounted for 17 per cent of the total Elementary schools in the country.[11]

The overall transition rate from Primary to Upper Primary level has

11. District Information System for Education (DISE, 2011-12).

increased impressively from 81 per cent in 2004-05 to 88 per cent in 2013-14. With the transition rate from Primary to Upper Primary levels for girls going up from 80 per cent to 90 per cent, SSA has already set a stage for Universalisation of Secondary Education (USE) and the demand for Secondary schools have increased tremendously in the rural areas.

High proportion of population lacking basic education even up to Primary level, or 'no schooling' population, obviously drags down the estimate of MYS. India's 'no schooling' population in the 15+ age group as per NSS estimate was 42.6 per cent in 2004-05. This came down to 34.5 per cent in 2007-08 and further to 30.2 per cent in 2011-12, the credit for which mainly goes to SSA. This 12 percentage points decline in the 'no schooling' population in conjunction with the accelerated growth of Secondary Education, had greatly helped in raising India's MYS from a measly level of 4.94 in 2004-05 to 6.28 in 2011-12. Had the school retention at Elementary Education improved significantly, India's MYS should have been averaging on par with that of developing countries (7.09 years). The Twelfth Plan had aimed to achieve this by 2016-17. India's MYS is expected go well past that of the average for developing countries when the full impact of SSA on 15+ age group of the population unfolds.

Another positive development is the decline in the number of child labour which was around 12 million in the 1980s and 1990s. It had halved to less than 5.3 million in 2009-10 (NSS, 66th Round) and a significant proportion of even those working children are covered under National Child Labour Projects supported by SSA. Studies show that rural households were withdrawing working children and adolescents of school-going age from workforce and sending them to schools. The implementation of MDMS has also played an effective supplementary role in increasing school enrolments and retention.[12] However, the Elementary dropout rates still remain unacceptably high; children are not yet seamlessly progressing through the education system. Accordingly, school retention needs considerable improvement.

With the sanction of about 2 million additional teachers, SSA has made a serious attempt to bring about a significant improvement on outcomes in terms of quality of education. There has been a modest improvement

12. Amartya Sen, 'The Importance of Basic Education', Speech given in Commonwealth Education Conference, Edinburg, UK, 28 October 2003. Also, Aparajita Goyal and Jean Dreze, 'Future of Mid-Day Meals', *Economic and Political Weekly (EPW),* vol. 38, issue no. 44, 1 November 2003.

in learning achievement of children by about 2 to 3 percentage points as per NCERT surveys. About half of the States have adopted Continuous and Comprehensive Evaluation System (CCES) in schools. The teacher training programmes have a special focus on improved classroom practices and child-centric processes including activity-based learning methods. Nevertheless, substantial efforts are required to continue teacher recruitment and capacity building under SSA. Learning outcomes need to be specifically targeted and accountability of teachers imparting education in publicly funded schools ensured. The unfinished agenda of raising the quality and standards of education was, therefore, the prime focus of the Twelfth Five-Year Plan (2012–17) and strategies have been evolved to provide specific cognitive skills expected of children in various stages of education, appointment of quality teachers through Teacher Eligibility Tests (TET), revamping governance system and professional cadre management of schools for quality outcomes.

The overarching goal of the Twelfth Five-Year Plan was to improve learning outcomes across the Elementary school years. To achieve this objective, there is a need for a system-wide effort to move the focus of all activity in Elementary Education from schooling to learning. This entails a shift at every level, macro and micro, whether in planning, resource allocation and implementation or measurement to processes and practices that are designed to achieve significant, substantial and continuous improvement in children's learning outcomes.

A shift from a decade-long project-based approach of SSA to a unified RTE-based governance system for universalisation of elementary education needs to be firmly established. Simultaneously, residual access and equity gaps in Elementary Education need to be addressed by adopting special measures to ensure regular attendance of children in schools and devising community-involved special strategy to tackle the problem of dropping out before completing the full cycle of Elementary schooling.

It is also essential to integrate pre-School Education with Primary schooling in order to lay a strong foundation for learning during Primary school. Focus on early-grade supplemental instruction is needed to ensure that all children achieve the defined age/class specific learning levels by the end of Class II. Clear learning goals that have to be achieved by the end of each class or set of classes should be articulated, explained to the parents and fully understood by the teachers.

There is a need to provide professionally qualified, trained, motivated competent teachers as per norms, recruited through mandatory Teacher Eligibility Test. Re-employment of quality teachers, particularly females, for Math, Science and English on contractual basis should be seriously considered up to the age of 65 years. Quality education is not a cost-less process and hence there is a need to invest in both top-down administrative oversight and bottom-up community-driven monitoring of schools including social audit. Improving teacher training with an emphasis on effective pedagogy, given the realities of Indian classrooms such as multi-age, multi-grade and multi-level contexts, is very important.

The RTE Act recognized the positive role for private sector and mandated certain social responsibility with regard to admission of 25 per cent of the seats to the disadvantaged groups in the neighbourhood. Several States/UTs have reported such mandatory admissions. Monitoring of RTE Act enrolments and reimbursement of fee to the schools are not yet satisfactorily handled in many States. A welcome development is the increased social awareness of this and NGOs are taking up the issues with States and the Central Government besides seeking legal remedies.

Effective implementation of this provision would not only open up opportunities for more and more public-private partnerships and enhanced parental choice but also underscore the imperatives of consolidation for better utilisation of available infrastructure facilities through resource mapping and leveraging private and non-governmental expertise and resources to improve the quality of education right from pre-Primary levels.

(C) Mid-Day Meal in Schools (MDMS)

In keeping with the constitutional provisions to raise the level of nutrition of children and enable them to develop in a healthy manner, the National Programme of Nutritional Support to Primary Education (NP-NSPE), commonly referred to as MDMS, was launched as a Centrally Sponsored Scheme in 1995.

MDMS was launched in 2,408 blocks as a dry ration scheme for Primary school children. In September 2004, the Scheme was universalised at the Primary level with hot-cooked meals. In 2008-09, the scheme was extended up to the Elementary level to cover all children in the government, local body, government-aided schools, Education Guarantee Scheme (EGS) and Alternative and Innovative Education (AIE) Centres,

Box 2.2: Status of Implementation of RTE Act, 2009 in 2015

- State Rules under RTE Act notified in 34 out of 35 State/UTs.
- All States/UTs have notified eight years Elementary cycle including 12 States which had seven years cycle.
- Thirty-four States/UTs have constituted School Management Committees (SMCs) and notified their roles and responsibilities and 91 per cent of schools have SMC.
- Decentralised grievance redressal mechanism has been constituted with the setting up of State Commission for the Protection of Child Rights (SCPCR) or Right to Education Protection Authority (REPA) in 33 States/UTs.
- No detention and no corporal punishments in Eementary Education notified in all State/UTs. Norms of 25 per cent admission in private schools at entry level has been notified by 27 States/ UTs.
- Thirty States/UTs have modules for Continuous and Comprehensive Evaluation (CCE) implementation in place, rest in process.
- Pupil-Teacher Ratio (PTR) in 2011-12 was 1:26 and professionally qualified teachers account for 80 per cent.
- Thirty-three States have completed revision of curriculum aligning it with NCF, 2005, and 25 States conducted Teacher Eligibility Test for recruitments.

Source: MHRD, 4th Year of Implementation of RTE Act (2015).

National Child Labour Projects (NLCP) schools, *Madrasas* and *Maktabs* supported under SSA.

The MDMS is now the world's largest school feeding programme, reaching out to about 100 million children in over 1.265 million schools/ EGS centres across the country.

MDMS is being implemented under various State-level arrangements such as SSA Society, Social Welfare Department and Panchayat Raj Department. In the metros and other cities, centralised cooking arrangements are made through NGOs. In non-centralised cooking 7arrangements, a wide variety of arrangements have been established such as involvement of Self-Help Groups (SHGs), Mahila Samakhya Sahyoginis, Mata Samitis, and Bhojan Matas. The hot-cooked meals for children are based on calorie requirements. Details of ingredients used and convergence with the Ministry of Health and Family Welfare can be

Box 2.3: Salient Features of MDMS

- MDM is being implemented in partnership with the States.
- The Government of India supplies food grains (wheat and rice @ 100 grams per child per school day for primary and @ 150 grams per child per school day for Upper Primary from the nearest Food Corporation of India (FCI) godown.
- The Government of India also provides transport assistance at par with Public Distribution System (PDS) rates prevalent in Special Category States and in all other States at the actual cost basis subject to ceiling of Rs 75 per quintal.
- The cooking cost is shared between the Centre and the States in the ratio of 75:25 (Special Category States 90:10).
- The assistance for procurement of kitchen devices is provided at an average cost of Rs 5000 per school.
- Besides, honorarium @ Rs 1,000 is provided to cook-cum-helper (one cook-cum-helper for 25 children; two cooks for 26 to 100 children and an additional cook for every additional 100 children).
- The honorarium for the cooks comes under fund-sharing arrangement between the Centre and the States.

Source: Planning Commission.

seen in Table 2.10.

There are some issues and concerns regarding MDMS which need to be addressed. One of the major concerns is the wide inter-State variation in enrolment, attendance and actual coverage of children. At the State level, the nodal departments vary such as Social Welfare, Panchayat Raj and Rural Development, besides Education Department. As such,

Table 2.10: Nutritional Content of Cooked Mid-Day Meals

S.No.	Item	Primary	Upper Primary
1	Calories	450 calories	700 calories
2	Protein	12 gm	20 gm
Ingredients			
1	Rice/Wheat	100 gm	150 gm
2	Pulses	20 gm	30 gm
3	Vegetables	50 gm	75 gm
4	Oil	5 gm	7.5 gm
5	Micro-nutrients	Adequate quantities of micro-nutrients like iron, folic acid, vitamin-A, etc. in convergence with the NRHM	

Source: Annual Report 2013-14, MHRD.

MDMS implementation is adversely affected on account of cumbersome State procedures towards release of funds for cooking costs. States like Bihar, Odisha and Nagaland are facing various problems due to the lack of adequate infrastructure (such as shortage of storage capacity of food grains), quantity and quality control, irregular and uncertain supply of meals and poor quality of grains. Though teachers and students are not supposed to be involved in cooking and other activities for which a separate helper is to be engaged, it has been found that in some States (viz., Bihar, Maharashtra, J&K) teachers/children are being engaged in procurement, cooking and cleaning activities. This diverts attention and affects the quality of education.

Some States like Tamil Nadu have prescribed students' health card for periodical health check-ups. Under school health programmes, Primary Health Centre (PHC) doctor is expected to visit Primary schools for periodical check-ups. This practice is now defunct in most of the States and needs to be revived. Micro-nutrient supplementation is not ensured in some States/UTs like UP, HP and Daman and Diu.

The MDMS also suffers from inadequate monitoring, supervision and management structures at the State and sub-State levels. Planning Commission's evaluation reveals that MDMS implementation witnessed a limited involvement of Gram Panchayats (GPs) in Arunachal Pradesh, Andhra Pradesh, Karnataka and West Bengal and no involvement in States like Bihar, Jharkhand and Meghalaya. In the centralised cooking arrangements with NGOs particularly, in some of the urban areas (viz., Hyderabad, Chandigarh), involvement of local bodies or school management committees is very limited.

Feedback on MDMS, however, shows a positive impact on enrolment and attendance of children, particularly from the weaker sections (Amartya Sen, 2003), elimination of 'classroom hunger' (A. Goel and Jean Dreze, 2003), retention of girls in schools and better learning achievement (NCERT, 2005). Sharing of common meal seemed to contribute to gender and social equity (UNICEF, 2005). Audit Evaluation of Comptroller and Auditor General (2009) noted overwhelming public support for continuation of MDMS, and majority of parents and teachers have reported a positive perception of its impact.

Food for education initiatives are the most widespread social protection programmes, and have reached 368 million children in 169 countries (World Food Programme, 2013). MDMS of India alone covers over 100 million children. School feeding programmes help ensure that children who attend school remain healthy. Initially expanded as the most effective means of reaching hungry children, they were galvanised by the consequences of severe food and financial crises, and the realisation that the policy could be scaled up fairly rapidly (Bundy et al., 2009; Lister et al., 2011; WFP, 2013). Popular demand for MDMS is very clear.[13]

Existing evidence suggests that school feeding programme participants have consistently better enrolment and attendance than non-participants (Behrman et al., 2013; Lister et al., 2011). Mid-day meals and school feeding programmes in rural India have had a sizeable impact on girls' enrolment (Afridi, 2011; Dreze and Kingdon, 2001). A study by National Institute of Public Cooperation and Child Development in Madhya Pradesh (2007) has noted the crucial role of MDMS in reducing dropouts, especially among girls. MDMS has a positive impact on increasing enrolment, averting classroom hunger and reducing the social discrimination (Dipa Sinha, EPW, 2008). Importantly, several studies have noted that three-fourths of children who benefitted by MDMS belonged to SC, ST and OBC categories and the Scheme had contributed to their improved attendance.

During the Twelfth Five-Year Plan, MDMS was expected to be expanded to cover pre-Primary schooling in a progressive manner, to private unaided schools, particularly in the SC/ST and minority concentrated

13. UNESCO, 'Education for all Global Monitoring Report (EFA-GMR),' 2015, p. 88.

areas, and to poor children admitted in the neighbourhood private schools against the 25 per cent earmarked seats as per provisions of the RTE Act. Convergence of the MDMS with the school health programme was also expected to be ensured during the Twelfth Five-Year Plan to benefit from synergy in two programmes. The progress, however, seems to be very slow and the States are complaining about poor funding by the Central Government for RTE children in private schools.

III. Secondary Education

Secondary Education serves as a bridge between Elementary and Higher Education and prepares young persons in the age group of 14 to 17 years for entry into Higher Education and also for the world of work. The government policy has been to ensure that Secondary Education of good quality is available, accessible and affordable to all young persons who pass out of Elementary schools.

As per Census 2011, the population of children in this age group is estimated at 96.94 million. The overall enrolment numbers by stages in Secondary Education and by sex in 2013-14 are presented in Table 2.11.

Table 2.11: Secondary & Higher Secondary Enrolments by Sex (million) (2013-14)

Schools	Boys	Girls	Total
Secondary	19.66	17.64	37.3
Higher Secondary	11.83	10.48	22.31
Sec. & Hr. Secondary	31.49	28.12	59.61

Source: Educational Statistics at a Glance, MHRD.

The decade-long implementation of SSA got a fillip with the enactment of the Right to Education Act (RTE) 2009, heralding a paradigm shift towards the rights perspective for universalisation of elementary education (UEE). The success of SSA in ensuring near full access to Primary schooling has increased the demand for Secondary schooling on an unprecedented scale. There has been significant acceleration in the growth of enrolments in Secondary Education. Relevant data on the number of Secondary and Higher Secondary schools and enrolments therein, classified by gender, are presented in Table 2.12. Between 2000-01 and 2011-14 Secondary

Table 2.12: Number of Secondary/Sr. Secondary Schools and Enrolments

Year	School	Enrolments (million)		
		Boys	Girls	Total
2000-01	1,26,047	16.9	10.7	27.6
2001-02	1,33,492	18.4	12.1	30.5
2002-03	1,37,207	19.5	13.7	33.2
2003-04	1,45,962	20.6	14.4	35
2004-05	1,52,049	21.7	15.4	37.1
2005-06	1,59,667	22.3	16.1	38.4
2006-07	1,69,568	23	16.9	39.9
2007-08	1,72,990	25.2	19.3	44.5
2008-09	1,93,200	25.6	19.9	45.5
2009-10	1,90,643	26.7	21.5	48.2
2010-11	2,00,184	28.3	22.9	51.2
2012-13	2,28,914	29	25.6	54.6
2013-14	2,37,111	31.5*	28.1*	59.6*

*Enrolment figures for 2013-14, include enrolment in Secondary/Higher Secondary schools and enrolments in courses offered by the National Institute of Open Schooling (NIOS)

Source: Educational Statistics at a Glance, 2011, MHRD; U-DISE, NUEPA.

and Higher Secondary enrolments increased at a compound growth rate of 6.10 per cent per annum.

We have already noted that the growth of female enrolments had significantly accelerated under Elementary Education, thanks to SSA. Its impact has been reflected in more than doubling girls' enrolment in Secondary Education with annual exponential growth rate of 7.69 per cent, much faster than that for boys (4.91 per cent per annum). It has, therefore, become very essential to plan for universalisation of secondary education in accordance with the World Education Forum's redefined concept of 'basic education' under Education for All (EFA). The world over, basic education now covers Secondary Education.

A sub-committee of Central Advisory Board of Education (CABE) examined a proposal for extending the Right to Education up to Secondary level or universalisation of secondary education. It may be noted, however, that it took nearly one and a half decade to universalise Elementary Education with RTE Act supported by massive DPEP, SSA and MDMS programmes preparing the ground work. At the Secondary level, on the other hand, the Government of India had only a couple of small-budget schemes like Access and Equity and Area Intensive Programmes and Madrasa Modernisation Programmes implemented through various NGOs besides Kendriya Vidyalaya (KVs) and Navodaya Vidyalaya (NVs). The KV and NV Sangathans were also reluctant to play the role of SSA as these were not geared for such a role and these high-profile schools preferred expansion in their own trajectory for the fear of dilution in terms of quality, performance and autonomy with States interference. (Expansion of Navodaya Vidyalaya Samiti (NVS) as recommended by the Group of Ministers (GoMs), with additional 292 schools in the districts of SC/ST concentration stood aborted due to the Sangathan's unwillingness and inaction despite Budget provisions in 2007-08.)

Moreover, historically, the management of Secondary Education has been predominantly with the private sector (private aided and private unaided). As such, the policy of universalisation of secondary education could not possibly be contemplated in isolation without their active involvement. The share of private unaided schools increased from 15 per cent in 1993-94 to 37 per cent in 2013-14. However, lack of viability, school autonomy and other socio-economic reasons may still hold up private sector in setting up of Secondary schools, particularly in disadvantaged areas including difficult terrains. The Eleventh Five-Year Plan (2007-12) had noted vast differences in terms of curriculum, syllabi and instruction material in Secondary Education (State Boards, Central Board of Secondary Education[CBSE], and Indian Certificate of Secondary Education [ICSE] and had recommended common curriculum and syllabi for the country as a whole.

Since around 71 per cent of institutions having Secondary sections and 63 per cent of those having Senior Secondary sections are located in rural India, the Government has the prime responsibility of providing access to Secondary schooling for disadvantaged regions and segments of population. The Secondary Education Management Information System (SEMIS) data showed school infrastructure in the State Government funded schools was poor with 11 per cent not having drinking water facility; 16 per cent not having urinals; 40 per cent not having library; and 72 per cent not having integrated science laboratory. Poor infrastructure, particularly science laboratory and library, adversely impacted the quality of education.

The need for a comprehensive Centrally Sponsored Scheme (CSS) for the Secondary Education, on the lines of SSA for Elementary Education, was felt strongly so as to support the State Governments to strengthen the progression of SSA pass outs. Rashtriya Madhyamik Shiksha Abhiyan (RMSA) filled this gap in the third year of the Eleventh Plan, i.e., in 2009-10.

(A) Gross and Net Enrolment Ratios

As can be seen from Table 2.13, the GER at Secondary (Grades IX-X) and Higher Secondary (Grades XI-XII) stages in 2013-14 was placed at 73.6 per cent and 49.1 per cent, respectively, giving a combined GER of 62 per cent. Notably, the enrolment of girls per 100 boys in Secondary and Higher Secondary was 63 and 62, respectively in 2000-01. With the accelerated growth of girls' enrolments in both Secondary and Higher Secondary, the gender gap however, has narrowed considerably and gender parity index was 1.0 for both Secondary and Higher Secondary Education in 2013-14.

Nevertheless, it may be noted that the national average tends to mask regional, social, economic and religious inequities, which are discussed in subsequent chapters. Besides, a big gap exists between GER and NER in Secondary Education as can be seen from Table 2.13. There could be some underage enrolments mostly through private unaided schools, which admit children in tender age. This was highlighted in 2015 in a Writ Petition filed in Madras High Court on underage students being denied admission for Medical courses in the preceding year as they had not completed 17 years when they cleared the Higher Secondary examinations.[14] Much of the gap between GER and NER in the rural areas, however, could be explained only by delayed access, poor classroom transactions and lack of remedial coaching/teaching.

14. A. Subramani, 'Previous years' students may bag over 1,000 MBBS seats', *The Times of India,* 23 June 2015, https://timesofindia.indiatimes.com/home/education/news/Previous-years-students-may-bag-over-1000-MBBS-seats/articleshow/47777392.cms?

Table 2.13: Total Enrolments, GER and NER in Secondary and Higher Secondary Education

Schools/ stages	Enrolments (Class IX-XII)(in million)			GER (%)			NER (%)		
	Boys	Girls	Total	Boys	Girls	All	Boys	Girls	All
Secondary	19.66	17.64	37.30	73.5	73.7	73.6	45.5	45.7	45.6
Higher Secondary	11.83	10.48	22.31	49.1	49.1	49.1	30.3	30.6	30.4
Sec. and Hr. Secondary*	31.49	28.12	59.61	61.9	62.1	62.0	38.3	38.6	38.4

Source: Educational Statistics at a Glance, 2014 (P).
*Derived from enrolment, GER & NER

It may be recalled that in the 15+ years age group population, those who completed educational level at Higher Secondary stage accounted for only 9 per cent. Nearly half of the enrolled children do not go beyond Class X. This obviously reduces the base for enrolment in Tertiary Education. Although school retention and transition rates have improved over the years, high dropout rates seriously hinder progress in transforming the country into a knowledge society.

(B) School Retention and Dropouts

There are several studies and national surveys (NSS/NFHS) identifying various reasons for high dropout rates in India's Educational System. Poor quality of schooling is an important reason for high dropout rates. Exercises carried out in the Planning Commission for preparation of the Twelfth Plan showed that the States with adverse Pupil-Teacher Ratio (PTR), higher Student Classroom Ratio (SCR), lower proportion of female teachers, higher ratio of single teacher schools, higher rates of repetition in schools and higher proportion teacher absenteeism had resulted in very high dropout rates.

In the North-Eastern States including Assam, high repetition rates and large proportion of single teacher schools appeared to be the most dominant factor for dropouts. In States like Bihar, Chhattisgarh, Madhya Pradesh, Jharkhand, adverse PTR, SCR, teacher vacancies/absenteeism and single teacher schools in tribal areas were dominant features resulting in high dropout rates. The problems were acute in Left Wing Extremism (LWE) affected districts in these States. Notably, socio-economic status of pupils has had an important bearing on school retention. Planning Commission exercises for the preparation of Twelfth Five-Year Plan showed that regions with higher degree of poverty are associated with high dropout rates and across social classification, a bulk of the dropouts were from disadvantaged communities such as the SCs, STs, OBCs and Muslim Minorities.

Studies also show parental education as an important determinant of school retention. Micro level studies undertaken by the Planning Commission suggest poor infrastructure of schools especially the lack of water and usable toilet facilities were responsible for female children getting dropped out in Minority concentrated districts, despite near full access to Elementary Education. An average village had two or more schools. However, female teachers accounted for a small proportion and even those teachers were commuting from other districts and States.

Some of the national agencies like NFHS and NSS have been historically identifying/eliciting reasons for dropping out from schools. For persons who were not currently attending any educational institutions, major reasons for not attending revealed by NSS[15] include: (i) school too far, (ii) to supplement household income, (iii) education not considered necessary, (iv) to attend domestic chores and (v) others.

The NFHS provides details on the reasons for dropouts, as summarised in Table 2.14. As per NFHS-3, the major reason for dropouts was 'children not interested in studies'. It stated that for children in the age groups 6 to 16, 37.2 per cent of boys and 22.3 per cent of girls dropped out of schools as they were not interested in studies. However, the attempts by national agencies to put the blame on the child for dropping out are misleading and therefore inappropriate. Repelling school environment, multi-grade teaching, utterly lacking joyful learning conditions in school cannot possibly be ignored. In this process, regrettably, the failure to ensure school preparedness with pre-Primary Education for ever-enrolled children does not get highlighted. Lack of primers in several Tribal

---

15. Ministry of Statistics & Programme Implementation, Government of India, 'Employment and Unemployment Situation among Social Groups in India', Report No. 563, 2014, p. 10.

languages making the classroom transactions uninteresting one-way communication forcing rote learning also gets overlooked. Therefore, an exceedingly large proportion of children reporting lack of interest in studies as a reason for dropping out is not acceptable at all.

The second major reason cited by NFHS-3, accounting for about 19 per cent dropouts each, among boys and girls, was high cost of education (Table: 2.14). With the RTE Act in place, this may not explain high Primary school dropout rates although the private cost of education remains high for a vast majority of poor segments of population as revealed by more credible NSS estimates on education expenditure (NSS-68th Round). Other reasons for dropouts as per NFHS include sibling care, domestic work, repetition, poor access and cultural reasons, including child marriage. Repetition and dropping out of schools is rampant among the children of migrant workers, brick-kiln workers and children of Denotified and Nomadic Tribes (DNTs).

Table 2.14: Main Reasons for School Dropout by the Sex of the Children (in %)

S.No	Reason	Boys	Girls	Total
1	Not interested in studies	37.2	22.3	29.8
2	Costs too high	18.9	18.6	18.8
3	Required for household work	7.8	16.1	11.9
4	Required for outside work for payment in cash/kind	9.2	3.4	6.3
5	Repeated failures	6.3	5.7	6.0
6	Required for work on farm/family business	7.6	3.3	5.4
7	School far away	1.2	5.9	3.5
8	Further education not considered necessary	2.8	4.0	3.4
9	Got married	0.2	5.6	2.9
10	Did not get admission	2.1	2.2	2.1
11	Not safe to send to school	0.2	2.7	1.1
12	Others	6.5	10.2	8.8
		100.0	100.0	100.0

Source: NFHS-3, 2005-06; Sample size: boys 6166 and girls 7400.

The Planning Commission's econometric studies showed that for every one per cent increase in the proportion of female teachers, dropout rates declined by about 0.61 per cent and the results were statistically significant explaining about 65 per cent inter-State variations in dropout rates. While SSA had stipulated that about one-third of new teacher recruits should be females, the Planning Commission suggested in States where the female teacher proportion was very low as in Bihar and Rajasthan, the reservation for females could be as high as 50 per cent. The real problem, however, is the lack of adequate number of qualified female teachers in these States for appointments under SSA.

The problem of dropouts largely pertains to publicly funded schools where a bulk of the poor children gets enrolled. SSA tried to bring down the dropout rates significantly but could not succeed despite the RTE Act. Although several strategies were designed to tackle the problem, most of these could not be implemented satisfactorily due to SSA lacking the flexibility of District Primary Education Programme (DPEP) and assured funding in educationally backward blocks/districts. In the absence of coordinators, School Management Committees (SMCs) could not be activated to deal with the problem locally as the bulk of SMC members hardly visited schools. The implementation of RTE Act suffered to some extent due to lack of adequate funding as planned and approved by the Government. As the bulk of the funding was going towards teachers' salary, infrastructure and other fixed grants, resources for innovative activities including hand-holding support for ever enrolled children, Tribal children, slum children, children of migrating parents and those belonging to disadvantaged social groups actually got squeezed out. State governments' activities like *Meena Manch, School Chalo* campaigns helped school enrolments to a great extent but more sustained efforts are needed locally for school retention. KGBV for girls helped school retention to some extent but the coverage was not more than 3 per cent of girls enrolled.

With the implementation of SSA, MHRD data as per apparent cohort method showed a somewhat higher rate of decline in dropout rates from historical trend rate of half a percentage point per annum in Primary Education. Recent estimates show that Primary dropout rate has declined to 22.3 per cent (23.4 per cent for boys and 21 per cent for girls) and at the Elementary level of education, it was 40.8 per cent (41.5 for boys and 40.0 per cent for girls). Educational statistics show that about half of the children enrolled in Class I get dropped out at Secondary level of education indicating a huge wastage in the educational system. The wastage was higher at 55 per cent for Scheduled Castes students and 66 per cent for Scheduled Tribes students.

Analysing regional dimensions, it has been observed that the dropout rates at the Primary level was higher than the national average in the entire NE region by a substantial margin and these rates were also very high in the eastern region (Bihar, West Bengal) and northern region (Rajasthan, Madhya Pradesh, Chhattisgarh, MP, Jharkhand and Uttarakhand). On the other hand, States like Tamil Nadu, Kerala, Karnataka, Goa, Maharashtra and the hilly states of J&K and HP have relatively low Primary dropout rates.

The Ministry of HRD in the recent years has been publishing data on dropout rates using a different methodology. It provides level-wise average annual dropout rate in School Education. The data for 2013-14 are given below:

It is observed from Table 2.15 that the dropout rates are higher for SCs (except for Classes I-V) and STs as compared to the national average. Data also show that dropout rates tend to increase for girls for higher classes. The dropout rates for STs at Elementary level of education (8.43 per cent) are more than twice that of the national average (3.77 per cent). Apparently, the progression of girls through the educational system is severely constrained and it is worse for Tribal girls. A very high rate of dropouts at Secondary Education also signifies a very poor quality of education. The dropout rates at Higher Secondary level are lower because of high dropout rates in Secondary Education (i.e., filtering effect).

Table 2.15: Level-wise Average Annual Dropout Rate in School Education (in per cent)

Level	All			Scheduled Castes			Scheduled Tribes		
	Boys	Girls	Total	Boys	Girls	Total	Boys	Girls	Total
Classes I-V	4.53	4.14	4.34	4.42	3.85	4.14	7.97	7.98	7.98
Classes VI-VIII	3.09	4.49	3.77	3.75	5.04	4.38	8.03	8.85	8.43
Classes IX & X	17.93	17.79	17.86	18.96	18.32	18.66	27.42	26.96	27.2
Classes XI & XII	1.48	1.61	1.54	2.20	1.38	1.81	3.09	2.77	2.94

Source: Min. of HRD, Educational Statistics at a Glance, 2014-15, Data pertains to 2013-14.

Table 2.16: Selected International Comparison of GERs (in %)

Countries	Primary	Secondary	Higher Secondary	Tertiary
India	106.5	82.0	56.8	20.8
Sri Lanka	98.4	99.1	99.6	17.0
China	127.9	103.5	76.6	26.7
South Africa	101.6	111.0	96.0	NA
UK	108.5	106.4	87.6	61.9
USA	98.1	98.0	89.5	94.3

Source: MHRD, Educational Statistics at a Glance, 2014.

Adequate efforts are not being made by the States and no specific targets have been set for reducing dropout rates in a time-bound manner. Even the RTE Act mandate remains unfulfilled in respect of children in the age group of 6 to 14 as several million children were not attending schools and a large number of them were ever-enrolled children (Census 2011).

In international comparison, India's GERs are much lower compared even to Sri Lanka and China, as can be seen from Table 2.16. The progression from Primary to Higher Education in India also leaves much to be desired.

In order to accelerate the Tertiary GER in India close to the developing countries' average of 30 per cent, broadening the base is a prime requirement. Both supply side and demand side constraints need to be eased simultaneously. The supply side constraints that limit access to Secondary Education include insufficient and uneven distribution of school infrastructure, inefficient teacher deployment, sub-optimal use of private sector enrolment capacity and an inflexible delivery system that does not allow for exit and re-entry. On the demand side, the biggest stumbling block is the low completion rate of Elementary Education (56 per cent), which limits the number of students ready for Secondary Education. While this is likely to improve significantly with RTE-harmonised SSA, there are also other factors limiting demand including the high direct and indirect costs of schooling borne by families, parents' misperceptions of the benefits about Secondary Education, especially for girls and among rural families, and poor quality and relevance of Secondary Education which needs to be addressed effectively. The RTE-harmonised SSA has to improve the internal efficiency and quality of Elementary Education for higher transition rates and support parents of disadvantaged children with entitlements for Secondary Education to offset the direct as well as indirect cost of education.

(C) Rashtriya Madhyamik Shiksha Abhiyan

Rashtriya Madhyamik Shiksha Abhiyan (RMSA) was launched in March 2009 with the objective to enhance access to Secondary Education and improve its quality. The schemes envisage, inter alia, to enhance the enrolment at Secondary stage by providing a Secondary school within a reasonable distance of habitation, with an aim to ensure GER of 100 per cent by 2017 and universal retention by 2020. The other objectives include improving the quality of education imparted at the Secondary level by making all Secondary schools conform to the prescribed norms, and removing gender, socio-economic and disability barriers, etc.

Important physical facilities are provided which include (i) additional classrooms, (ii) laboratories, (iii) libraries, (iv) art and crafts room, (v) toilet blocks, (vi) drinking water provisions, (vii) electricity/telephone/ Internet connectivity and (viii) disabled-friendly provisions. Improvement in quality aspects is sought inter alia through (i) appointment of additional teachers to improve the PTR (ii) in-service training of teachers, (iii) ICT-enabled education, (iv)curriculum reforms and (v) teaching-learning reforms. The equity aspects are addressed through (i) special focus in micro planning, (ii) preference to areas with concentration of SC/ST/ Minority for opening the schools, (iii) special enrolment drive for the weaker sections, (iv) more female teachers in schools and (v) separate toilet blocks for girls.

The funding pattern under RMSA in respect of normal States is 75:25 and in the case of North-Eastern States it is 90:10. The Scheme is being implemented by a Society set up by the State Government for implementation. With a view to ensuring efficient utilisation of funds and greater coordination, other Centrally Sponsored Schemes (CSS) of Secondary Education, i.e., ICT@School, Inclusive Education for the Disabled at Secondary Stage (IEDSS), Vocational Education (VE) and Girls Hostel (GH) Scheme have been subsumed under the existing RMSA.

For enhancing the quality of Secondary Education, RMSA, in association with the National Council of Educational Research and Training (NCERT) and the National University for Educational Planning and Administration (NUEPA), has taken several initiatives including school leadership development programme, national achievement survey at Class X, development of framework for school standards, and performance evaluation and national repository of open education resources. RMSA has sanctioned 9,799 new schools and strengthening of 35,547 existing schools besides appointing 52,352 additional teachers. In addition, residential quarters for teachers in difficult areas, major repair of classrooms, school annual grants, minor repair grants, in-service training of teachers, etc. were approved. RMSA has sanctioned annual grants to 75,394 government Secondary schools besides sanctioning minor repair grants to 62,221 schools. Despite a delayed start, the programme has been welcomed by the States and has posted some credible achievement in strengthening Secondary school infrastructure in the country.[16]

(D) Model School Scheme, JNVs and KVs

In addition to RMSA, the Government also launched a Model School Scheme to be set up at the rate of one school per block in two categories—educationally backward blocks (EBBs) and Non-EBBs, with the latter soliciting private partnerships. The objective of the Model School Scheme is to have at least one good quality Secondary school in every block that will work as a pacesetting institution and provide support to other Secondary schools in that area (mostly rural) addressing the issues of contextual curriculum and pedagogic practices for Secondary-stage learners. The funding pattern for model schools in EBBs managed by States is 75:25 between the Centre and States except Special Category and NE States for which a 90:10 fund sharing ratio has been set. The Government has approved 3,500 model schools on KV template to be set up in each EBB. MHRD has sanctioned 2,266 schools so far and 1,184 Model schools have been made functional in 12 States. The setting up of 2,500 Model schools in PPP Mode in non-EBB has also been approved for phased implementation @ 500 schools in the first year of the Twelfth Plan (2012–17) and @ 1000 schools each, in the succeeding two years.

There are five apex-level national institutions for Secondary Education, viz., National Council of Education Research & Training (NCERT), Navodaya Vidyalaya Samiti (NVS), Kendriya Vidyalaya Sangathan (KVS),

16. Planning Commission, 'Twelfth Five Year Plan (2012 -17),' vol. III, (New Delhi: Sage Publications India Pvt Ltd, 2013), p. 70.

National Institute of Open Schooling (NIOS) and Central Tibetan School Administration (CTSA).

The Kendriya Vidyalayas primarily cater to the educational needs of the wards of transferable Central Government employees. There are 1060 KVs with an enrolment of over a million students.

There are 576 Jawahar Navodaya Vidyalayas (JNVs) functional in 34 States/UTs with more than 2.1 lakh students on roll. These are pacesetting schools providing quality modern education to talented children from rural areas. The NVs are fully residential co-educational institutions up to Higher Secondary stage providing free boarding, lodging, textbooks and uniforms to all students. The percentage of students belonging to SCs, STs, female gender and coming from rural areas was well above the national norm: SCs–24 per cent; ST–18 per cent; Girls–36 per cent and Rural–78 per cent. The pass percentage was 97.84 per cent in Class X and 94.1 per cent in Class XII in 2009, well above the CBSE overall pass percentage of 88 per cent and 81 per cent, respectively.

The JNVs and KVs need to engage in pacesetting activities in the district. Presently, the JNVs and KVs remain isolated schools. Their mandate and role need to be revisited to forge these premier schools as pacesetters for neighbourhood schools in government and government-aided schools.

The National Institute of Open Schooling (NIOS) is an autonomous organisation pursuing its mission of reaching the unreached by providing opportunities for continuing education, from Primary to pre-Degree, to those who have missed mainstream School Education. Currently, it has more than 1.5 million students on roll, 15 regional centres, 2,700 study centres, 1,943 accredited institutions for academic courses and 1002 Accredited Vocational Institutes (AVIs) for programme delivery through Open Learning and Distance Learning. Besides study centres in India, centres have been set up in the UAE, Kuwait, Nepal and Canada. NIOS has introduced the facility of on-line admission; its salient features include: (i) direct access to admission and (ii) freedom to select the study centre. NIOS should be slated for expansion with functional State Institutions in all the States/UTs.

(E) Quality and Efficiency of Secondary Education

As indicated earlier, the quality and availability of teachers, access to learning tools (such as, ICTs) so as to enhance the delivery of information, the course curricula, the approach of pedagogy applied, conducting regular examinations, quality assurance and suitable supervision are the key elements of educational quality.

Several issues persist in teachers' pre-service education at the Secondary level (university degree plus teacher education), including poor standards, inadequate monitoring, weak accreditation framework, outdated and traditional pedagogical methods, insufficient supply of basic learning and teaching material, and little or no incentive for improvement. Despite the exponential expansion of Secondary Education, publicly funded Secondary teachers seem to be unaccountable to parents and educational administration.

In a stark contrast to the international standards, the Indian curricula for languages, arts, mathematics and sciences rewards rote learning instead of developing thinking skills of students. Moreover, there is an overload of curriculum with little focus on the quality of learning materials in Secondary Education. Central Board textbooks lay somewhat more emphasis on conceptual understanding compared to State-level textbooks, which generally tend to address examination needs of students. There is a deficit in learning tools, such as ICTs, fully equipped laboratories, visual aids, audio-visual equipments, library and reference books, which are required to supplement textbooks for learning purposes.

It is crucial to improve the quality of Secondary Education. Some necessary strategic interventions may be as follows:

- Improving Secondary Education Teacher Training Colleges, with rigorous institutional accreditation, assessments and reforms. Competition should be encouraged for larger investments into improved facilities as well as faculty and equipment upgradation. There should be an increase in intake of trainess for subjects that are inadequately served.
- Creation of a network of teachers across schools for a peer-based, mentor-led and subject-specific professional development of teachers and their mutual exchange of resources and effective pedagogical approaches.
- Clearly defining teacher performance standards and disseminating information about their use, periodically evaluating teacher performance, and conducting research on the correlation between teacher incentives and improved student learning.

- Increasing incentives for State Boards, in terms of funding and technical assistance, so as to align curriculum and examination pattern with the National Curriculum Framework.
- Bringing reforms in development and procurement of textbooks and their revision by inviting suggestions from teachers is essential. Permitting private textbook suppliers to compete will end monopolies of certain textbook providers. Additionally, larger investments into ICTs to draw from a wide range of resources available on the Internet will enable student-centred learning.
- Increasing investments and reforming the quality assurance mechanisms, so as to emphasise innovative and tested pedagogical approaches, as well as links to in-service teachers' professional development.
- Transformation of examination patterns with a view to stimulate problem-solving and information-reasoning skills, instead of rote learning. What is taught and how it is taught will not change until the examination pattern undergoes a metamorphic change.
- Developing and efficiently administering standardised tests and assessments for Grade X and XII at the national level.
- Encouraging and preparing students to participate in international assessments of achievement at the Secondary level.

IV. Vocational Education

The vocationalisation of Secondary Education provides for diversification of educational opportunities so as to enhance individual employability, reduce the mismatch between demand and supply of skilled personpower and an alternative for those pursuing Higher Education. Vocational Education programmes are being implemented by the HRD Ministry at school, college/university community levels. A Centrally Sponsored Scheme (CSS) initiated in 1988 and revised in 1992-93, provided for financial assistance to the States to set up administrative structures, area-vocational surveys, preparation of curriculum guides, training manual, teacher training programme, strengthening technical support system for research and development, training and evaluation, etc. It also provided for financial assistance to NGOs. The Government of India has been supporting about 19 activities in areas like agriculture, engineering and technology, business and commerce, home science, health and paramedical, humanities, science and education and offering around 150

Vocational courses. The coverage was 9,583 schools, 21,000 sections with one million students.

The Scheme went for yet another revision in 2014 and is aimed at enhancing the employability of youth through demand-driven, competency-based, Modular Vocational courses; to maintain their competitiveness through provisions of multi-entry, multi-exit learning opportunities and vertical mobility/interchangeability in qualifications; to fill the gap between educated and employable; and to lower the dropout rate at the Secondary level and reduce pressure on academic Higher Education.

The Scheme was merged with RMSA to partly remove the social stigma attached to Vocational Education as it is widely believed that those enrolling in Vocational Education programmes were mostly low-performing students. The Central Government has launched a pilot project in Haryana for four industry sectors, i.e., Information Technology (IT)/ Information Technology Enabled Services (ITeS), Automotive, Security and Retail. The sectors have now been expanded to include Travel and Tourism, Healthcare and Beauty and Wellness. Further expansion is contemplated and a template has been developed based on the experience which States could adopt with modifications suiting their requirements on the basis of the emerging demand pattern.

The National Vocational Education Qualification Framework (NVEQF) is a descriptive framework that classifies qualifications according to various levels of knowledge along with skills. These levels focus on the competencies which the learners must mandatorily possess irrespective of the nature of education acquired and training received (formal, non-formal or informal means). Different levels are defined in terms of learning outcomes. Qualifications are made up of occupational standards for specific areas of learning units. This enables learners, education and skill training providers and employers to be informed about the broad equivalence of qualifications across specific skill sectors.

Therefore, a nationally integrated education and competency-based skill framework will be effective in providing a multitude of pathways within Vocational Education as well as between general and Vocational Education. It will ensure that learners can progress from any starting point to an advanced level in the education and/or skill system.

The key elements of the NVEQF include: (a) guidelines for providing Vocational Education towards achieving international equivalency, (b) multiple entry and exit between Vocational Education, general education and job markets, (c) progression within Vocational Education, (d) transfer between Vocational Education and general education, and (e) partnership with industry/employers. The NVEQF was expected to be assimilated into the National Skills Qualification Framework (NSQF) once that framework is notified for the country.

NVEQF has been developed by the Ministry of Human Resource Development (MHRD). Under the NVEQF, the level one of skill development, pre-Vocational stage starts in Grade IX. Flexible learning pathways are envisioned to integrate schooling with Higher Education. Vocational curriculum is aligned and integrated with academic curriculum and has modules on various generic and specific skills. The courses at school levels need to be aligned to the existing job market demand. Replication of the course offered by the ITIs has to be avoided. This requires a contact with the Sector-specific Skill Councils. The new emerging employment areas need to be identified. Curriculum development should take place in consultation and active involvement of the Industry. Also, each course should undergo accreditation by the Industry.

There was another framework developed, i.e., the National Vocational Qualification Framework (NVQF). Envisaged by the Ministry of Labour, it starts at zero level education, with or without any School Education. With RTE Act and universalisation of RMSA, in the longer term, a student will enter the labour force after the year 2016-17 with a minimum of eight years of education. However, in the shorter term, 35 per cent labour pool, which has zero-level education, needs skilling for employment now. They need to be skilled at whatever levels of education they are at. This is where NVQF becomes applicable.

At the government level, efforts were made towards synthesising and synchronising the two frameworks in the backdrop of addressing skilling needs of those who are currently 'out of school' with a minimum zero level of education attainment at one level and at the other end where Vocational course starts in Grade IX.

It may be noted, however, that there is a need for a large-scale pruning of the number of courses offered in Vocational Education and Training (VET). The courses of skill development and training offered have not kept pace with the emerging demand pattern. There is a need to carefully select trades and disciplines keeping in view the employment potential and demand by the industry. Curricula, including practical training, must meet the demand for specific skills.

The Vocational Education stream in schools aim at developing courses which do not require expensive infrastructure for practical training and do not replicate the training in specialised institutions like the ITI/ Polytechnics/KVKs which puts the Secondary Board Certification at a discount in the job market in relation to the diploma of these specialised institutions. New emerging areas such as information technology and IT-related services, tourism, hospitality, banking and insurance, retail trade, community services, BPO, media services, etc. are the areas of expanding high quality jobs. Courses in such areas require less investment in infrastructure and could be successfully carried out in two or three rooms within the school premises. There should be a greater linkage with Vocational training and academic education to provide for vertical mobility for students aspiring for higher professional programmes in polytechnics, universities and engineering colleges.

The first step to learning any skill faster requires deconstructing the skill one wants to learn. Deconstruction means taking something that is very large or complex and breaking it down into smaller pieces. Most, if not all, of the skills one wants to learn are just bundles of smaller sub-skills that occur in combinations simultaneously. By breaking these sub-skills down to their minimal components, one can figure out exactly what you need to learn, which sub-skills are important, and therefore which should be learnt first. Modern skill imparting approach relies more on deconstructing the skills for raising the capacity for rapid learning. Such an approach invariably applies the Pareto Principle or 80/20 rule which states that 20 per cent of the invested input is responsible for 80 per cent of the results obtained. Careful selection of key sub-skills and efforts put on that 20 per cent should lead to 80 per cent of the desired outcome.[17]

Conventional Vocational Education and Training programme curricula and classroom/workshop transactions do not identify the principal factors or elements that need to be the focus for various trade skills but hand out the whole theory and practical of the chosen or offered trade. This not only slows down the knowledge skill acquisition but also results in wastages.

Flexibility needs to be provided at different levels of the school

---

17. Sean Kim, 'How to Deconstruct Any Skill You Want to Learn Faster', *Lifehack*, https://www.lifehack.org/324939/how-deconstruct-any-skill-you-want-learn-faster.

curriculum; marks can be awarded for Vocational subjects and wherever applicable, credits can be carried forward. At present, the colleges/universities are not giving weightage to the marks scored in Vocational subjects for admission of the student to Higher Education.

Vocational Education through schools works well in the United States, Sweden, France, South Korea and Taiwan. The apprentice system works well in Germany. Reviewing the global experience, the National Commission for Enterprises in the Unorganised Sector (NCEUS) had concluded:

> It has been seen that comprehensive systems of skill development that exist internationally are primarily for the formal sector, as it is the economies that are dominated by the formal sector that have evolved such systems. In countries of East Asia, which have been characterised as State-led, demand-driven systems, it is the universalisation of basic education, enlarging the coverage of Secondary Education and developing a vibrant system of Vocational Education that has laid the foundation towards specifically targeted skills designed for the workplace. Strengthening the educational system and universalising access is thus an essential prerequisite for widespread skill development, particularly when the skill mix needs to change to accommodate the needs of greater integration with the knowledge economy.[18]

The NIOS offers Vocational Education courses through Accredited Vocational Institutes (AVIs) in the major areas of agriculture, business and commerce, engineering, etc. The NIOS offers 70 Vocational Education courses through 1,000 AVIs with an enrolment of 22,000 students per annum. Indira Gandhi National Open University (IGNOU) has been offering Vocational Education courses for the last 15+ years. The courses are offered at the Certificate and Diploma levels. The enrolment for Vocational Education courses therein is about 1.20 lakh per annum.

The scheme of polytechnics provides both Vocational Education and Training. The aim of the Polytechnic Education is to create a pool of skill-based personpower to support shop floor and field operations. There are three types of polytechnics—government, private aided and private unaided (self-financing). The total number of all polytechnics is

18. National Commission for Enterprises in the Unorganised Sector (NCEUS), Government of India Report.

1,752 (Polytechnics–1,244, Institutions for Diploma in Pharmacy–415, Institutions for Diploma in Hotel Management–63, Institutions for Diploma in Architecture–25). About 40 per cent of the polytechnics are in four States viz. Tamil Nadu (210), Karnataka (205), Maharashtra (172) and Andhra Pradesh (100). The total enrolment in polytechnic institutes is 2.95 lakh.

The major constraints of Polytechnic Education system include non-availability of technicians in new and emerging areas, obsolescence of equipment, inadequacy of financial resources, lack of State policy for training and retraining of faculty and staff, lack of flexibility to students, autonomy to the institutions and static curricula, poor industry participation and lack of reliable technical personpower forecast.

The Government of India launched the National Policy for Skill Development and Entrepreneurship in 2015.[19] For the first time, the national scheme for skill development is integrated with promoting entrepreneurship on a large scale. The vision of the Policy is 'to create an ecosystem of empowerment by skilling on a large scale at speed with high standards and to promote a culture of innovation-based entrepreneurship which can generate wealth and employment so as to ensure sustainable livelihoods for all citizens in the country'.[20]

The Policy has four focus areas to achieve this vision. First, it deals with the main impediments to skill development, including low aspirational value, weak integration with formal education, inadequate emphasis on the outcomes, and inferior quality of training infrastructure and the trainers. Secondly, the Policy seeks to strike a balance between supply and demand for skills by addressing the prevailing skill gaps, promoting industry engagement, designing an operationally meaningful quality assurance framework, leveraging technology and providing greater opportunities for apprenticeship training.

Third, the Policy seeks to achieve equity using targetted skilling opportunities for disadvantaged as well as socially/geographically marginalised groups. Lastly, there is a focus on Skill Development and entrepreneurship programmes for women. In the arena of

19. *PTI*, 'PM Narendra Modi likely to unveil new National Skills Policy on July 15', *The Economic Times,* 8 July 2015, https://economictimes.indiatimes.com/news/politics-and-nation/pm-narendra-modi-likely-to-unveil-new-national-skills-policy-on-july-15/articleshow/47991947.cms

20. Ibid.

entrepreneurship, the Policy seeks to educate and equip potential entrepreneurs, both within and outside the formal education system. In addition, it seeks to connect entrepreneurs to mentors, incubators and credit markets so as to foster greater innovation and entrepreneurship.

Jan Shikshan Sansthan

The scheme of Jan Shikshan Sansthan (JSS) is an adult education programme aimed at improving the Vocational skills and quality of life of neo-literates. There are 194 JSS offering around 284 different types of Vocational courses—from candle making to computer and health care. About 65 per cent of the beneficiaries are women.

It has been proposed to increase the number of JSS to 400 and prune and tune Vocational courses only in respect of those skills which are in demand locally and training be imparted to the beneficiaries. The course curriculum will have to be improved and the training formalised. In high-tech areas like computer training, etc., certification system will have to be initiated. Apart from imparting skills, the programme content should also include some atleast rudimentary knowledge of business management, accounting, marketing as well as some administrative exposure so as to enhance the likelihood of success of the beneficiaries' self-employment ventures.

V. Tertiary Education

(A) Status of Higher Education

Undoubtedly, India's Tertiary Education is not only one of largest but also the fastest growing system in the world. At the time of the Independence, there were about 27 universities and 578 colleges. Subsequently, its growth has been phenomenal as can be seen from Table 2.17. This unprecedented growth has greatly contributed to economic development and social progress, and has anchored the growth of a vibrant political democracy.

It is stated that the relationship between economic growth and growth in the Tertiary Gross Enrolment Ratio (GER) is particularly strong for economies with lower levels of GDP (purchasing power parity) per capita.

Table 2.17: Number of Colleges and Universities in India, 1950-51 to 2013-14

Year	Colleges	Universities
1950-51	578	27
1960-61	1,819	45
1970-71	3,277	82
1980-81	6,963	110
1990-91	5,748	184
2000-01	10,152	254
2010-11	32,974	621
2013-14	36,671	712

Source: Educational Statistics at a Glance 2014.

As was noted long ago by the University Education Commission,[21] the 'admission of a large number of students in response to popular demand without the necessary staff, classroom and hostel accommodation and equipment makes it impossible for most colleges and universities to give full education to their inflated undergraduate population'. The Commission felt quite uneasy about the inadequacy of Higher Education system, particularly in terms of quality and standards. Another Commission observed that 'the situation in Higher Education was unsatisfactory and even alarming in some ways, that the average standards have been falling and rapid expansion has resulted in lowering the quality'.[22]

The marked deterioration of standards in teaching and examinations and increasing dissatisfaction with the conduct of university administration and selections of university authorities continue to be matters of great concern for the last six decades. Over a large area of education, the content and quality are inadequate for our present needs and future requirements and compare unfavourably with the average standards in other educationally advanced countries. What is worse, the large gap between standards in India and those in advanced countries is widening rapidly. 'Unless we ensure the highest standards of teaching in our universities, our degrees will not command recognition and respect

21. S. Radhakrishnan Commission, 1948-49.
22. Kothari Commission, 1964–66.

either in our own country or abroad. The average standard of our degree still remains on the low side', the Kothari Commission had stated.[23]

In the temporal context, in view of very low base, expansion in the number of Tertiary sector institutions and, consequently, Higher Education enrolments appear to be quite impressive. However, the university and college enrolments accounted for only 21 per cent of the eligible age groups (18 to 23) population of 141 million which underscores the gross inadequacy of the system to meet the large and growing magnitude of demand for Tertiary Education in any meaningful way. It also compares very unfavourably with 50 per cent enrolments in the developed countries and the world average of 31 per cent for the corresponding age groups.[24]

The National Knowledge Commission noted that India's GER in Higher Education was only half the Asian average. The Census data[25] shows that the proportion of total graduates and postgraduates in general and professional streams account for just 6.2 per cent of the working age population (15 to 59 years). Apparently, those with professional qualifications not even account for 1 per cent of the working age population. India boasts of a country with the largest cattle population but the number of veterinarians is only around 37,000. There are only 1.4 million doctors for a population of 1.28 billion. There is an acute shortage of nurses (over 2.0 million). India has about 6.5 million teachers and not even half of them have professional education after graduation. The details provided in Table 2.18 are thus quite revealing.

Thus, the phenomenal growth of institutions and enrolment in Tertiary Education has just not been adequate for India's current requirements and also for future needs of establishing a knowledge society. A large segment of India's population just does not have access to Higher Education.[26]

As India's economy continues to grow, a huge number of first-generation learners will demand access to Higher Education.[27] A vibrant democracy can ill afford to ignore their legitimate demand and perpetuate social,

23. Ibid.

24. UNDP, Human Development Report, 2014.

25. Census, 2011, Cultural Tables, August, 2015.

26. National Knowledge Commission, Government of India 'Report to the Nation 2006-09', March 2009.

27. The McKinsey Global Institute Report (2007) cited in 'The Emerging Middle Class in Developing Countries', OECD Development Centre, Working Paper No. 285, January 2010.

Table 2.18: Census-2011- India's Higher Education Attainments

Streams (General and Professional)	Number	Percentage to Working Age Population
Graduates (non-technical)	38,742,338	5.307
Postgraduates (Non-technical)	13,607,951	0.186
Engineering & Technology	6,925,177	0.095
Medicine	1,399,696	0.192
Agriculture & Dairy	137,436	0.019
Veterinary	36,862	0.005
Teaching	27,42,346	0.376
Others	21,891	0.003
Total	63,613,697	6.182

Source: Census 2011, C Tables. Working Age Population—730 million.

economic and regional inequities which had characterised the system all along. Today, access to Higher Education for masses is imperative—politically, economically and demographically. A significant driver for educational change is population growth and the demographic profile. More than 50 per cent of India's population is under the age of 25. By 2020, India will have one of the youngest populations in the world, with an average age of 29 years.[28] India will outpace China in the next 10 years as the country with the largest Tertiary-age population and its relative success in boosting Primary enrolment, access to Secondary Education and improved retention rates would mean India would have the largest growth in Tertiary enrolment in the world in 2020-28. It has been projected that by 2020, 200 million of the world's 25–34-year-olds will be university graduates and 40 per cent of these will be from China whereas only 13 per cent will come from India, together representing a huge proportion of the global talent pool.[29]

Growth, however, is likely to be uneven; India will be challenged by a growing disparity between those who have access to better education and

28. ILO, 'Estimates and Projections of the Economically Active Population: 1990–2020', October 2011.

29. OECD, 'Education Indicators in Focus', May 2012, http://www.oecd.org/education/50495363.pdf

those who do not. Despite remarkable strides in Primary enrolment rates, India still has the largest number of OoSC in the world, more than the whole of sub-Saharan Africa, and 69 per cent of India's population still lives on less than \$2 a day.[30] No wonder, the World Bank categorises India as 'an extreme dual economy'.

India is aware of the acute regional and social imbalances in Higher Education and has been consciously addressing these with inclusive policies, including reservation of seats for the disadvantaged social groups, liberalising scholarship regimes, easing educational loans with interest subsidy, accelerating access in over 370 districts which had GER much lower than the national average and expanding hostel facilities especially for girls. There is a considerable progress in temporal context in girls' enrolments in Higher Education but much more needs to be done.

India's Tertiary Education System could broadly be classified under three categories, viz., (a) universities and its equivalents, (b) colleges and (c) institutions granting diplomas. The structure of Higher Education institutions in the country is presented in Table 2.19.

A striking feature of the Higher Education in India is the system of affiliated colleges. A recent study noted that a vast bulk of students study at public and private colleges which are affiliated to State Universities. These colleges do not have their own degree awarding powers; they deliver the courses, curricula and examinations specified and regulated by their parent State University. The affiliated college sector is huge, enrolling over 90 per cent of undergraduates, 70 per cent of postgraduates and 17 per cent of doctoral students. Some universities have as many as 1000 colleges affiliated to them. There are considerable challenges in regulation and quality control; and while there are notable exceptions, many are perceived to be sub-standard.[31]

The affiliation system served the purpose in olden days when there were only a handful of universities with concentration of talents for setting standards, developing curriculum, syllabi, assessment, research capabilities and managerial abilities. The universities in the three Presidencies, viz., Madras, Bombay and Calcutta had the bulk of affiliated colleges. The physical distance between the university and the affiliated

30. World Bank (2010), http://data.world bank.org/indicators/SI.POV.2 day on 05/11/2013.

31. British Council, 'Understanding India: The future of higher education and opportunities for international cooperation', February 2014.

Table 2.19: Indian Universities and Colleges

University and Higher Education	Institutions	Percentage Distribution
1. Central Universities	42	5.9
2. State Public Universities	310	43.5
3. Deemed Universities	127	17.8
4. State Private Universities	143	20.1
5. Central Open Universities	1	0.1
6. State Open Universities	13	1.8
7. Institutes of National Importance (Central)	68	9.6
8. Institutes of National Importance (States)	5	0.7
9. Others	3	0.4
TOTAL (1–9)	**712**	**100.0**
Degree Colleges	**36,671**	-
Institutions Granting Diplomas		
i. Diploma Level Technical	3,541	30.9
ii. PGDM	392	3.4
iii. Diploma Level Nursing	2,674	23.4
iv. Diploma Level Teacher Training	4,706	41.1
v. Institutes Under Ministries	132	1.2
TOTAL (i–v)	**11,445**	**100.0**
Total Tertiary Education Institutions	**48,828**	-

Source: MHRD, Educational Statistics, 2013-14.

colleges were at times, over 1,000 kilometres. Gradually the system had degenerated and universities took very little interest in affiliated colleges and were, at times, conducting annual ritual of examination, collection of fees, declaring results and holding convocations. Examining the deteriorating quality and standards of university education, S. Radhakrishnan had once observed that 'an educational institution, like an organic cell, could grow up to an optimum level and then split as otherwise they tend to decay'.

India's Higher Education enrolment is placed at 29.6 million (ASHER

Chart 2.4: Structure of Higher Education Enrolments in India

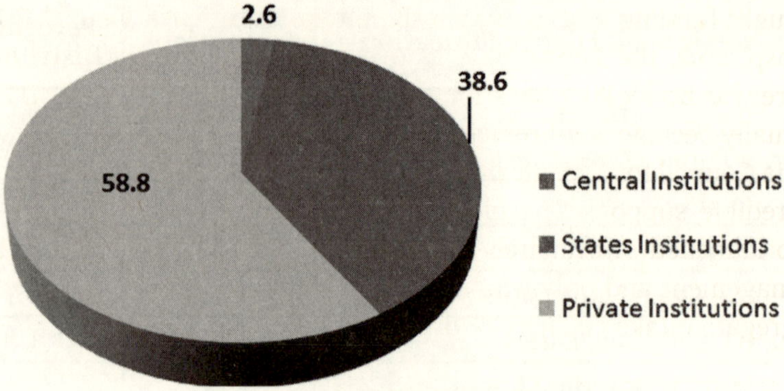

Source: British Council, 2014

2013). The structure of enrolments is given in Chart 2.4:

Evidently, the State institutions are the mainstay of Higher Education sector in India, especially if it is noted that thousands of private colleges are actually affiliated to the State Universities.

(B) Status of Technical Education

At the time of Independence, India had 46 engineering colleges and 53 polytechnics imparting Technical Education to 6,240 students. When India ushered in an industrial revolution during the Second Five-Year Plan, the Planning Commission lent great support for accelerating the growth of technical institutions in the country and kept the tempo in successive Five-Year Plans. However, the resource crunch during the 1980s, both at the Centre and the States, and in the wake of rising demand for Technical Education, some States like Karnataka, Maharashtra, Tamil Nadu and Andhra Pradesh took initiatives to permit private registered trusts and societies to establish and run technical institutions on self-financing basis, unlike in the past, where private initiatives were mostly from charitable endowments.

These States witnessed a spate of new institutions coming up.[32] Initially, some of the States like Tamil Nadu were too cautious and were gauging

32. AICTE, 'Technical Education in Independent India: 1947–1997, A Compendium to Commemorate the 50th Year of Anniversary of Independence', (New Delhi: All India Council for Technical Education, 1999).

the progress in Maharashtra and Karnataka. When they found the system brought funding and increased the intake capacity to meet the demands of aspirants, the hesitation was overcome by joy in the mid-1990s and there was no looking back for them ever since. The Engineering colleges virtually became self-financing, controlling about 95 per cent of seats. All India Council for Technical Education (AICTE) and State Boards provided a credible support. The phenomenon went viral to other States which also launched self-financing institutions in engineering and technology, management and polytechnics. There are about 10,300 institutions with aggregate intake capacity of over 3.70 million seats (Table 2.20).

Table 2.20: Technical Education Institutions

S.No.	Programme	No. of Institutions	Intake
1	Engineering and Technology	6,214	2,934,580
2	Management	3,764	449,829
3	MCA	1,571	22,644
4	Pharmacy	1,419	168,287
5	Architecture	165	12,870
6	HMCT	119	9,337
7	Applied Arts and Craft	67	4,866
	TOTAL	**10,298**	**3,702,413**

Source: MHRD.

Privatisation of Technical Education led to an acute regional imbalance. The States looked upon IITs to provide faculty and set benchmark for quality and standards of Technical Education. When IITs were unable to do the needful, several institutions went astray. There were serious ethical issues with some of the new institutions. There was absolutely no transparency whatsoever in the fees charged. Malpractices could not be controlled. Some unscrupulous private institutions started charging capitation fees under the table. All sorts of development funds were raised from the students. The deposits collected at the time of joining from students were seldom returned. AICTE could not maintain quality standards of these institutions and it had no credible faculty development plan either. The institutions often engaged graduates who had just passed out, without any teacher training, to undertake undergraduate teaching and were paid a paltry sum. This was often very exploitative. The AICTE and State Departments of Technical Education remained silent and many investors became Chancellors and developed a clout with State Governments.

Some of the problems in this regard which need to be addressed are:

- Excess capacity in most of the Southern States and Maharashtra,
- Regional imbalance within the States,
- Acute faculty shortage,
- Lack of transparency and misuse of autonomy, and
- Acute imbalances within the Technical Education (A study noted that 70 per cent of enrolments were in 20 per cent branches)

(C) Tertiary Education: Regular vs. Distance Mode

Table 2.21 presents data on Tertiary Education in regular vis-à-vis distance mode.

Table 2.21: Tertiary Education Enrolments in Regular and Distance Modes (in million)

Mode	Male	Female	Total	Percentage
Regular	14.3	11.7	26.0	88%
Distance	2.0	1.6	3.6	12%
Total Enrolments	16.3	13.3	29.6	100%

Source: All India Survey on Higher Education 2012-13 (Provisional) Report.

The distance mode of education covers about 3.6 million students accounting for only about 12 per cent of Tertiary Education enrolments. Even in distance mode, boys outnumber girls in enrolment. However, female enrolments have been accelerating in the recent years. While IGNOU has been very popular at the national level, some State institutions like Annamalai University have set standards. IGNOU runs many courses but not all of them are recognized by respective professional councils. For example, the Maternal Child Health programme has no approval of Medical Council of India (MCI). There is a tremendous scope for expanding Tertiary Education in the distance mode.

VI. Recent Developments and Policy Issues

(A) School Education

(i) Major Achievements

Some of the major achievements of the Department of School Education and Literacy may be summarised as under:

- The number of Elementary schools has expanded to 1.45 million, offering access to as many as 197 million students.
- Habitations having access to Primary schools rose to 97.2 per cent whereas those with access to Upper Primary schools expanded to 97.7 per cent. As many as 24 States have reported universal access to Elementary Education.
- 'Out-of-school children' (OoSC) have been brought down from around 135 million in 2005 to 8.1 million in 2010 and further to 6.1 million in 2015.
- The number of teachers increased to 4.67 million with pupil to teacher ratio (PTR) of 29:1 at Primary level and 27:1 at Upper Primary level.
- Average annual dropout rate for Primary Education came down from 9.9 per cent in 2005 to 4.71 per cent in 2016-17.
- The transition rate from Primary to Upper Primary has improved from 83.5 per cent in 2009-10 to 90.1 per cent in 2015-16.

These achievements, as reported by the Department of School Education and Literacy to the Parliament, are certainly praiseworthy, and so are the major new initiatives.[33]

(ii) Major New Initiatives

- A non-lapsable fund called Prarambhik Shiksha Kosh (PSK) in the Public Account of India has been set up where proceeds of Primary Education cess would be credited. These proceeds would be spent exclusively

33. Parliament of India, Rajya Sabha. '305th Report: Demands for Grants 2018-19 (Demand No. 57) of the Department of School Education & Literacy,' March 2018.

on the SSA and MDMS. Similarly, Madhyamik and Uchchtar Shiksha Kosh (MUSK) has been created where all proceeds from Secondary and Higher Education cess would be credited.

- A School Education Quality Index (SEQI) is being developed jointly by HRD Ministry and NITI Aayog in consultation with States and UTs. This index is expected to capture the status of education outcomes (i.e., access, learning and equity) for any State or UT. Future release of funds to States/UTs may be linked to their performance as measured by this index.
- National Repository of Open Educational Resources (NROER) is being created. The Repository aims at making digital resources available for students and teachers as free and open source material.
- A web portal and mobile app styled *e-Pathshala* has been created as a repository of all e-books and other audio and video resources for students and teachers.
- A platform of Massive Open Online Courses (MOOCs) called SWAYAM (Study Webs of Active Learning for Young Aspiring Minds) was launched in August 2016. The portal offers various online courses for School Education and Higher Education.
- An Innovation Fund had been created (Rs 100 crore) under RMSA with a view to support innovative projects for Secondary Education. These projects submitted by States/UTs would be aimed at enhancing access, improving gender parity, quality and learning outcomes in educationally backward blocks (EBBs).
- Under Swachh Vidyalaya initiative, around 136 million children in 1.108 million government schools were given access to gender-segregated toilets. Thus, every government school, now, has separate functional toilets for girls and boys.

Notwithstanding these achievements and new initiatives, there are several issues that continue to need serious policy attention, to which we turn next.

(iii) Budgetary Allocation

The details of budgetary allocation for and the actual expenditure of the Department of School Education and Literacy for the last five years are presented in Table 2.22.

As can be seen from Table 2.22, budgetary allocation as well as the

Table 2.22: Budgetary Allocation and Expenditure on School Education and Literacy (FY 2013-14 to FY 2017-18) (Rs Crore*)

Year	Budgetary Allocation	Actual Expenditure
2013-14	50,701	46,989
2014-15	55,115	45,757
2015-16	42,219	41,809
2016-17	43,554	38,786
2017-18	46,356	38,331

Source: Report of the Parliamentary Standing Committee on Human Resource Development, 305th Report (March, 2018) *1 crore = 10 million.

actual Central Government expenditure on School Education has taken a dip even in absolute terms from the year 2014-15 onwards, which is unfair and undesirable. The counter-argument offered that under the 14th Finance Commission, devolution of funds to the States has been raised substantially (from 32 per cent to 42 per cent) is not convincing. As a ratio of GDP, budgetary allocation for School Education has come down from a measly level of 0.47 per cent in 2013-14 to barely 0.28 per cent in 2017-18. This is exceedingly poor in comparison with the combined target (for School Education and Higher Education) of 6 per cent recommended by Kothari Commission way back in 1966.

(iv) Quality Issues

As the Finance Minister admitted in his Budget Speech of 2018-19 'we have managed to get children to school, but the quality of education is still a cause of serious concern'.

There are at least three dimensions to the quality issues:

- Assessment of quality,
- Quality of teachers, and
- Improvement in technology of education

As far as the assessment of quality is concerned, it is heartening to note that the Central Rules to the RTE Act have now been amended to include reference on class-wise, subject-wise learning outcomes. The learning outcomes have been finalised for every class up to the Elementary stage.

The National Council of Educational Research and Training (NCERT) has started conducting periodical national surveys of learning achievements—i.e., National Achievement Survey (NAS).

Expeditious completion of NASs at all levels of School Education would enable generation of district-wise learning report cards. These learning progress cards would be very helpful in planning and implementation of interventions for improving learning levels of children from classroom setting right up to the national level.

As far as the teachers are concerned, there are several issues that need urgent attention. First, in Elementary schools, there are more than 9 lakh vacancies of teachers lying vacant (as of end of March 2017). Secondly, according to U-DISE data for 2015-16, more than 15 per cent Elementary schools had a single teacher and more than 33.9 per cent schools had an adverse pupil-teacher ratio, which is well beyond the acceptable standards. Thirdly, absenteeism among teachers is also unacceptably high—more than 15 per cent at Primary level and around 17 per cent at Upper Primary level. Fourthly, more than 1.3 million untrained teachers in service need to be trained on priority.

Moreover, as indicated by the Finance Minister in his Budget Speech 2018-19, it is imperative that technology becomes the biggest driver in improving the quality of education. In this regard, the Indian Education System needs to move from 'blackboard' to 'digital board' and the digital intensity in education needs a significant upscaling. Teachers also would have to upgrade their technology skills through the digital portal 'DIKSHA' launched recently.

(B) Higher Education

(i) Major Achievements

Some of the major achievements of the Higher Education sector, as reported in Report 302 of the Parliamentary Standing Committee on Human Resources Development (March 2018), include:

- Operationalisation of Rashtriya Uchhatar Shiksha Abhiyan[34] (RUSA)

34. As Member of the Planning Commission, in-charge inter alia of Education, I had an opportunity to take the lead in the formulation of the ambitious RUSA Scheme. Simultaneously, my being a Member of National Advisory Council (NAC) also did help in getting the Scheme through.

as a Centrally Sponsored Scheme (CSS). This overarching scheme is operated in a Mission Mode, funding the State Governments so as to achieve the goals of equity, access and excellence in Higher Education. The Central Government's funding which goes to State Universities and colleges through State governments is based on critical appraisal of State Higher Education Plans (SHEPs).

- Creation of State Higher Education Councils in 34 States/UTs.
- Creation of State Project Directorates in 31 States/UTs.
- Improvement in accreditation status in respect of universities and colleges. State level Quality Assurance Cells have been constituted in almost all States and UTs to facilitate the process.
- Academic reforms such as choice-based credit system and examination reforms have been initiated.

(ii) Major New Initiatives

- As indicated earlier, a platform of MOOCs called SWAYAM has been launched. UGC and AICTE have issued 'Credit Framework for Online Learning Courses through SWAYAM, Regulation 2016', which facilitates transfer of credits for students using SWAYAM. National MOOCs Coordinators (NMCs) have been constituted so as to ensure developing and delivering MOOCs in various disciplines.
- Higher Education Financing Agency (HEFA) is being set up as a not-for-profit organisation that will leverage funds from the market and supplement them with donations and CSR funds. These funds will be used for financing improvement in infrastructure in our top institutions (Report 302, March 2018, cited above).
- A major initiative is to be launched by 2022, titled, 'Revitalising Infrastructure and Systems in Education (RISE) with a total investment of Rs 1 lakh crore. RISE will help step up investments in research and related infrastructure in premier educational institutions, including health institutions (Report 302, cited above).
- Another initiative called the Global Initiative of Academic Networks (GIAN) in Higher Education has been launched. This initiative seeks to invite distinguished academicians, entrepreneurs, scientists and experts from premier institutions across the world to teach in the Higher Education institutions in India. The Scheme essentially envisages garnering the international expertise into the Indian

Education System.

- Yet another noteworthy initiative is to create 20 world-class institutions, both in the public and private sector.
- A platform called e-Shodh Sindhu (e-SS) has been launched with a view to provide access to high quality electronic resources including full text bibliographic and factual databases to academic institutions at lower rates of subscription. This initiative has been promoting scholarly communication among academicians and researchers.

Notwithstanding these achievements and new initiatives, there are several issues that merit attention:

(iii) Funding of Education

As can be seen from the snapshot in Table 2.23, India spends about 4.3 per cent of its GDP on education. States' contribution was 3.13 per cent and that of the Central Government was 1.16 per cent. The Public expenditure (Centre and the States) on Higher and Technical Education was 1.43 per cent of the GDP. The Central Government's share of investment in this Tertiary Education Sector was 0.61 per cent of GDP.

Historically, the Central institutions gobbled up over 65-67 per cent of Central budgeted expenditure on Higher and Technical institutions depsite the fact that their share in the total enrolment in Higher and Technical Education was exceedingly small. Thanks to *Rashtriya Uchchatar*

Table 2.23: Expenditure on Education (BE 2012-13)

Education Sectors	**Education Expenditure (Rs Crore)**			**Expenditure as a Percentage GDP**		
	Centre	States/UTs	Total	Centre	ST/UTs	Total
Elementary	41,022	128,228	169,250	0.44	1.37	1.80
Secondary	10,468	88,376	98,844	0.11	0.94	1.05
Univ. and Higher	32,739	50,820	83,559	0.35	0.54	0.89
Adult Education	709	479	1,188	0.01	0.01	0.01
Technical	24,283	26,109	50,393	0.26	0.28	0.54
Total	**1,09,223**	**2,94,013**	**4,03,236**	**1.16**	**3.13**	**4.29**

Source: Analysis of Budgeted Expenditure, 2012-13.

Shiksha Abhiyan (RUSA), however, the funding for the State institutions has increased during the recent years and the share of Central institutions had come down somewhat. The Government of India should increase its investments in the State sector institutions whose enrolment is over 11.5 million while the enrolment in Central institutions is about 0.77 million only. RUSA funding needs to be stepped up significantly.

The private sector has outpaced the State sector in Tertiary Education and is rapidly expanding. The private sector will continue to be crucial in the growth of Higher Education in India and already comprises 64 per cent of the total number of institutions and 59 per cent of Tertiary enrolment across the country.[35] Private Higher Education Universities were growing at 40 per cent per annum and were worth $6.5 billion in 2011-12.[36]

India does not promote educational institutions by 'For Profit' establishments in the private sector. It is argued that 'For Profit' institutions will charge cost-based fees and will ensure quality of education. Self-regulatory mechanism would ensure accountability and outcomes will commensurate for the value of money invested by the parents and students. It is believed that the market force would ensure only best institutions to survive and institutions with poor outcomes will lose 'business'. The point, however, is when even the so-called non-profit institutions running colleges and universities resort to capitation fees and very unethical practices in fleecing the students, what the 'For Profit' institutions would do is anybody's guess. Studies show that 'the quality of education at "For-Profit" colleges is far lower than even second-tier non-profit colleges. The "For-Profit" institutions are blamed for poor quality on allegedly questionable marketing practices and high spending on executive compensation'.[37]

(iv) Research and Faculty Development

India has not been producing enough PhDs. Very few students continue

---

35. FICCI and Ernst & Young, 'Higher Education in India: Twelfth Five Year Plan (2012–17) and beyond', FICCI Higher Education Summit 2012, (New Delhi: FICCI, 2012).

36. The Parthenon Group, 'Private Universities in India: An investment in National Development', Indian Education Congress, 2012.

37. Rafiq Dossani, 'The Cost of Higher Education: The Big Picture', *RAND Center for Asia Pacific Policy,* 12 July 2013, https://www.rand.org/blog/2013/07/the-cost-of-higher-education-the-big-picture.html

on to research degrees compared to other countries. Only 140,000 (1 per cent) students are enrolled as postgraduate researchers. The lack of enquiry-based learning and early researcher skills is limiting the capacity of Indian institutions to engage in vital research and innovation activity.[38] In several quarters, it has been lamented that despite possessing the world's largest cadres of agricultural scientists and nationwide network of institutions on research and education, India could not take the Green Revolution to other parts of the country. The premier Institutions such as IITs produce world-class scientists and engineers but the national research stream has rarely produced world-class results.

One possible reason is the missing link between scientists in universities and the research institutes and practitioners in agriculture and industry. Another reason is that non-teaching research institutes lack continuous inflow of young talented research scholars. At another level, the quality of research produced in the universities/technical institutions is also not up to the mark when it comes to additions to the existing body of knowledge in the subject chosen. Most of the Supervisors/Guides seem to be satisfied with the output of the scholars in the course work and often lack capabilities to inspire stretching the imagination of young scholars.

One of the serious consequences of limited enrolments for PhD and poor-quality outcomes in research results in universities facing acute shortage of quality faculty. Therefore, faculty shortage in Higher and Technical Education needs to be met with increased fellowships for PG/ research degrees and also compulsory UG teaching assignments for Junior Research Fellows (JRFs) so that Readers and Professors devote more time to PG and research scholars.

The UGC/AICTE should evolve a faculty development plan inviting services of the scientists in public and private sector research institutions outside the domain of the university system, for teaching assignments. There is a need to revamp Teacher Education institutions in Higher Education and Training, both in service and pre-service training. Knowledge capital infusion should be promoted in Academic Staff Colleges (ASCs) in the first instance with specialised package, outside existing university norms through contractual engagements from reputed institutions, national and international, in a wide range of disciplines. This should be opened to government research organisations/specialised institutions. Poor quality

38. British Council, 'Understanding India', 2014.

pre-service training has been wrecking the quality of education in publicly funded institutions. No amount of in-service training could improve the calibre of a teacher if his or her pre-service training is dismal. The results of National Eligibility Test (NET) are anything but encouraging. However, the NET candidates are better than State Level Education Test (SLET). A large number of institutions have come up including District Institute for Education and Training (DIETs) for providing degrees and diplomas. It is essential that all Teacher Education institutions including those imparting Certificate/Diploma in Early Childhood Care and Education (ECCE) should be brought under the university system.

(v) Governance Issues

Many State Universities spend much of their time in administering the examinations and admissions to their affiliated colleges. Enrolments at State Universities are highly sought after by students for the simple reason that the fees charged are very low; there is transparency in the system with the government and better campus environment with fewer restrictions and scholarships are easier to obtain than in private institutions. As it happens, those who score high in the Board examination or entrance tests get seats in government institutions for Technical Education. They are mostly urban students from affluent sections with public school background. However, those poor rural children, who have all along studied in government schools suddenly find themselves in quandary as they are shoved out in the high cut-off marks/or poor scoring in entrance test. The affluent classes manage the best of both worlds. The poor rural children are directed to private institutions where they get fleeced in most cases.

The difficulties in regulating the Higher Education System have been compounded by structural issues, including a national quality assurance system which has struggled to adequately monitor standards in colleges and universities, and which has been particularly problematic in the burgeoning private sector. This situation is changing, however. Accreditation of all colleges and universities became mandatory in 2013 and thousands of institutions have registered for accreditation in the recent past. There is a new impetus to strengthen national systems through mechanisms which grant more autonomy and funding to States linked to greater accountability. The Washington Accord (WA) had admitted National Board of Accreditation, India, as its 17th member. This gives some global recognition for Tier 1 institutions providing engineering courses accredited by NBA through Outcome Based Accreditation criteria.

Currently, the pressure is on Higher Education to deliver. Earlier, there was unspoken acceptance that universities were the best places to judge the quality of Higher Education. As a corollary, there was an acceptance that Higher Education should not be regulated nor its quality assessed by anyone other than academics themselves. The concept of peer review was ingrained in this paradigm. Such an approach is no longer deemed to be sufficient in the current context. There are four primary forms of regulation and thus accountability — national regulation by government bodies; professional accreditation; the market demand from students, and most importantly, self-regulation by the institution itself. For Higher Education institutions to maintain quality and indeed to improve, there must be an acceptance of these broader demands for accountability and a willingness to engage in the debates around them.[39]

(vi) International Collaborations

Except a few big institutions, many in India operate in seclusion. International institutions often avoid collaborative work with them. For example, most research collaborations between India and the UK formed through UK Research Councils and the UK-India Education and Research Initiative or UKIERI are focussed on the 'best' research institutions in India, primarily the Centrally-funded Universities and Institutes of National Importance, where only 2.6 per cent of Indian students are enrolled. While Phase 2 of UKIERI has encouraged broader participation with 'tier 2 and 3' institutions, forming over 20 per cent of the partnership awards, this is still a very small representation. There remains limited international research collaboration with State universities and Private institutions, with a few notable exceptions such as Savitribai Phule Pune University in Maharashtra.[40]

39. Carol Nicoll, 'How can Higher Education maintain and improve quality?', Tertiary Education Quality and Standards Agency, Australia, IMHE General Conference, Attaining and Sustaining Mass Higher Education, Paris, 17–19 September 2012.

40. As Vice-Chancellor of Pune University during 2006-09, I promoted international collaborations to such an extent that in the year 2008, as many as 45 per cent of all foreign students coming to India came to Pune University alone!

(vii) Accreditation

Recently, accreditation through the National Assessment and Accreditation Council (NAAC) and the National Body for Accreditation (NBA) of all universities and colleges was made mandatory. A huge exercise is currently underway to accredit the two-thirds of universities and four-fifths of colleges that do not have accredited status.

State Universities, through their activities, form by far the largest segment of Higher Education in India. They are run and funded through their respective State governments. There is a wide variation in the amount of funding they receive but, in general, they have been critically underfunded over the last 20 years. State Universities depend on affiliation fees paid by the colleges for their survival. These fees, supplemented by State government funding, are generally used to pay salaries and little else; most of these universities have poor infrastructure and conduct little research, although pockets of excellence do exist. Again, Savitribai Phule Pune University is one such exception.

(viii) Scholarships and Educational Loans

Scholarship regime should be expected to cover at least one-third of Higher, Technical and Professional Education enrolments. Common family income criteria should be set in consultation with the States. The Education Loan Scheme should be reformulated by the government and should not be left to the bankers who attempt to make business out of educational loans. Moratorium periods and subsidy for interest does not really help much. Capitalisation of interest on educational loans should be done away forthwith. This is simply compounding liabilities like credit card outstanding amount. In fact, no interest should be charged on educational loans, like in the Australian system. The loans should come with a flat rate fee of 15-20 per cent. This would be far cheaper than recurring interest liabilities of eight years or more. This should be uniformly applied to all educational loans.

Currently, different banks in India charge different interest rates for education loans. It is reported that banks are facing a lot of problems with mounting non-performing assets (NPA). In order to reduce NPA some banks (e.g., SBI) sold out Education Term Loans (ETL) to Corporates by the way of 'asset reconstruction'. Other private banks appoint collection agents. Both are the same in effect. SBI is reported to have sold out NPA for 45 per cent.[41] It is quite possible that the actual loan amount provided to students was near about this proportion and the rest of NPA could have arisen on account of interest dues and capitalisation of interest which the poor unemployed or grossly under-employed students could not repay.

The Australian Government has noted that the cost of the education loan at 20 per cent itself was very much on the higher side discouraging students from taking educational loans.[42] The loans should be serviced at 15 per cent fee and prompt repayments may have a rebate of 3 per cent fee concession. The Twelfth Plan (2012–17) had envisaged reduction in interest rate and the rate was to be comparable to Government Securities for 10 years.

The intention of education loan schemes is to support students in pursuing Higher Education and banks should be entitled to recover cost and a little margin. Banks should look for viability funding from the government, if need arises. The future of India should not be left languishing in debt, which the current system invariably does. There are press reports of poor students unable to repay the education loan committing suicides[43] and also banks insisting on collaterals for educational loan despite instructions to the contrary. What collateral a poor farmer can give to his son's educational loan save for a milch animal or two and the land that sustains the poor family? Banks which insist on collateral do not accept agricultural land as collateral and the courts have to come to the student's rescue.[44] It is not fair to entrust the job of formulating the educational loan scheme to the banks.

---

41. Sruthisagar Yamunan, 'The "bad" side of education loans', *The Hindu,* Chennai Edition, 22 June 2016, https://www.thehindu.com/todays-paper/tp-national/tp-tamilnadu/The-%e2%80%98bad%e2%80%99-side-of-education-loans/article14394716.ece

42. Department of Education, Australian Government, 'Transforming Australia's Higher Education System', 2010.

43. Unable to repay education loan engineering student commits suicide A civil engineering student, son of a poor mason, had taken an educational loan of Rs 1.90 lakh from a nationalised bank in Madurai, Tamil Nadu. He was getting frequent calls from the bank for recovery of loan. He was reportedly warned that his original certificates would be seized for non-repayment. The unemployed student got depressed and committed suicide. 'Engineering student commits suicide', *The Hindu,* Madurai Edition, 16 July 2016.

44. The Madras High Court directed Indian Overseas Bank to accept agricultural land as collateral security and grant a poor farmer's son educational loan to pursue MBBS in a medical college in Navi Mumbai. *PTI*, 'HC directs bank to accept farm land as collateral for edu loan,' *Business Standard,* 26 June 2017.

This should be formulated by the Ministry of HRD in consultation with the Ministry of Finance.

In sum, there is a lot that needs to be done in the field of Higher and Technical Education in India to meet the global demands in terms of quality, reach and access. Some key elements that need to be addressed in Higher Education are as follows:

- The quality of teaching faculty has been a key concern, possibly due to dilutions of selection standards.
- The curriculum, content, teaching methods, assessment standards and methods have all to be revamped and upgraded.
- In order to make Higher Education competitive and global, the credit system needs to be introduced.
- Research facilities have to be improved and students attracted to take up research work without any hurdles.
- The regulatory authority be least interfering, more supportive and follow well-defined assessment criteria for accreditation so that the Indian Universities are globally accepted.
- There is a wide gap between the industry expectations and the university standards, on account of which millions of people are unemployed/unemployable, while thousands of jobs are lying vacant for want of the right personnel.
- The role of private operators in the field of Higher Education has increased and a meaningful private-public partnership is a must to cater to the increasing number of users. At the same time, there should be proper regulatory mechanism to ensure that unethical practice of fleecing the students with capitation fees by Deemed Universities/ Institutions is put to an end with fair transparent admission and fee structure published on the Institution's website.

3

Demographic Dividend, Education and Skill Development: Temporal and Spatial Dimensions

Having examined India's overall attainment in education and skill development in the previous chapter, attention is focussed in this chapter on the Demographic Dividend, fortuitously said to be available to India, say, up to the year 2030.

This chapter is organised as follows. Section I offers a cross-country perspective on the concept of Demographic Dividend—how it is expected to work and what are the actual experiences across the world. Section II deals with the estimation of the quantum of Demographic Dividend available in India and its social dimensions. In this regard, detailed projections of India's population up to the year 2030 have been made. Section III covers spatial dimensions of the potential Demographic Dividend for India. Section IV then analyses the current state preparedness in India, especially in terms of education, skill development and health, for harnessing and leveraging the Demographic Dividend currently available. The final Section, i.e., Section V, surveys recent policy initiatives in respect of Skill Development by the Modi Government and identifies policy issues that merit urgent attention.

I. Demographic Dividend: A Cross-Country Perspective

A striking feature of India's demographic transition is undoubtedly its youthfulness with steadily increasing working age population (15–59 years). The average age of India's population is expected to be around 29 years by 2020 as against 48 years in Japan, 45 years in Western Europe and 37 years each, in China and the United States of America. As most of the developed countries of the world imminently face the burden of rapidly ageing population, the inevitable shortage of young working age population estimated around 56 million by 2022 has been casting a long shadow on the global economy. Even the recent easing of single child norm in China is unlikely to correct the imbalances engendered through decades of restrictive policies. The fortuitous circumstance is that India would be the only country in the world brimming with a surplus of 47 million youth.[1] This is precisely the basis for India's claim to the so-called Demographic Dividend, which occurs only once in the entire lifetime of a nation.

A review of literature on Demographic Dividend[2] indicates that the potential gain to the economy involved, accrues as a combined result of at least five distinct forces:

- Swelling of the labour force as the large and growing young population reaches the working age;
- Possibility of enabling the government to divert public resources from investing in children to investment in physical capital, job

1. Labour Bureau, Ministry of Labour and Employment, Government of India, 'Education, Skill Development and Labour Force 2013-14', Fourth Employment & Unemployment Survey Report (2013-14), vol. III, November 2014.

2. David E. Bloom ('Population Dynamics in India and Implications for Economic Growth', 2011); Bloom and David Canning ('Global Demographic Change: Dimensions and Economic Significance', 2008); and Bloom, Canning and Jaypee Sevilla ('The Demographic Dividend: A New Perspective on the Economic Consequences of Population Change,' 2003) are particularly important.

training and technological progress;

- Declining fertility among women and consequent possibility of the rise in their workforce activity;
- Since working years also happen to be the prime years for savings, the swelling of the workforce can give a boost to savings, which in turn, could be the bedrock for accumulation of physical and human capital as well as technological innovation; and
- With greater longevity, the retirement years tend to be longer, which, in turn, provides a bigger incentive to save thereby promoting savings further, leading possibly to acceleration of economic growth.

It may be noted, however, that there is nothing automatic about the effects of demographic change on economic growth. Relevant literature, in fact, emphasises that 'demography is not destiny'. Changes in age structure of a country simply affect the supply-side potential for economic growth. Capturing that potential depends on numerous other factors, especially public policy on education, skill development, health as well as the overall macroeconomic management and governance.

Against this background, it would be interesting to look at the actual evidence from different countries at different stages of economic growth and development.

Evidence has been recorded regarding unprepared and under-prepared governments missing their chances of reaping their 'Demographic Dividend'. The opportunity to reap a Demographic Dividend, in fact, occurs only during a finite window that gradually closes as the working generation ages. For example, the late 20th century saw Demographic Dividend in Asia. The Gross Domestic Product (GDP) increased sevenfold — an economic boom that was described as the 'Asian economic miracle'. On the other hand, in Latin America around the same time, growth was only two-fold, reflecting unequal access to investments in education and health, including the reproductive health and rights of women and girls.[3]

Elsewhere in the world, a low dependency ratio has been extremely beneficial for China's unprecedented period of economic growth since 1978. However, China denied itself the opportunity of Demographic Dividend with one child family planning norms and is, of late, facing a serious problem with large and growing proportion of aged people with the attendant overburdening of health and social security programmes.

3. UNFPA, 'Demographic Dividend', 2016.

According to some studies, China is heading for a difficult situation in near future as the quality of human capital has been materially getting altered with aging population. It is being argued that the skill-quotient is determined not merely by experience and expertise but also with actual ability and fitness of the workforce to be productive on the factory floors.

East Asia provides some of the most compelling evidence of the Demographic Dividend to date. The demographic transition in East Asia occurred over 5–15 years, during the 1950s and 1960s, a shorter time period than anywhere else earlier. During this time, East Asian countries invested in their youth and expanded access to the means of family planning encouraging people to start families later and have fewer children. More resources were released for investment in infrastructure and other productive investments as fertility rates fell resulting in unprecedented economic growth. In fact, the UNFPA stated that 'the Republic of Korea saw its per capita gross domestic product grow about 2200 per cent between 1950 and 2008, and Thailand's GDP grew 970 per cent'. Needless to say that East Asia was able to benefit from the knowledge, experience and technology of other countries that had already passed through the demographic transition. Nevertheless, there is no denying that the Demographic Dividend played a key role in the 'economic miracle' of the East Asian Tigers.

Another example of Demographic Dividend and its transition is the Irish government initiative in 1979 of legalising contraception as a measure to counter the high birth rate. The policy resulted in a reduction in the fertility rate and a lower dependency ratio. The resultant increase in the share of the working age group population has been regarded as an important contributing factor to the economic boom of the 1990s. During this period, the decline in the dependency ratio also emanated from increased female labour market participation and a reversal from outward migration of working age population to a net inflow.

In Africa, on the other hand, fertility rates have remained relatively high, even though significant progress has been made in respect of bringing down the mortality rates. This has led to a continuing population explosion rather than an increase in the share of working age population, which contributed to economic stagnation in much of Sub-Saharan Africa. The African example clearly shows that the magnitude of the Demographic Dividend seems to be dependent on the ability of the economy to absorb and productively employ the additional workers.

In fact, according to the UN Population Fund, 'if sub-Saharan African countries are able to repeat the East Asian experience, the region could realise a Demographic Dividend amounting to as much as $500 billion a year for 30 years' (UNFPA, 2016).

As mentioned earlier, demography is not destiny; growth of the working-age share of the population does not automatically lead to an acceleration of economic growth. Demographic Dividend may provide a boost to economic growth, but appropriate policies must be in place to allow this to happen. Without such policies, a country may instead find itself with large numbers of unemployed or underemployed working-age individuals. In that case, the situation could become a 'demographic disaster' or 'demographic nightmare' instead of Demographic Dividend.

II. Potential of Demographic Dividend in India

In order to quantify the potential of Demographic Dividend, a detailed analysis of demographic trends in India would be necessary. In particular, projections of India's overall population and relevant parameters such as fertility rates and dependency ratios would have to be worked out. A meaningful and operationally relevant quantification of India's Demographic Dividend could be made on the basis of an estimated share of working age group population during the period up to the year 2030.

India's population increased at an exponential rate of 1.64 per cent per annum to reach 1,211 million in 2011 from 1,029 million in 2001. The net addition of 182 million people during the decade was only marginally lower than the entire population of Brazil, the fifth most populous country in the world.[4] India's population has been projected to be at 1,419 million by 2025 (medium variant) and in the subsequent three years, it is slated to overtake China's population of 1,450 million.[5] India's population is currently growing at a rate far surpassing that of China's 0.7 per cent per annum. The differential population growth rates between India and China (as projected in 2011) will result in India surpassing China's

4. K.S. James, 'India's Demographic Change: Opportunities and Challenges', *Science*, 29 July 2011, vol. 333, issue no. 6042.

5. UN, 'World Population Prospects, the 2012 Revision', (New York: UN Population Division, Department of Economic and Social Affairs, 2013).

population in less than 20 years.[6] The BBC reports that India would be the world's most populous country from 2028 onward.[7] According to the United Nations Population Fund (UNFPA), India's population is expected to reach 1,523 million by 2030, accounting for 18.3 per cent of the world population, then estimated to be of 8,321 million.[8] Some estimates project India's population to overtake that of China by 2023 itself and reach 1,500 million by 2030.[9] On the other hand, McKinsey Report seems to project India's population somewhat lower at 1,470 million by 2030.[10]

India is still working its way through the demographic transition with the gradual decline in fertility and mortality rates in the temporal context. However, spatial variation continues to be wide. Analysis of Sample Registration System (SRS) data show that the annual birth rates declined by about 1.4 percentage points since 2008; the rural birth rates being distinctly higher than those in urban areas. Estimate of birth rates are provided in Table 3.1.

Table 3.1: Annual Estimates of Birth Rates, 2008–13

	2008	2009	2010	2011	2012	2013
All India	22.8	22.5	22.1	21.8	21.6	21.4
Rural	24.4	24.1	23.7	23.3	23.1	22.9
Urban	18.5	18.3	18.0	17.6	17.4	17.3

Source: Sample Registration System (SRS), Registrar General of India, 2013.

In bigger States, the annual birth rates tend to be substantially higher—Uttar Pradesh (29.1 per cent), Bihar (28.9 per cent), Madhya Pradesh (28.9 per cent), Rajasthan (27.5 per cent) and Chhattisgarh (26.1 per cent)—than the national average, reflecting continued high fertility rates on account of several factors including illiteracy, universal marriage often at younger ages, high infant mortality and limited outcomes of family

6. Bloom, 'Population Dynamics in India and Implications for Economic Growth', 2011.

7. 'UN: India to be world's most populous country by 2028', *BBC News,* 14 June 2013, https://www.bbc.com/news/world-asia-22907307.

8. Most Populous Nation by 2030, Demographics of India.

9. Euromonitor International reports.

10. McKinsey Report on 'Urban India 2030'.

welfare programmes.

In India, the twin demographic goals of National Population Policy (NPP) 2000, viz., achieving the population replacement level. Total Fertility Rate (TFR) of 2.1 by 2010 and a stable population by 2045, would apparently call for a revised time frame. Recent trends in fertility decline show a deceleration. The TFR declined by 1.6 (from 5.2 to 3.6) between 1971 and 1991. In the following two decades or so, i.e., 1991–2009, however, it declined by merely 0.7 to 2.9. Therefore, time-over runs are most likely in achieving the projected TFR of 2.1. The population projections based on Census 2001 and long-term indicators of fertility etc. now appear to be underestimates, thereby calling for a revision to set a more realistic goal in the temporal context.

Long-term trends in the composition of the Indian population reveal that there has been a gradual decline in the share of population in the age group 0–14 from 41.2 per cent in 1971 to 38.1 per cent in 1981, 36.3 per cent in 1991 and further to 30.8 per cent in 2011. At the other hand, on account of better education, health facilities and increase in life expectancy, the population in the age group of 60+ has gone up from 5.3 per cent in 1971 to 8.9 per cent in 2011. The main feature of the demographic change, however, is in the proportion of economically active population (15–59 years) that has increased from 53.4 in 1971 to 56.3 per cent in 1981, 57.7 per cent in 1991 and 60.3 per cent in 2011. Projected age structure of the Indian population in 2013 is depicted in Chart 3.1.

The latest structure of the population (as per Census 2011) not only

Chart 3.1: Age Structure of India's Population (2013)

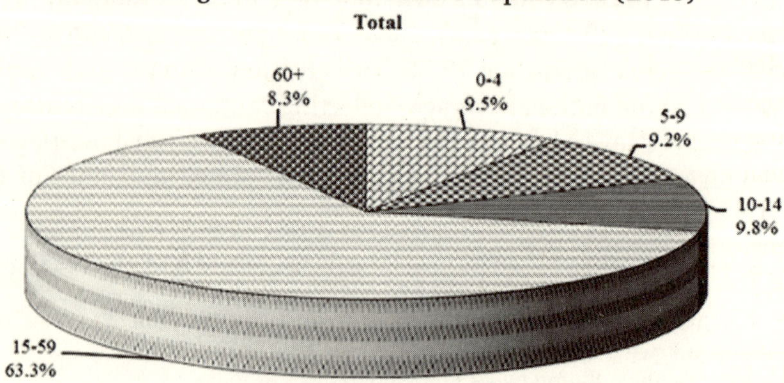

Source: O/o Registrar General of India, SRS, 2013.

shows India's vast human resources at present but also a grand continuum in the pipeline for the next two decades which contrasts with the ageing population in most of the developed and developing countries. The adolescent and youth population (10–24 years) at 365 million accounted for a solid 30.1 per cent.

It is being argued that population stabilisation even with the existing regional, social and gender imbalances, is not expected before the country's total population exceeds 1,700 million. Going by the Chinese experience, even after replacement level fertility is attained, it would take more than three decades for the population to stabilise. According to the population projection released by the United Nations Population Division,[11] the ultimate size of India's population when the population stabilisation is achieved will be about 1.72 billion around 2060. Their more recent projection (2017), however, shows that India's population would reach 1.66 billion by 2050 and would decline to 1.52 billion by 2100 (Table 3.2).

Table 3.2: Population Projections India and the World (in billion)

Year	India	World
2017	1.34	7.55
2030	1.51	8.55
2050	1.66	9.77
2100	1.52	11.18

Source: United Nations Population Division, 2017.

Technical Group set up by the National Commission on Population projected (in 2006) India's population by 2026 to be at 1,400 million and these estimates are widely used for perspective planning in the country. A linear extrapolation of this estimate would place the country's population at 1,454 million by 2030. However, as can be seen from Table 3.3, Census 2011 revealed that the actual population had actually exceeded the Technical Group's projected population estimates at 1,191 million in

11. UN, `World Population Prospects: The 2010 Revision', (New York: UN Population Division, Department of Economic and Social Affairs, 2011), available at http://esa.un.org/undp/wpp/index.htm

Table 3.3: Technical Group's Population Projections and Census Estimates, 2011

Technical Group's Projection 2011				Census 2011			
Population by Age Groups (million)				Population by Age Groups (million)			
0–14	15–59	60+	Total	0–14	15–59	60+	Total
347	746	98	1,191	372	730	108	1,210
29.1%	62.6%	8.3%	100.0%	30.8%	60.3%	8.9%	100.0%

Source: National Commission on Population, May 2006; Census 2011.

2011 by around 19 million. An analysis of Census 2011 data shows that over 60 per cent of this variation is accounted by two States, viz., Tamil Nadu and Bihar, where the actual population in 2011 turned out to be significantly higher than the ones projected earlier. On the other hand, the actuals in Kerala and Uttar Pradesh were somewhat lower than the preceding projections.

While projecting India's population by 2030, here the Technical Group's population estimates were utilised together with the underlying population growth rates. Also taken into account were the Census 2011 population estimates to rework the growth rates and linearly extrapolate the population for various age groups for 2030 using exponential functions. Accordingly, for Tamil Nadu, Bihar and a few other States where the actual estimates of Census 2011 varied with a wide margin as compared to Technical Group's projections, exponential growth rates were reworked on the basis of 2011 Census instead of the Census 2001. The estimates for 2006 and 2016 were derived through interpolation and extrapolation, respectively, on decennial growth rates for various age groups using single age population data released by the Registrar General of India.

It turns out that our projection of India's population at 1,538 million by 2030 is strikingly close to the latest USAID estimates.[12] Alternatively, the United Nations Population Division has released its projections (2017) of world population at 8.6 billion and that of India's at 1.51 billion by 2030 (as indicated in Table 3.2) which is also fairly close. As per these

12. According to 2018 World Population Data Sheet, Population Reference Bureau, USAID, India's population by mid-2030 would be 1,532 million and in mid-2050, around 1,680 million.

projections, India's population by 2050 is placed at 1.66 billion and is expected to fall to around 1.52 billion by the turn of the century. The marginal difference of 28 million in population projected by us and that of UN Population Division (2017) for the year 2030 could be explained by our assumption of accelerated growth of population in States like Bihar experiencing *population momentum* in view of most youthful population. Given the current trends in various parameters usually considered in population projections, perhaps, McKinsey Report (2010) appears to have given a low-end projection of India's population in 2030 to be 1,470 million. However, the usual caveat would apply for all population projections.

Our projections of India's population by States during the period, 2011–2030 are presented in Table 3.4.

Table 3.4: Projected Population by States, 2011–2030

	STATES	**INDIA'S POPULATION BY 2030 (millions)**						
		2001	**2006**	**2011**	**2016**	**2021**	**2026**	**2030**
	***EAG STATES**							
1	Uttar Pradesh	166.2	181.8	199.8	220.6	237.9	252.9	266.4
2	Bihar	83	92.8	104.1	117	129	133.4	137.5
3	Jharkhand	26.9	29.7	33	36.7	40.5	42.4	44.1
4	Madhya Pradesh	60.3	66.1	72.6	80	86.4	91.2	95.6
5	Chhattisgarh	20.8	23	25.5	28.4	31.1	32.5	33.8
6	Uttarakhand	8.5	9.2	10.1	11.1	11.9	12.4	12.9
7	Odisha	36.8	39.2	41.9	45	48.1	49.4	50.7
8	Rajasthan	56.5	62.1	68.5	75.9	84.8	88.9	92.6
	NE STATES							
9	NER (Excluding Assam)	12.2	13.2	14.3	15.5	16.1	16.8	17.5
10	Assam	26.7	28.8	31.2	33.9	36.9	38.3	39.7
	OTHER STATES							

	STATES	INDIA'S POPULATION BY 2030 (millions)						
		2001	**2006**	**2011**	**2016**	**2021**	**2026**	**2030**
11	Jammu and Kashmir	10.1	11.3	12.5	14	15.1	15.6	16
12	Himachal Pradesh	6.1	6.4	6.9	7.3	7.6	7.8	8
13	Punjab	2.4	2.6	2.8	3	31.1	32.2	33.2
14	Haryana	21.1	23.1	25.4	28	30	31.7	33.4
15	West Bengal	80.4	85.5	91.3	97.9	101.8	105	108
16	Gujarat	50.7	55.3	60.4	66.2	72.6	75.7	78.5
17	Maharashtra	96.8	104.1	112.3	121.7	133	140	146.1
18	Andhra Pradesh (including Telangana)	76.2	79.9	84.6	90.1	97.3	100.5	103.4
19	Karnataka	52.8	56.6	61.1	66.2	68.8	71	73.1
20	Kerala	31.8	32.6	33.4	34.3	35.1	35.8	36.4
21	Tamil Nadu	62.4	67	72	77.7	81.8	82.6	83.5
	ALL India	1028.6	1114	1210.5	1320.7	1421.9	1484.5	1537.6

Source: All India estimates include all left-out small States/UTs.
*Empowered Action Group

Our data analysis indicates that the number of children in the age group of 0–14 would decline by 25 million (from 372 million in 2011 to 347 million in 2030) and their proportion to total population by 8.2 percentage points (from 30.7 per cent to 22.5 per cent). However, the population in the 60+ age group is set to increase by 118 million (from 108 million in 2011 to 226 million, by 2030) and their proportion to population by 5.8 percentage points (from 8.9 to 14.7 per cent) for the corresponding period. Thus, the net increase in dependent population, assuming that all the 60+ age groups are dependents as such, would be around 93 million between 2011 and 2030.

According to our projections, by 2030, India would add 327 million to its 2011 population of 1211 million. In this incremental change, the share of dependent population would be 28.4 per cent. Conversely, the bulge in the working age population would account for the rest. More specifically, **the working age population (15–59 years) in India is set to increase by 234 million (327 million minus 93 million)** from 731 million in 2011 to 965 million by 2030 and their share to total population by 2.4 percentage points from 60.3 per cent to 62.7 per cent. Thus, **the incremental addition to the working age population of 234 million would account for as much as 71.6 per cent of the net increase in total population between 2011 and 2030.**

India's demographic changes between 2001 and 2030 would result in a net increase in population by 509 million. The child population (0–14) would decline by 17 million. On the other hand, the 60+ age group population is set to increase by 156 million. Thus, the net increase in dependent population would be 139 million during the period 2001–2030. This would account for 27.3 per cent of the net increase in total population. Conversely, the bulge in the working age population would account for 72.7 per cent of the incremental change in population between 2001 and 2030.

This bulge in the working age population would alter the age structure of the population (see Chart 3.2) resulting in reduced dependency ratio from 0.73 in 2001 to 0.66 in 2011 and further to 0.59 in 2030. This clearly shows the tremendous potential for reaping Demographic Dividend in India.

Chart 3.2: Structure of India's Population in 2001 and 2030

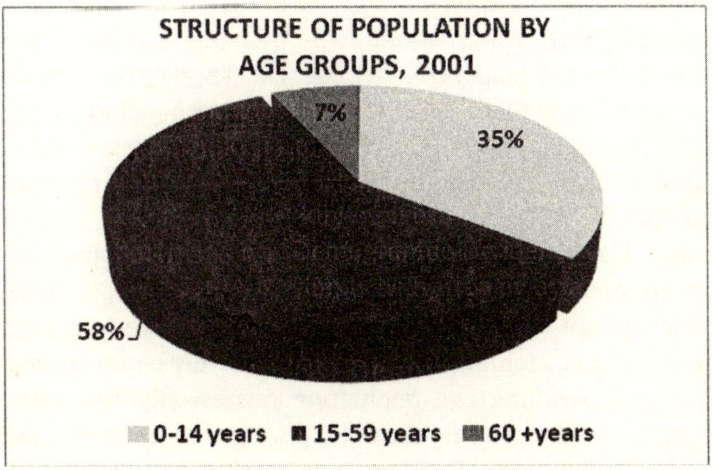

Source: Planning Commission.

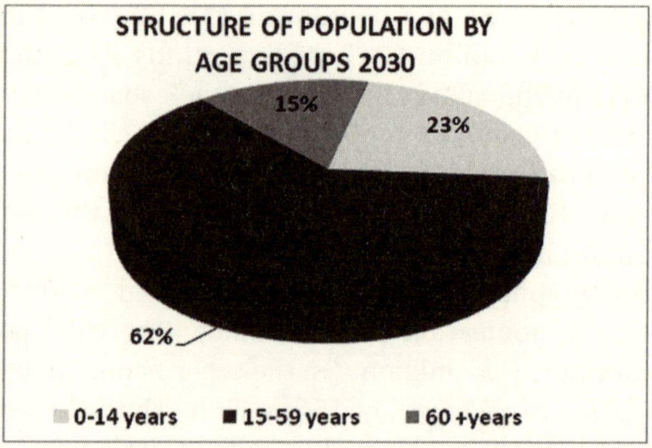

III. Spatial Distribution of Demographic Dividend

Given the size and diversity of India with differential fertility and mortality rates, the decline in the overall dependency ratio is unlikely to be uniform across the country. Accordingly, there would be a great deal of variation in the opportunities of Demographic Dividend across the States.

In the net addition to India's population, 509 million between 2001 and 2030, the share of Uttar Pradesh would be 19.5 per cent followed by Bihar (10.6 per cent), Rajasthan (7 per cent) and Madhya Pradesh (6.9 per cent). In other words, these four States would share around 44 per cent of the incremental addition to India's population between 2001 and 2030. The combined share of the eight so-called Empowered Action Group (EAG) States would be 54 per cent in 2030 as against the population share of 44.6 per cent in 2001. On the other hand, although the four Southern States (Tamil Nadu, Andhra Pradesh including Telangana, Karnataka and Kerala) accounted for nearly 21.7 per cent of the country's population in 2001, they would share only 14 per cent of the net increase in population by 2030.

In States like Tamil Nadu, Karnataka and Kerala, which are better equipped to capitalise on the Demographic Dividend with relatively better governance system, strong social security safety nets, sound education and health care system, training systems, and relatively better infrastructure, the increase in working age population ranges only between 1.0 and 4.0 per cent. In other words, those States which are better equipped to harness the Demographic Dividend are likely to have relatively smaller increases in their ratio of working age population.

The regional imbalance in the potential for Demographic Dividend in India becomes abundantly clear from our estimates of dependency ratios by States during the period 2001–2030, presented in Table 3.5.

Table 3.5: Quantitative Indicators of Demographic Dividend: State-wise Dependency Ratios

	States	DEPENDENCY RATIOS						
		2001	2006	2011	2016	2021	2026	2030
	EAG STATES							
1	Uttar Pradesh	0.89	0.84	0.79	0.76	0.74	0.70	0.68
2	Bihar	0.91	0.91	0.92	0.93	0.85	0.81	0.79
3	Jharkhand	0.81	0.79	0.77	0.76	0.69	0.69	0.69
4	Madhya Pradesh	0.81	0.76	0.71	0.67	0.65	0.63	0.62
5	Chhattisgarh	0.77	0.71	0.67	0.62	0.58	0.57	0.56
6	Uttarakhand	0.78	0.72	0.67	0.63	0.61	0.58	0.57
7	Odisha	0.69	0.66	0.63	0.60	0.54	0.56	0.57
8	Rajasthan	0.86	0.79	0.74	0.69	0.63	0.60	0.58
	NE STATES							
9	NER (Excluding Assam)	0.72	0.76	0.81	0.87	0.79	0.72	0.68
10	Assam	0.74	0.70	0.65	0.62	0.55	0.55	0.56
	OTHER STATES							
11	J&K	0.72	0.71	0.70	0.70	0.60	0.58	0.56
12	Himachal Pradesh	0.66	0.61	0.57	0.53	0.53	0.54	0.55
13	Punjab	0.67	0.61	0.56	0.52	0.52	0.52	0.53
14	Haryana	0.75	0.68	0.63	0.58	0.56	0.55	0.55
15	West Bengal	0.66	0.60	0.56	0.52	0.53	0.56	0.59
16	Gujarat	0.65	0.62	0.59	0.57	0.52	0.53	0.54
17	Maharashtra	0.68	0.63	0.58	0.55	0.49	0.50	0.50
18	Andhra Pradesh	0.65	0.60	0.57	0.56	0.52	0.54	0.56
19	Karnataka	0.64	0.60	0.56	0.53	0.53	0.55	0.56
20	Kerala	0.58	0.57	0.56	0.56	0.58	0.60	0.63

	States	DEPENDENCY RATIOS						
		2001	2006	2011	2016	2021	2026	2030
21	Tamil Nadu	0.56	0.54	0.52	0.50	0.48	0.49	0.51
	India	0.73	0.69	0.66	0.63	0.60	0.59	0.59

Source: Own projections.

At the national level, the dependency ratio is set to decline from 0.73 in 2001 to 0.59 in 2030. Among the EAG States, Rajasthan promises the fastest decline (0.28) in the dependency ratio. The dependency ratios in Uttar Pradesh, Uttarakhand, Madhya Pradesh and Chhattisgarh would decline by about 0.20 each between 2001 and 2030. Bihar's dependency ratio would decline from 0.91 to 0.79 and that for Jharkhand from 0.81 to 0.69 for the corresponding period. In the North-Eastern Region, Assam's dependency ratio is set to decline from 0.74 in 2001 to 0.56 in 2030.

It may be noted that despite a perceptible decline in the dependency ratios for some States, i.e., Uttar Pradesh, Bihar, Jharkhand and Madhya Pradesh and North-Eastern Region excluding Assam, the levels of the dependency ratios remain well above the national average, which would tend to limit their potential for Demographic Dividend.

Among other States, Maharashtra's dependency ratio would decline from 0.68 to 0.50 and that for Haryana from 0.75 to 0.55. Perhaps, these two States with better infrastructure facilities are capable of reaping rich Demographic Dividends in the country.

In the States of Tamil Nadu and Kerala, whose Total Fertility Rates (TFRs) are around 1.7 each—much lower than the national replacement level target of 2.1—and dependency ratios have either declined modestly (i.e., Tamil Nadu) or in fact increased (i.e., Kerala), there would hardly be any Demographic Dividend.

IV. Demographic Dividend: State of Preparedness in India

The potential of Demographic Dividend for India is clearly evident. This discussion couched in terms of dependency ratios essentially involves the basic changes in age structure which merely affect the supply-side potential for economic growth. As mentioned earlier, actually capturing that potential depends on numerous other factors, especially public policy on education, skill development, health and employment. In other words, the fortuitously available Demographic Dividend in India can be harnessed and reaped only by ensuring that every adolescent and youth, both men and women, have good health, high-quality education, opportunities for acquiring marketable skills and decent employment (including self-employment). What is the state of preparedness in this regard as far as India is concerned? This is the main issue to which we turn next.

(A) Demographic Dividend and Education

Education has a major role to play in India's ability to capitalise on the Demographic Dividend. Education, especially Secondary and Tertiary Education may be expected to equip India's youth with the skills they need to be productive in an increasingly competitive environment.

The implementation of RTE Act should have positive impact on higher transition rates in basic education leading to universalisation of Secondary Education. Pursued wholeheartedly, this could effectively eliminate the possibility of teenage youth entering workforce without adequate education and skills. Vocational Education and Skill Training should be an integral part of School Education. Expansion of Higher, Technical and Professional Education so as to enhance the GER in Tertiary Education from the existing level of 20 per cent plus to 30–35 per cent in the next one and a half decade would be imperatively needed. Accordingly, much larger investment is called for in Education and Skill Development.

Some realignment of investments is possible as the number of children in the youngest age group of 0–9 would decline from about 245 million in 2001 to 210 million by 2030. However, this realignment would be possible more in Southern States and in some Western States, and not so much in other parts of the country where the existing budgets for children are already grossly inadequate, especially in a vast majority of Northern and Eastern States.

Educating girls serves a dual purpose: it acts as a development indicator and also as an instrument to promote decline in fertility rate. Women who are educated tend to have fewer children, since their employability improves substantially. Educated women choose not to forgo employment opportunities by bearing more children. Moreover, education empowers women to express their views and take decisions on their lifestyle and fertility. Families with fewer children facilitate greater investment into health and education of each child, thereby contributing to higher productive capacity of future generations. The positive effects of education—girls' education in particular—are extremely powerful.

While India has made an impressive achievement in bridging gender gaps at the Primary Education level much ahead of the Millennium Development Goals (MDG) deadline, i.e., 2015, girls' education in Secondary schools needs to be accelerated with further incentivisation. Secondary Education for girls will bring a sea change, particularly in some of the educationally lagging States. In this regard, thought needs to be given to extending MDMS up to Class X. Several States now provide bicycles to girls in Secondary schools and this has brought about a tremendous change in perception and outlook of parents, and has given a lot of confidence to the girl children. It has been observed that households provide a bicycle to boys on their own, squeezing their own resources, when the girl child has been provided with a bicycle by the government.

KGBV has made a remarkable progress in providing residential schools for girls belonging to disadvantaged sections, although the total coverage is very limited in terms of numbers enrolled. RMSA provides for girls' hostels. RUSA provides grants for hostels for girls at university levels. Efforts are being made in respect of polytechnics to provide for hostels for girls to focus on greater participation of women under Sakshar Bharat. However, there is a need to set up ITIs/ITCs exclusively for women in the States that show faster decline in the dependency ratio, i.e., the whole of Northern and Eastern India. Kerala should be a good model for educating and providing marketable skills in diverse fields, especially in the services sector, and also in lending employment support services.

No one can disagree with the proposition that every girl and young woman should have 'the chance to go through life's critical transitions—from childhood to family formation to old age—without risk of being derailed by child marriage or unplanned childbearing, maternal morbidity, exposure to violence or displacement, the pain of discrimination or the risk of early death'.[13]

A recent survey showed that Indian women in the age group of 20–24 years married before 18 years of age accounted for 24.9 per cent. In rural

13. Daniel Schensul, Kathrin Weny and Rachel Snow, 'Foundation for the Future', UNFPA, May 2016.

areas, this proportion was higher at 31.5 per cent, whereas in urban areas it was 17.5 per cent. Women in the age group of 15–19 years who were already mothers or were pregnant accounted for 7.9 per cent. Again, this proportion was higher at 9.2 per cent in the rural areas as compared to 5 per cent in urban areas.[14] Although, the incidence of child marriage has been declining, it is still widespread in educationally lagging States. Such social customs and traditions act as a serious impediment for harnessing the Demographic Dividend.

In India, while significant gains have been made in Primary Education and child health, gaps do widen and barriers tend to grow as children become adolescents and youth. This, in turn, sets the stage for long-term costs in respect of working life and ageing. Gender inequality and harmful practices mean that life's chances are undermined for millions of girls by discrimination at home and in school; by expectations of servitude in marriage; by early, risky and numerous pregnancies; and by poor health care and early death.[15]

The NSS 61st Round (2004-05) showed that about 50 per cent of the rural households did not have a single literate woman and this proportion was 62 per cent in Uttar Pradesh, 63 per cent in Madhya Pradesh, 65 per cent in Bihar, 66 per cent in Jharkhand and 70 per cent in Rajasthan. As per NSS 68th Round, there has been some improvement and the proportion of such households had declined from 50 per cent in 2004-05 to 38.3 per cent in 2011-12. Nevertheless, these States are nowhere near the national average.

In the States where female educational levels are low, girls get married in teenage, leading to a very long span of fertility. The DLHS-3 (2007-08) showed that the proportion of currently married rural women who got married before the age of 18 years was as high as 70 per cent in Bihar, 62 per cent in Rajasthan, 59 per cent each in UP and MP and 58 per cent in Jharkhand. On the other hand, where female education is relatively higher as in Himachal Pradesh, Kerala and Tamil Nadu, this proportion ranged between 9 per cent and 26 per cent only. The mean age at marriage for women in Bihar and Rajasthan was 17.6 and 17.7, respectively. At the national level, more than one-fifth (22 per cent) of marriages were below

14. Ministry of Health and Family Welfare, Government of India, 'National Family Health Survey 2015-16 (NFHS-4): India, Key Indicators', (Mumbai: IIPS, December 2017).

15. Schensul, Weny and Snow, 'Foundation for Future', 2016.

the legal age and about 6 per cent of total deliveries relate to teenage groups putting young mothers at a considerable risk.

The State-sponsored family planning programme has not met with adequate success after its disruption in the mid-1970s. The contraceptive prevalence rate showed a very marginal improvement from 52.5 per cent in 2002-04 to 54.0 per cent in 2007-08. For Indian couples, protection continues to be heavily dependent on female sterilisation, which happens mostly at higher order of births. Male sterilisation has not yet found widespread acceptance. Social marketing of contraceptives had limited impact. Unmet need for family planning (with spacing and limiting) remained around 21 per cent during 2002–08. This ranged between 32 per cent and 36 per cent in Bihar, Jharkhand and Uttar Pradesh. Higher order of birth of 4 and above is around 20 per cent or more in these States as compared to 1-2 range in the Southern States of Tamil Nadu, Andhra Pradesh and Kerala (SRS, 2013).

As can be seen from Table 3.6, TFRs are inversely related to the level of education.

Table 3.6: Total Fertility Rates by Levels of Education

Level of Education	TFR	Level of Education	TFR
Illiterates	3.1	Upper Primary	2.2
Without Any Formal Education	3.2	Secondary	1.8
Below Primary	2.8	Higher Secondary	1.6
Primary	2.5	Graduate and Above	1.7

Source: Registrar General of India, SRS, 2013.

The complementary nature of health and education is well known. Public investment in these sectors is very essential in order to reap the Demographic Dividend, failing which the demographic transition will be simply be fretted away as it is happening in some of the African countries.

(B) Demographic Dividend and Skill Development

The Census 2011 has revealed a rather dismal picture of Vocational Education in quantitative terms. At the all-India level, the number of persons in the age group of 18–23 was 138 million—males 72 million and females 66 million. Of these, the number of persons attending Vocational institutions was merely 4.1 million—2.7 million males and 1.4 million females, hardly accounting for 3 per cent of the youth population in this age group. Moreover, nearly half of these youth getting vocational skills were from the States of Kerala, Karnataka, Andhra Pradesh and Tamil Nadu.

A North-South regional picture on Vocational Education of the youth is even more distressing. For example, Bihar with a youth population of over 10 million in the age group of 18–23 years hardly has 70,000 enrolled and attending Vocational institutions. The RG office has not yet fully released the Census 2011 Cultural Statistics. The number of Scheduled Tribes, Scheduled Castes, Muslim minorities attending these institutions should reveal acute imbalances in regional and gender comparisons across these social groups. While complete data for Castes Census have not become available as yet, the released information of 'others' tends to conceal a great deal on inequity as this would club Muslim minorities with SCs and STs. This would invariably affect the preparedness for benefitting from the limited window of opportunity of Demographic Dividend for this segment of population.

It is increasingly being realised that the provision of Vocational Education and marketable skills is the only panacea for all the economic and social ills of the disadvantaged strata of the society. There are 6100 odd ITIs/ ITCs in the country, but 60 per cent of these are located in the four Southern States and two Western States (Maharashtra and Gujarat). On the other hand, Bihar, Chhattisgarh, Jharkhand, West Bengal and Assam have hardly 7 per cent of these institutions. Even the existing ITIs/ ITCs in these States have lower intake capacity as compared to those in Southern States, and institutions for women account for a very negligible proportion.

The National Skill Development Council (NSDC) has been mandated to accelerate setting up of new institutions in disadvantaged locations and a new Ministry has already been created—Ministry of Skill Development and Entrepreneurship (MSDE), to provide infrastructure support also in States/regions suffering inadequate access for skill development and training of youth.

Skill Development is vital not only for reaping the benefits of Demographic Dividend, but also for more inclusive growth and to bridge the demand-supply mismatch of skilled persons. The transition of the economy from Primary to Tertiary sector implies migration of a large portion of workforce from the Primary sector to the Tertiary sector. It is the lack of education and skills that drives migrant workforce to urban areas in very adverse conditions, swelling the menial workforce in unorganised sector often leading to sub-human living conditions in urban slums. There is a large skill gap in the process of transition from the Primary to Secondary and on to the Tertiary sector. This calls for skill development for the existing workforce as well as for the new entrants to the workforce.

The current size of India's formally skilled workforce is woefully small, around 2 per cent as compared to 96 per cent in South Korea and 80 per cent in Japan. The poor skill levels among India's workforce are attributed to the dearth of an elaborate Vocational Education framework, very large school dropouts, inadequate skills training capacity and negative perception towards skilling and lack of 'industry-ready' skills, even in professional courses.[16] Limited participation of the private sector has also been one of the major reasons for the exceptionally small size of the formally skilled workforce.

Table 3.7 presents details of Mean Years of Schooling (MYS) of non-agricultural workers in India.

Table 3.7: Mean Years of Schooling of Non-Agricultural Workers

Category of Workers	Rural		Urban	
	Male	Female	Male	Female
Casual workers in unorganised sector	3.6	1.5	4.3	2.1
Regular workers in unorganised sector	7.0	5.6	7.1	4.8
Self-employed in unorganised sector	5.3	2.9	7.7	5.1
Unorganised workers in organised sector	5.3	4.0	7.4	7.3
Regular workers in organised sector	7.9	7.2	8.8	9.6
Organised sector	7.6	5.7	10.1	10.1

Source: ISAS Working Paper No.103, December 2009.

It is evident from Table 3.7 that the organised sector has higher MYS than the unorganised sector and regular workers have better MYS than

16. FICCI and Ernst & Young, 'Reaping India's promised demographic dividend — industry in driving seat' (New Delhi: Ernst and Young, 2014).

casual workers. The self-employed category has MYS midway between those who are casual and those who are regular. The MYS of organised sector workers was above the unorganised workers for both men and women, in rural and urban areas, across the States.

Obviously, education is an important asset that helps entry into the preferred organised sector jobs. Entry into the organised sector even as unorganised workers required higher MYS. Women with higher education are able to compete with men for jobs in the organised sector. Low access to education and, consequently, lower levels of education keep the women mainly in the unorganised sectors. Low levels of education create vulnerability at two levels: first, it denies access to preferred jobs in the organised sector; secondly, it confines the workers mostly as casual workers in unorganised sector or unorganised workers in the organised sector. Women workers seem to be the worst victims of this double disadvantage, as can be seen from Table 3.7. Admittedly, education does not necessarily lead to the development of marketable skills. However, it does provide a general background and makes it easier to access both formal and informal Vocational Education.

Results from a Labour Bureau Study (2013-14), regarding Vocational Training status of the States are presented in Table 3.8. It is disheartening to note that at the national level, only 6.8 per cent of persons aged 15 years and above reportedly have received/are receiving Vocational Training. The formal system accounted for 2.8 per cent and the informal for 4.0 per cent. In the formal system, among the major States, Kerala leads the nation with 11 per cent, while the big States like Uttar Pradesh and Madhya Pradesh account for merely 1.7 per cent and 1.2 per cent, respectively. It is somewhat surprising that some of the most industrialised States such as Tamil Nadu and Gujarat are below the national average in Vocational Training. Apparently, the private sector which dominates the industry in these States offers very little facilities for Vocational Training and Skill Development. The situation is no better in the informal Vocational Training.

Table 3.8: Vocational Training Status (15+ age group) (per 1000 persons)

S. No	States/UTs	Formal			Informal			None		
		M	FM	P	M	FM	P	M	FM	P
1	Andhra Pradesh	32	15	23	80	24	51	888	962	925
2	Arunachal Pradesh	11	3	7	16	-	8	972	997	984
3	Assam	24	14	19	35	10	23	941	976	958
4	Bihar	18	6	12	28	11	20	954	984	967
5	Chhattisgarh	30	9	20	189	164	177	781	828	804
6	Delhi	42	21	32	23	3	13	935	977	954
7	Goa	122	5	65	10	13	12	867	982	923
8	Gujarat	32	12	22	44	9	27	923	980	950
9	Haryana	54	25	40	52	17	36	895	958	924
10	HP	56	53	55	33	26	29	911	921	916
11	J&K	17	13	15	33	21	27	951	966	958
12	Jharkhand	61	26	45	169	18	98	770	956	857
13	Karnataka	55	24	40	34	12	23	911	964	937
14	Kerala	126	97	110	139	57	96	735	846	794
15	MP	17	6	12	23	6	15	959	987	973
16	Maharashtra	51	28	40	31	11	21	918	961	938
17	Manipur	14	11	13	86	83	85	900	906	903
18	Meghalaya	43	52	47	36	7	22	921	941	931
19	Mizoram	35	21	28	30	4	17	935	975	955
20	Nagaland	51	39	46	44	42	43	905	919	912
21	Odisha	36	11	24	35	12	24	929	977	952
22	Punjab	23	16	20	19	9	14	958	974	966
23	Rajasthan	39	12	26	62	14	39	899	974	934
24	Sikkim	287	62	186	49	11	32	664	927	782
25	Tamil Nadu	35	11	23	39	13	26	926	976	951
26	Telangana	27	12	19	56	20	38	917	968	942

S. No	States/UTs	Formal			Informal			None		
		M	FM	P	M	FM	P	M	FM	P
27	Tripura	39	17	28	20	2	11	941	981	961
28	Uttarakhand	79	32	56	60	17	38	861	952	906
29	UP	20	9	17	65	13	49	915	978	934
30	W. Bengal	48	25	37	77	29	54	875	946	909
	All India	**36**	**19**	**28**	**56**	**19**	**40**	**907**	**962**	**932**

Source: Labour Bureau, Employment Unemployment Survey (2013-14).

As can be seen from Table 3.8, Assam, which has more than two-thirds of the looms in the country, shows Vocational Training proportion of barely 2.3 per cent in the informal sector. On the other hand, Vocational Training in the informal sector was the highest, ranging between 9.8 per cent (Jharkhand) and 17.7 per cent (Chhattisgarh). These newer States seem to have taken some concrete steps for promotion of skill development in traditional activities such as textiles, silver jewelleries, wood carving and some non-traditional food processing activities in village and cottage industries. In the rest of the States, the picture is not very encouraging and is in fact worrisome, since a significant proportion of those trained people remained unemployed and, sadly, not even in the workforce.

It is observed that about 51 per cent of employed females have had some Vocational Training, formal or informal. However, a recent study by Labour Bureau has brought out that about 40 per cent of those who had some Vocational Training were simply not in the labour force and another 6.1 per cent remain unemployed. Thus, a significant proportion of females have not joined the labour force even after receiving Vocational Training in different fields. As many as 46 per cent of females under the 'Others' category have reported to be 'not in labour force' classification after receiving Vocational Training in different fields.[17] Apparently, those who could be trained have been trained and not those who could be ready to plunge in the world of work with the acquired new skills. This wastage of skill training needs to be addressed. It is also necessary to

17. Labour Bureau, 'Report on Education, Skill Development and Labour Force: 2013-14', vol. III, (Chandigarh: Labour Bureau, November 2014). https://labour.gov.in/sites/default/files/Report%20Vol%203%20final.pdf

assess the aptitude of the beneficiary for the particular vocation that they are trained for. Trained people should also be provided with post-training support for employment through career guidance centres.

At the national level about 17 Ministries and Departments of the Government of India are engaged in skill development for about 3.1 million persons every year. Individually, these Ministries and Departments were able to reach only a segment of the new entrants to the labour force. It is observed that even collectively, they provided training to only about 20 per cent fresh entrants to the labour force. Each Ministry/Department in charge has set up training establishments in its field of specialisation. But there is not much coordination; often they were operating in silos.

Some institutions like the ITIs, formerly under the Ministry of Labour and Employment (MoLE), were operating, although successfully, in areas ('trades') which were beyond the scope of these institutions originally envisaged. In fact, the institutions were struggling to keep pace with the technological changes with outdated equipment and grossly under-equipped workshops. At the same time, the vacuum created due to inevitable decay of commercial institutes for typing, stenography, etc. caused by computer revolution has been filled by ITIs successfully. These courses in new 'trades' offer more employability than traditional training in trades like fitter and turner as repair services. Hands-on experience is simply not available for a vast majority of trainees in industrial trades in modern plant and machinery. Lack of industry involvement meant lower quantum of apprenticeships and low exposure to fast-track automated assembly line production systems in the industrial sector. In fact, industries lack training facilities too. A World Bank Study indicates that in-service training is received by only 15 per cent of workers in the manufacturing sector,[18] which is far below what is observed in many countries.

The National Policy on Skill Development, 2009, aimed at training 500 million people by 2022, by empowering all individuals through improved skills, knowledge as well as nationally and internationally recognised qualifications to gain access to decent employment and ensure India's competitiveness in the global market. It also aimed to increase workforce in organised and unorganised sectors especially among youth, women, disabled and disadvantaged sections. The Policy clarified the roles that different stakeholders—government, industry, trade unions, and civil

18. World Bank, 'India Country Strategy (CAS) 2009–12', April 2010.

society—would need to play for the creation of a skills ecosystem in India.

The Skill Development Policy, 2009 specified that skills-related training should focus on outcomes, and be linked to jobs and employability. With regards to access to training, the Policy stated that it should be available to everyone, especially to those at the lowest level of the pyramid. It suggested that the various private sector initiatives in the Skill Development sector should be complemented by the Government and emphasised the need for short duration industry-relevant courses. The Policy also suggested establishing a framework for effective assessment and credible certification, along with giving publicity to information on training institution outcomes so as to ensure greater transparency. A larger role for State Governments in the skilling initiative was also contemplated. All States have set up State Skill Development Missions and many have put together a strategy to equip millions of persons with skills over the next few years.

Against this backdrop, the Twelfth Five-Year Plan (2012–17) embarked on a relatively modest target of skilling 80 million people until 2019, which leaves around 400 million people to be trained in the Thirteenth Plan by 2022.[19] However, some experts have raised concerns over the ambitious magnitude of the target. In this regard, the erstwhile Institute of Applied Manpower Research (IAMR) had computed new skill gap figures to arrive at a 'realistic' overall target of people to be trained—ranging between 249 and 290 million—across differing skill requirement scenarios.

Studies by consulting firms ICRA Management Consulting Services Ltd (IMaCS) and Aon Hewitt have forecast an incremental shortfall of 347 million people by 2022 in about 20 high-growth sectors of the Indian economy. The biggest shortfall is projected at 103 million in the infrastructure sector. Building and construction, automobile and textile industries are likely having substantial skill gaps, as indicated in Table 3.9.

The NSDC's interventions are indeed laudable and are playing a significant role for the cause of skills promotion. However, there is no room for complacency. A lot more work remains to be done for a culture of skill development to take roots in India. It is said that 'skill development is a Chief Executive Officer (CEO) agenda but often left to HR & Training component'. The industry leaders have to start taking ownership of

19. Labour Bureau, Employment and Unemployment Survey, 2013-14.

Table 3.9: Incremental Skill Gap across Various Industries in India in 2022

Sl No.	Industry	Incremental Requirement (million)
1	Building and Construction Industry	33.0
2	Infrastructure Sector	103.02
3	Real Estate Services	14.0
4	Gems and Jewellery	4.6
5	Leather and Leather Goods	4.6
6	Organised Retail	17.3
7	Textiles and Clothing	26.2
8	Electronics and IT Hardware	3.3
9	Auto and Auto Components	35.0
10	IT and ITES	5.3
11	Banking, Financial Services and Insurance	4.2
12	Furniture and Furnishings	3.4
13	Tourism and Hospitality Services	3.6
14	Construction Material and Building Hardware	0.4
15	Chemicals and Pharmaceuticals	1.9
16	Food Processing	9.3
17	Healthcare	12.7
18	Transportation and Logistics	17.7
19	Media and Entertainment	3.0
20	Education and Skill Development Services	5.8
21	Select Informal Sectors (Domestic Help, Beauticians, Security Guards)	37.6
	Incremental Skill Gaps	**347**

Sources: ICRA Management Consulting Services Limited (IMaCS) reports 'Human Resource and Skill Gap Requirements (2022)' (2008), Aon Hewitt Report 'Talent Projections and Skill Gap Analysis for the Infrastructure Sector (2022)', 2011, National Skill Development Corporation (NSDC), 2011.

driving the Sector Skill Councils (SSCs) and the National Occupational Standards (NOS) exercise in their respective domains through greater involvement. Without the occupational standards, accreditation system and certification in place, Skill Development would be reduced to a futile exercise.

Similarly, it is advisable for the various Skill Development programmes run by the different Ministries and States to streamline their requirements through Sector Skill Councils (SSCs). To make the system scalable and sustainable, there should be uniform focus along the entire value chain of Skill Development, right from mobilisation to placement and also post-placement support.

Although Skill Development is essentially State-engineered, the private sector in India has the opportunity to play a significant role in the country being able to produce job-ready and industry-ready professionals in large numbers.[20]

(C) Demographic Dividend and Work Participation

The structure of Indian workforce is noteworthy. The NSS data show that more than two-thirds of our workforce in 2009-10 was in the age group of 15–44; male workers accounted for 67 per cent in rural areas and that in urban areas they accounted for an even larger proportion of 71 per cent. About one-fifths of workers were in the age group of 45–59 years. In the oldest age group of 60+, urban workers accounted for 4-5 per cent but in rural areas it was 9 per cent for males and 7 per cent for females.[21]

A large part of workforce is still engaged in self-employment and unless they become invalid, there is hardly any retirement for them. A vast majority of self-employed workforce is in agriculture and allied activities, household industry, artisan-based industry, etc. There is hardly any retirement benefit that could plough into savings, leading to an accelerated capital formation. In fact, a majority of agriculture-labour households and small and marginal cultivating farmer households are indebted as revealed by successive Rural Labour Enquiry Reports released

20. Dilip Chenoy, 'Skill Development in India: A Transformation in Making' in *India Infrastructure Report 2012,* (Routledge, 2012), pp. 199-207.

21. Ministry of Statistics & Programme Implementation, Government of India, 'Employment and Unemployment Situation in India: 2009-10', NSS Report No. 537 (66/10/1), November 2011, p. 78.

by the Labour Bureau.

Another major problem is the large-scale induction of very young people in the workforce without even basic education. As can be inferred from Table 3.10, based on the Usual Principle Status in NSS 68th Round, around 4.4 per cent of rural boys and 11.0 per cent of rural girls get inducted in labour force at a tender age of less than 14 years. These proportions are higher at 5.5 per cent for urban boys but lower at 4.5 per cent for urban girls.

In the age group of 15–19, the proportion of rural boys and girls in labour force is substantially higher at 30.8 per cent and 11.3 per cent, respectively. In urban areas, these rates are 24.3 per cent for boys and 7.2 per cent in girls.

This uneducated and unskilled part of the labour force subdues the impact of Demographic Dividend since their earnings are much lower

Table 3.10: Age-Specific Labour Force Participation Rates (2011-12) (millions)

	Rural		Urban	
(Years) (1)	**Male (2)**	**Female (3)**	**Male (4)**	**Female (5)**
5–9	0	1	0	1
10–14	24	20	31	6
15–19	308	113	243	72
20–24	767	203	654	178
25–29	961	242	949	223
30–34	989	300	988	224
35–39	991	349	989	239
40–44	986	357	988	239
45–49	987	365	979	212
50–54	964	338	945	196
55–59	931	304	867	153
60 and above	639	159	360	67
All	**547**	**181**	**560**	**134**

Source: NSS Report No. 554, Employment and Unemployment Situation in India (2011-12).

as compared to those in skilled employment. Schemes like MGNREGS provide much-needed avenues for local employment for such unskilled labour force but this is not a permanent solution for enhanced earnings or skilling the uneducated youth. Thus, the impact of Demographic Dividend is likely to be sub-optimal in many States where this young workforce has not been provided with basic education and employable skills, as yet.

One of the implications of Demographic Dividend is that on account of reduced fertility, households' earning strength tends to go up with increased female work participation. Perhaps, this is the toughest outcome of Demographic Dividend to materialise in the short run. In India the female work participation rates actually show a decelerating trend as captured by various NSS estimates. Female workers accounted for about just one-third of total workforce in 2004-05. This has declined to 27.4 per cent in 2011-12. As compared to 2004-05 estimates, in absolute terms, the decline in the female workers was over 20 million as can be seen from Table 3.11.

The decline could be partly attributed to increased enrolment of girls in educational institutions which is also borne out by narrowing gender gap in Elementary and Secondary Education and steep increase in girls GER at all stages of education in the country. This is a welcome development as education would substantially improve the quality of workforce.

Table 3.11: Work Participation by Male and Female in India (2004-05 to 2011-12)

Rates/ Ratio and Actuals	**NSS 61st Round (2004-05)**			**NSS 66th Round (2009-10)**			**NSS 68th Round (2011-12)**		
	Male	Female	Persons	Male	Female	Persons	Male	Female	Persons
LFPR	559	294	430	557	233	400	556	225	395
WPR	547	287	420	546	228	392	544	219	386
Labour Force	316.4	152.6	469.0	338.4	130.4	468.8	351.3	132.4	483.7
Workforce	309.3	148.6	457.9	331.7	127.3	459	343.8	129.1	472.9

Source: NSS data quoted in Planning Commission documents.

Note: LFPR: Labour Force Participation Rates; WPR: Worker Population Ratio; While LFPR and WPR are per 1000, the labour force and workforce numbers are in millions.

Labour Bureau studies give hope that the work participation increases with education although unemployment rate is also reported to have increased with higher levels of education.

The NSS data (Table 3.12) show that employment of household members is strongly correlated with the household income (Mean Per Capita Expenditure – MPCE used as a proxy). The Worker Population Ratio (WPR) for males increases more or less steadily with increase in MPCE decile class in both rural and urban areas. In rural areas, for males, WPR was 48 per cent in the bottom decile class whereas it was 60 per cent in the top decile class. The corresponding figures for urban areas are 49 per cent and 56 per cent. For rural females, the WPR for the bottom decile class was 23 per cent and that for top decile, 30 per cent. The corresponding figures for urban females were 14 per cent and 17 per cent, respectively. The relatively better sex ratio of workers in the bottom

Table 3.12: The WPR according to Usual Status (PS +SS) and Sex Ratio per 1000 among workers by decile classes on MPCE

Decile Classes on MPCE	Worker Population Ratio (WPR)			Sex Ratio of the Population	Sex Ratio among Workers
		(per 1000)		(per 1000)	(per 1000)
	Male	Female	Persons		
1	2	3	4	5	6
	RURAL				
0–10	476	233	354	1015	497
10–20	497	233	366	992	465
20–30	520	218	371	972	408
30–40	518	255	390	947	466
40–50	544	251	403	931	429
50–60	546	261	410	913	436
60–70	583	272	432	941	439
70–80	579	282	435	942	459
80–90	599	303	457	918	464
90–100	603	302	460	902	452
All Classes	547	261	408	947	452

Decile Classes on MPCE	Worker Population Ratio (WPR)			Sex Ratio of the Population	Sex Ratio among Workers
		(per 1000)		(per 1000)	(per 1000)
	Male	Female	Persons		
1	2	3	4	5	6
	RURAL				
	URBAN				281
0–10	485	143	315	987	291
10–20	514	150	336	962	281
20–30	539	145	344	980	264
30–40	544	142	350	935	244
40–50	544	129	346	912	216
50–60	556	140	361	881	222
60–70	554	113	346	895	183
70–80	562	129	364	838	192
80–90	566	120	360	856	181
90–100	558	166	377	860	256
All Classes	543	138	350	909	231

Source: NSS Report No. 537, Employment and Unemployment Situation in 2009-10

MPCE decile, i.e., 49.7 per cent in rural areas and 29.1 per cent in urban areas, suggest the necessity for females in low-income groups to engage in gainful economic activities. On the other hand, relatively better sex ratio in the top decile of MPCE, i.e., 45.2 per cent in rural areas and 25.6 per cent in urban areas, could probably be reflecting a better access to education and training for females.

It may be noted that low female work participation, both in the rural and urban areas, acts as a barrier in garnering the Demographic Dividend.

(D) Demographic Dividend and Health Sector

There are several ways in which India can maximise its chances of success in reaping the Demographic Dividend, including making larger investments into the public health sector. Greater investments into health will result in socio-economic development. Through programme-based financial commitments to the health sector and its significant potential, India can promote higher income. Establishment of the Public Health Foundation of India and the National Rural Health Mission are notable steps in this direction, as they seek to fill India's urgent need to train and deploy medical and public health professionals at a large scale, for disease prevention, treatment and care.

The National Rural Health Mission (NRHM) and the subsequently launched National Urban Health Mission (NUHM) are the two sub-missions within the larger National Health Mission (NHM). The main components of the programme include enhancing the health system in rural and urban areas especially in the areas of Reproductive, Maternal, Neonatal, Child and Adolescent Health (RMNCH+A), and Communicable and Non-Communicable Diseases. The NHM aims at achieving universal access to equitable, affordable and quality healthcare services that are accountable and responsive to people's needs.

After decades of stagnation, there is a 4.1 percentage point fall in the growth rate of population in the EAG States (UP, Bihar, Jharkhand, Madhya Pradesh, Chhattisgarh, Rajasthan, Odisha and Uttarakhand) from 24.99 per cent in 2001 to 20.92 per cent in 2011. Sustained efforts are needed to accelerate fertility decline in these populous States. There is a need to expand family-planning services in a way that is respectful of people's reproductive rights. Approximately 13 per cent of Indian women (10 per cent in urban areas and nearly 15 per cent in rural areas) report unmet need for contraception, meaning that many currently married women who desire to postpone or forego childbearing are not using contraception. Spacing between two childbirths is less than the recommended period of 3 years in 57.4 per cent of births (Sample Registration System, 2012). About 46 per cent of women have spacing less than 30 months.

The limitations of family planning programme in India have been revealed, time and again, by National Family Health Survey, District Level Household and Facility Survey and National Sample Survey. These show that a large proportion of eligible couples are turning to private providers of healthcare services (50 per cent) as compared to government services (23 per cent) for child-spacing methods. There is a need to recognise and support private providers of family planning services. Overall, 56 per cent of married women in India (64 per cent in urban areas and 53 per cent in rural areas) report that they use contraception (either modern or traditional methods), with female sterilisation by far the most common method. Satisfying unmet needs for contraception will help achieve the Government's commitment of bringing TFR to the long-run replacement fertility level of 2.1, at least by 2025.

There is a considerable scope for improving contraceptive prevalence, education and quality of service in public sector healthcare institutions. Reducing unwanted pregnancies benefits maternal health. It is essential to promote healthcare services during the phase of Demographic Dividend. The focus should be on promoting and supporting productive capacity of the disadvantaged sections that generally depend on public sector services.

Current 'high focus approach' through categorisation of States in terms of TFR levels, such as 2.1 and below; 2.1 to less than 3.0; and more than 3 should actually get down to sub-State level categorisation as per the original exercise carried out by the National Commission of Population, and erstwhile Planning Commission. The State average conceals wide intra-State variations in TFR. The special focus districts should be identified and supported in an approach similar to that of SSA in the Elementary Education sector.

The national average urban TFR has already reached 1.9. The rural average, on the other hand, is as high as 2.8. In about 250 rural districts including 100 odd districts with concentration of Muslim minorities, it could be over 3.0. These should be the special focus districts where extra efforts are needed to support private providers of family planning services as well. The population of Muslims in India is growing at a faster rate. Fortunately, *Madrasas* are opening up for State curriculum and their children have started getting the benefits of SSA. Instead of making an issue with regard to their population growth, there are better ways to address family welfare for the Muslim Minorities. Perhaps, the Government can step back and support private providers of health and family welfare services and build awareness through trusted NGOs within the community. It should be realised that in the transition period, it is necessary to build confidentiality of family welfare service which is simply not possible with public sector Community Health Centre (CHC), Primary Health Centre (PHC) and sub-centre set up.

Improving infant and child survival rates have a significant impact in reducing the fertility rates. The infant mortality rate (IMR) for the country has come down to 40 in 2013 from 53 in 2008, a decline of 13 points over 5 years and an annual average decline of about 2.6 points. The corresponding decline in rural IMR has been to the tune of 14 points (from 58 in 2008 to 44 in 2013) as against a decline of 9 points in urban IMR (from 36 in 2008 to 27 in 2013). Despite this decline, one in every 25 infants at the national level, one in every 23 infants in rural areas and one in every 37 infants in urban areas still die within one year of life.[22]

Vaccines against childhood diseases are one potent way to realise an improvement in child survival, which leads to more than proportionate fertility reductions. The assessed need for immunisation has not been fully achieved even under Polio. In 2013-14, the DPT immunisation for children had reportedly a shortfall over 25 per cent.[23] Immunisation record should be cent per cent as it is essential for the very survival of a child in need. Immunisation gaps must be taken far more seriously. Partnerships with private providers of healthcare services, individual professionals and institutions are essential. In fact, there should be a role for every registered medical practitioner and every healthcare and nursing institution in the country with regard to family welfare and immunisation programmes.

There is an acute shortage of skilled paramedical and nursing personnel. India is short of 2.3 million nurses. There is an imperative need to accelerate the enlargement of the pool of qualified nurses and paramedical staff. Every district hospital should have a nursing training institution attached, and their Council should gear up and perform a proactive role and also involve private institutions.

V. Skill Development: Recent Developments and Issues

1. India's largest skill certification scheme titled *Pradhan Mantri Kaushal Vikas Yojana* (PMKVY)—the flagship outcome-based skill training scheme of the newly created Ministry of Skill Development and Entrepreneurship (MSDE)—was launched in July 2015.[24]

The Scheme being implemented through National Skill Development

22. Vital Statistics Division, Office of the Registrar General, Sample Registration System (SRS) Survey 2013.

23. Ministry of Health & Family Welfare, Government of India, 'Annual Report 2013-14', 2014.

24. A part of this Section is drawn from a brief prepared by the Ministry of Skill Development and Entrepreneurship (MSDE) (2018).

Corporation (NSDC) at the Central and State Governments level, has two components: (i) Centrally Sponsored, Centrally Managed (CSCM) which receives 75 per cent of the PMKVY funds, and (ii) Centrally Sponsored, State Managed (CSSM), claiming the remaining 25 per cent.

Salient Features of the Scheme

A. The CSCM component comprises three parts:

- Short-Term Training: School/college dropouts or unemployed youth are trained at training centres (TCs) according to the National Skills Qualification Framework (NSQF), in areas of soft skills, entrepreneurship, financial and digital literacy.
- Recognition of Prior Learning: Individuals with prior learning experience or skills are assessed and certified with a view to align the competencies workforce to the NSQF. Sector Skill Councils (SSCs), among others, are being incentivised to implement such projects.
- Special Projects: Training in special areas/job roles not defined under the National Occupational Standards (NOSs).

B. The CSSM component enables States Skill Development Missions to assist in the formation of institutional capacities at State/local level.

C. A process, based on online portal SMART, has been delineated for accreditation and affiliation of training centres (TCs).

D. Sector Skill Councils (SSCs) have been entrusted with the task of standardisation of course content. Trainers have to mandatorily undergo the Train the Trainer programme of the relevant Sector Skill Councils.

E. Candidates trained under the Scheme and possessing entrepreneur zeal are encouraged and supported in availing Mudra Loans through the portal *Udyami Mitra*.

Cumulative Achievements under the Scheme

Cumulatively, a network of 7,800 training centres (TCs) and 2,300 training providers have been imparting skill training (as of end of March 2018). So far 17 lakh candidates have been placed with leading industry players.

2. Ministry of Skill Development and Entrepreneurship (MSDE) has initiated setting up of *'Pradhan Mantri Kaushal Kendra'* (PMKK) as a state-of-the-art model training centre in every district of India.

PMKK aims at transforming the short-term training ecosystem from a mandate-driven footloose delivery model to a sustainable institutional model. The initiative envisions creation of standardised infrastructure for delivery of skill development training which is equipped to run industry-driven courses of high quality with focus on employability as well as generating an inspirational value. Six hundred PMKKs were expected to be set up across the country by end of March 2019. When fully operational, PMKKs would be expected to train around six lakh candidates annually.

3. In August 2016, a new Scheme was launched titled National Apprenticeship Promotion Scheme (NAPS) aimed at promoting apprenticeship training and to cumulatively enhance the engagement of apprentices to 50 lakh by 2020.

Under the Scheme, the Central Government bears 25 per cent of the stipend paid by employers (subject to a maximum of Rs 1,500 per month). In respect of those coming directly to apprenticeship training, the Central Government shares the basic training cost (subject to a maximum of Rs 7,500). Here again Sector Skill Councils, Industry Chambers and Associations are expected to play a major role in developing curriculum and implementation.

4. Industrial Training Institutes (ITIs) have been the backbone of the Skill Development system in India for the last six decades. There are around 14,000 ITIs spread across the country, with cumulative enrolment capacity of around 30 lakh candidates (with actual cumulative enrolment of around 20.4 lakh).

Directorate General of Training (DGT), which regulates ITIs, has been shifted from the Ministry of Labour and Employment to the new Ministry of Skill Development and Entrepreneurship (MSDE). With a view to ensuring that 'ITI ecosystem' remains up to date and relevant to emerging industrial requirements, several new initiatives have been taken. These include ISO 29990 certification for ITI training, revised curriculum, upgradation of infrastructure, more even geographical distribution, capacity utilisation, improvement in the quality of trainers, industry connect through apprenticeships and quality differentiation of ITIs through robust grading system. Revised new norms have been notified as 'Affiliation Norms for ITIs (2017) under the aegis of the National Council for Vocational Training (NCVT), with a view to curb the mushrooming of substandard institutes across the country. Importantly, MSDE aims to identify at least 500 ITIs to become 'world-class' training institutes which could act as Model Institutes for others to emulate and also provide strategic in industrial training in the country. Notably, an MOU for cooperation in the area of 'Skill Development and Vocational Education and Training' has been signed between India and Germany.

5. Notwithstanding these encouraging recent developments, it is being argued in influential quarters that 'Skill India is ailing'.[25] In their view, the 'optimism over the launch of Skill India in July 2015 and the roadmap for skilling 400 million people by 2022' has disappeared.

According to Thakur and Mantha, the 'fatal flaw' lies in not making Vocational Education as the centre-piece of the education system, as was recommended by Kothari Commission (1964–66). There were few takers for Vocational Education, essentially on account of 'deep-rooted social prejudices' against working with own hands, which was considered 'lowly and demeaning'.

The National Policy for Skill Development and Entrepreneurship 2015 actually did highlight the importance of NSQF and the necessity of linkages between skills and education. NSQF is, in fact, a framework under which skills are mainstreamed into the education system at the national level. It has several advantages. First, while the modular courses offered by ITIs are terminal in nature, NSQF allows vertical mobility. For example, a student can have a bachelor's degree in Vocational Education (B.Voc.). Second, it provides seamless horizontal pathways between education, skills and the job market. This de-stigmatises Vocational Education by making it part and parcel of School and Higher Education.

Thakur and Mantha go on to argue that those strengths of NSQF have been lost in 'translation' and in 'the petty turf games which ministries and bureaucrats are so prone to playing'.

---

25. Ashok Thakur and S.S. Mantha, 'Skill India is ailing', *The Indian Express,* 17 November 2018, https://indianexpress.com/article/opinion/columns/skill-india-is-ailing-world-youth-skill-day-2022-narendra-modi-5450627/

It is stating the obvious when they say that 'MSDE's success as a Ministry depends largely on its capacity to work closely with the other 18 ministries (which deal with Skill Development)'. But they are hitting the nail on its head when they argue that 'the mind-boggling target of skilling 400 million... would have been less daunting with the MHRD's capital and human resources of more than 900 universities, 6,000 technical institutions, 3,200 polytechnics, 36,000 colleges and 1.55 million schools, compared to the MSDE's 10,000 (actually 14,000) ITIs'.

Skill India has not been as successful as was expected also because of 'insufficient industry partners' and the failure to attract genuine skill knowledge providers'.... 'The Apprenticeship Act, which has enormous potential, has also failed to enthuse industry'.

The Indian Higher Education System can certainly bring in uniformity throughout the country in terms of enforcing the National Occupation Standards and NSQF. In recent years, Skill Universities are coming up in many States. There is, therefore, a need for an apex body so as to ensure standardisation across the country. Some thought could also be given to the idea coming up, time and again, to create a National Skills University which could possibly do the same fundamental groundwork that IGNOU did in the 1980s for spreading Open and Distance Learning.

4

Equity Issues in Education and Skill Development

Having extensively discussed India's educational attainments and skill development status (Chapter 2), followed by a detailed analysis of the state of preparedness in India for harnessing and leveraging the fortuitously available Demographic Dividend (Chapter 3), the present chapter takes up the all-important equity issues in Education and Skill Development in India.

Chapter 4 is organised as follows: Section I dilates briefly on the importance of equity issues in India in terms of the Constitutional provisions on one hand and the prevalence of an exceptionally large number of out-of-school children (OoSC) on the other. Section II, which forms the bulk of this chapter, discusses in some details various dimensions of inequity in Education and Skill Development especially in the context of socio-economic conditions. These include issues of poverty and income inequality, gender and social inequities and regional inequities in Education and Skill Development. Sections III and IV then deal with inclusive education for *Divyang* or Persons with Disabilities (PwDs) and for Muslim Minority, in that order.

I. Relevance of Equity Issues

Social sector policy statements on equity issues have always been appealing in India as these are purported to fulfil the Constitutional mandate that guaranteed equality and equal opportunities without any discrimination. Since the policies derive their legitimacy from the supreme law of the land—the Constitution of India—irrespective of the Party in power, there has been a remarkable consensus that ensured a strong temporal and spatial continuum throughout the country despite strong regional, linguistic and cultural diversities. A remarkable feature of the Indian Constitution is that it provides for an effective insulation mechanism for policies aiming at social justice, and makes provisions for a positive discrimination in favour of the disadvantaged. However, both at the Centre and States, the fundamental problem has always been with the actual implementation of the policies to move towards achieving social democracy.

Poor translation of policies into programme implementation, perhaps, has something to do with the evolution of the historical process of social, economic, political, religious and cultural development over centuries that has had an effect of reinforcing inertia to pursue vigorous action to achieve equality. In a society that evolved with subjugation and subordination as social norms for centuries, the word discrimination or inequity has always been an outlier, easily brushed aside or returned with stoic silence and virtual inaction. The issues of equity are often raised in the temples of democracy—the Parliament and State Assemblies. However, affirmative action on equity moves at a slow pace gradually undermining effectiveness of the policy prescriptions, probably due to 'lack of awareness' or 'vested interests' or both.

It is increasingly realised that equality strengthens the democratic process although levelling involves the giving up, by the privileged, of some sort of traditional rights enjoyed earlier. For example, in India, education was denied to certain segments of population from time immemorial. When the country achieved political Independence in 1947, establishment of social and economic democracy became an integral part of the Republic that India became in 1950. Nevertheless, poverty, illiteracy and dependence on the privileged ensured that the lapses in pursuing the agenda for social justice often got delayed which, at times, amounted to a virtual denial.

It is for this reason that Dr Babasaheb Ambedkar, the Principal Architect of the Indian Constitution had warned the young nation while presenting the final Draft of the Indian Constitution to the Constituent Assembly (25th November 1949). He said:

> On 26th January 1950, we are going to enter into a life of contradictions. In politics, we will have equality and in social and economic life we will have inequality. In politics, we will be recognising the principle of one man one vote and one vote one value. In our social and economic life, we shall, by reason of our social and economic structure, continue to deny the principle of one man one value. How long shall we continue to live this life of contradictions? How long shall we continue to deny equality in our social and economic life? If we continue to deny it for long, we will do so only by putting our political democracy in peril. We must remove this contradiction at the earliest possible moment or else those who suffer from inequality will blow up the structure of political democracy which this Assembly has so laboriously built up.

The fastest and the most sustainable leveller for social and economic equity is education because it does not suppress the existing elevations but pushes up the capabilities of the depressed through knowledge and skills. The Directive Principles of State Policy enshrined in the Indian Constitution provided for free and compulsory education for children of 6–14 years age group right from the beginning (1950). Six decades lapsed with very little progress. A provision had to be made as a justiciable Fundamental Right by moving it from Part IV to Part III (Fundamental Rights) of the Constitution. This process itself took almost a decade to culminate into the Right of Children to Free and Compulsory Education (RTE) Act, 2009, which became operational in April 2010. This Act is hailed as a major achievement establishing Constitutional and legal underpinnings for achieving universalisation of elementary education (UEE). The Central and State governments have framed implementation rules under the RTE Act and set up sub-State level institutional arrangements to give effect to the crucial legislation. National and State-level Commissions for protection of the rights of children have also been set up to closely monitor the implementation process and assess the outcomes.[1]

1. MHRD, Government of India, 'Implementation of RTE Act, IVth Year Report', 2014.

Against this backdrop, it was shocking when the Census 2011 revealed that an alarming number of as many as 42 million children in 6–14 years age group were not attending educational institutions! The total number of OoSC in the world was then reported to be around 58 million. The figure reported for India by UNESCO was just 1.3 million,[2] while in reality over 42 million children were languishing without basic education, and the worse is that 36 million children had never been enrolled in schools at all, despite a decade-long implementation of Sarva Shiksha Abhiyan (SSA) and two years of RTE-harmonised SSA. This grave situation has put an enormous pressure on the implementation of RTE Act, 2009.

A few social activists complain that several million children in the school-going age are in an utter state of destitution and not attending schools despite the Constitutional guarantee of compulsory education for up to 14 years. The responses were twofold: the first was to show statistics for progress in the temporal context that are impressive, and the second was to divert the attention to other problems in education. Diversion from the basic issue of providing access to schooling for poor and destitute children sometimes takes the form of *quality* in education, the country's poor standing in international assessment or not achieving world-class status in Higher Education.

International studies clearly show that expanding access is essentially *inclusive* while quality-related interventions border on *selectiveness* or *restrictiveness* in enhancing the average years of schooling.[3] The usual question often posed is about what is the point in attending school when children learn very little. Needless to say that education imparted should have acceptable quality and standards. However, languishing 42 million odd children left in lurch must be of atleast equally serious concern as they are children belonging to disadvantaged social groups in villages and urban slums.

Access to schooling is fundamental and should be the first charge on education expenditure. Failure on this count has made India the most illiterate nation in the world and the country might also have the dubious distinction of being a nation with the largest number of OoSC. No wonder our 'no schooling' population in the 15+ age group is over 40 per cent.[4]

2. UNESCO, 'EFA-GMR 2015', Statistical Tables.

3. Braga, Checchi and Meschi, 'Institutional Reforms and Educational Attainment in Europe', 2011.

4. Census 2011.

Under these circumstances, the choice between access and quality must not be mutually exclusive.

In a country of continental size where income and wealth are unequally distributed and majority of the population lives in rural areas engaging in self-employment in agriculture and allied activities, educational attainments actually determine the employability of the workforce in any gainful economic activity in the non-agricultural sector. This is because commercialisation has already turned agriculture into labour-saving. Although income transfer programmes and other social safety nets are in vogue for many decades the world over to tackle the problem of poverty of the disadvantaged segments of population or social groups, these are often much less efficient as compared to investing in education and skill development of the poor people.

There are many reasons for this. First, the resource constraints limit the quantum and spread of doles which are often not sustainable. Second, social sector programmes attempt to provide relief to the beleaguered sections but often sustain poverty as they fail to eradicate poverty on a permanent footing. Third, such programmes restrict mobility of workforce and regional inequity gets perpetuated over the years. Lastly, besides poor outcomes and unplugged leakages tending to benefit the undeserved, such programmes also develop dependency syndrome and undermine or suppress the desire for self-development. Thus, governments all over the world attempt to tackle the problem of poverty and unemployment through investing in education and marketable skill development of adolescent and youth population so as to enhance the opportunities for their employability in quality jobs.

In this context, not enabling a very large number of poor children to attend even the Primary schooling is not only a serious violation of the RTE Act, but it is actually a denial of social justice.

II. Dimensions of Inequity in Education and Skill Development

While China is far ahead of India in basic education with comfortable Mean Years of Schooling (MYS) of a little over[5] 8 years, India's 'no

5. Barro and Lee, 'A New Data Set of Educational Attainment in the World, 2010.

education' working age of population of over 40 per cent pulls down the mean. The Indian illiteracy is largely confined to females, SCs, STs, OBCs and Minorities whose economic activities are basically in wage-labour, mostly in casual and seasonal employment, suffering income as well as non-income poverty. In addition to poverty, barriers to education includes children's gender, caste, ethnic and linguistic background, race, disability, geographical location and livelihood. Marginalised children often suffer from multiple disadvantages that are mutually reinforcing leading to acute education deprivation in particular populations.[6]

Table 4.1 provides a snapshot of MYS in India differenciated by income, gender, region (i.e., rural-urban) and social categories (SCs, STs, OBCs and Muslims).

Table 4.1: India's MYS by Income, Gender, Region and Social Categories (NSS 66th Round, 2004-05)

All	**Male**	**Female**	**Rural**	**Urban**	***MPCE Q1**	**MPCE Q5**
5.08	**6.07**	**4.04**	**4.08**	**7.58**	**2.84**	**9.95**
STs	SCs	OBCs	Others	Muslims		
3.25	3.79	4.69	6.91	3.89		

Source: NSS Data (66th Round)

***MPCE:** Monthly per capita consumption expenditure in quintiles.

As can be seen from Table 4.1, the MYS for the Monthly Per Capita Consumption Expenditure (MPCE) classes of the lowest quintile was as low as 2.84 years. The same for the highest quintile was 9.95 years and the gap between these two quintiles was as much as 7.1 years.[7] Moreover regional, gender and social gaps in MYS were unacceptably high. Subsequent National Sample Survey (NSS) data indicate that India's MYS has improved to 5.48 and the regional and gender gaps are on the decline.[8]

6. UNESCO, EFA-GMR (2015).

7. Ministry of Statistics & Programme Implementation, Government of India, 'Employment and Unemployment Survey 2004-05', NSS 61st Round, September 2006.

8. Ministry of Statistics & Programme Implementation, Government of India 'Education in India 2007-08 – Participation and Expenditure': NSS 64th Round, Report No. 532 (May 2010).

(A) Poverty and Income Inequality

Research findings on the relationship between economic and education variables show that while socio-economic status exerted a major influence on educational outcomes, some studies also demonstrate that education levels strongly impact earnings. A World Bank Study (2002) observed that working Secondary School graduates earned 2.9 times higher than illiterate workers, and 1.7 times higher than workers with only Primary Education. The benefits were higher for female workers with Secondary Education. No wonder, in India, education is widely seen as panacea—the key to getting out and staying out of generational poverty.

It is widely agreed that the relationship between poverty and education operates in two directions. Poor people are often unable to obtain proper access to good quality education and, as a result, they are constrained to a life of poverty. Multidimensional interpretation of poverty has since moved far beyond the notion that poverty is solely related to a lack of financial resources. Probability of finding employment and better-quality employment greatly increases with education. Research has shown that investment in education has high returns.[9]

There is an overwhelming evidence of a continuing decline in the incidence of absolute poverty in the developing world. Temporal studies show that the overall proportion of people living below international poverty line of $1.25 a day declined from 52 per cent (or 1.9 billion) in 1981 to 22 per cent (or 1.3 billion) in 2002. Although progress has been uneven, all regions have witnessed a falling head count ratio (HCR) in the first decade of the new millennium, and India is no exception.

Various estimates of poverty in India, particularly rural poverty, showed that the HCR which had remained high and unabated at around 50 per cent till the mid-1980s relented thereafter. Our analysis here is focused on how and to what extent the decline in poverty or HCR have impacted the social sector development in India, particularly in the education outcomes across the States.

It is well known that educational indicators are influenced by several factors such as access, equity and quality, besides the socio-economic

9. Servaas van der Berg, 'Poverty and Education', Education Policy Series 10, The International Academy of Education, The International Institute for Educational Planning and UNESCO, 2008.

status of students. Several studies including that of Organisation for Economic Co-operation and Development's Programme for International Student Assessment (OECD-PISA) have noted that socio-economic status of the children have a strong bearing on educational outcomes.[10]

Multivariate regressions conducted, as detailed in Annexure A show that the HCR, per capita expenditure on education and female literacy explain about 88 per cent of the inter-State variation in educational attainments (MYS) and the coefficients of independent variables are statistically significant.

This confirms the imperative need to accelerate public investment in the education sector and also the necessity of focussing on bridging the gender gap in literacy. While the accelerated growth of the economy may bring down HCR, public investment in education sector with emphasis on educating rural girls is very essential so as to achieve an MYS of 8 years, comparable to that of China's achievement. Education holds the key to achieving most of the Sustainable Development Goals (SDGs) by 2030. Economic growth can be a powerful actor in education development, but only if governments are able and willing to mobilise resources and divert them to education.[11]

Increased female literacy seems to have a significant impact on enrolments in Primary Education. A literate mother tends to be more inclined to send her children to schools than an illiterate one, so that the family gets the benefit of education in terms of better quality non-farm employment or at least opportunities for 'working in shade' as the villagers put it. The thrust on rapidly increasing GERs for girls belonging to weaker sections and reducing gender gaps in enrolment have been reflected in the improvements in female literacy as revealed by the last two Census Rounds.

Analysis of gross enrolment ratio (GER)[12] or for that matter changes in GER at two different points of time has certain limitations. In view of

10. 'Knowledge and Skills for Life: First Results from the PISA 2000', (OECD, 2001).

11. UNESCO, 'Education 2030: Equity and Quality with a Lifelong Learning Perspective', Education for All Global Monitoring Report (EFA-GMR) Policy Paper 20, May 2015.

12. GER: Gross enrolment ratio is a statistical measure used by the UN in its Education Index to determine the number of students enrolled in a specific level of education, regardless of age, expressed as a percentage of the population in the official age group corresponding to that level of education.

underage/ overage enrolments and repetitions, the GER tends to be higher. In some of the smaller States, the GER figures are unreasonably high, e.g., when enrolments are twice that of children in the eligible age groups. This also explains the delay in providing access to schooling. Therefore, the decline in GER need not necessarily be taken as an adverse development but GER getting closer to Net Enrolment Ratio (NER) could be a positive sign that more and more age-specific children are in school at appropriate levels of education.[13] Accordingly, another multivariate regression was attempted, using NER as the dependent variable (Annexure B).

Here again, multivariate regression results confirm the causal links between education outcomes and a range of socio-economic factors. The inter-State variation in NER appears to be explained better by HCR1, public investment in Elementary Education and nutritional support (MDMS). All the three independent variables in the equation are statistically significant.

The latest Global Monitoring Report states that India has made marked progress, increasing its NER significantly as Gross National Product (GNP) per capita improved, suggesting a more equitable distribution of economic gains.[14] This augurs well for the Education and Skill Development sector.

Privatisation and Affordability Issues

India Human Development Survey (IHDS) had estimated once that 51 per cent of children in urban areas and 21 per cent in rural areas were enrolled in private schools.[15] The enrolments for 6–14 age group children in private unaided institutions (PUI) increased from 10 per cent in 1996 to 28 per cent in 2005. Perhaps these included enrolments from unrecognised institutions as well. There are 2,60,000 schools imparting Elementary Education under private unaided managements. The share of aided institutions has been declining with the expansion of government schools, private unaided schools and with the State Governments' support

13. NER: The Net Enrolment Ratio (NER) is defined by the United Nations Educational, Scientific and Cultural Organisation (UNESCO), Institute for Statistics, as the enrolment of the official age group for a given level of education expressed as a percentage of the corresponding population.

14. UNESCO, 'EFA-GMR', 2015, p. 81.

15. Anuradha De, Claire Noronha and Meera Samson, 'Private Schools for Less Privileged: Some Insights from a Case Study', *Economic and Political Weekly (EPW),* 28 December 2002, vol. 37, issue no. 52, 5230-36

for publicly subsidised private education.[16]

Government-aided schools accounted for only 5 per cent of the total enrolments.[17] DISE (2010-11) placed private unaided institutions' (PUIs) enrolment at 22 per cent for both Primary and Upper Primary Education. However, in as many as 19 States/UTs, this proportion has been much above the national average. ASER (2012) reported rural enrolments in private schools at 28.3 per cent and projected 50 per cent enrolments by 2018 if the then prevailing trend continued.[18] A recent State Report Card at the national level shows total enrolment in private schools at 75 million or 38 per cent. Historically, Secondary Education had a dominant presence of private schools, particularly in West Bengal, UP, Gujarat, Maharashtra, Tamil Nadu and Kerala. However, some studies indicate a rapid growth of private schools in Punjab and Haryana even at the Elementary level of education in the rural areas, unlike in the past when such growth took place mostly in urban areas.

UNESCO's Education for All Global Monitoring Report (EFA GMR) (2015) has noted that the role of private schooling has grown over the past two decades and in South Asia, its growth has been explosive with approximately one-third of 6–18-year-olds attending private schools. The reason for and the merits of the expansion of the private sector's role in the overall education system are a subject of much debate. The UNESCO Report further states that private schools are likely to have helped in at least two ways. First, where the public sector supply of schools, classroom and teachers did not keep pace with population growth, private schools may have filled up the gap, providing education for the mainstream population. Second, where public schools have failed to provide education access to the disadvantaged populations such as the children in slums, low-fee private schools have entered the market. In many contexts, parental preferences have increased the demand for private schools.[19]

The first observation may not apply in the Indian context since one of the long-standing demand of the private institutions in India is to dismantle

16. World Bank (2003), Discussion Paper.

17. Sonalde B. Desai et al., 'Human Development in India: Challenge for a Society in Transition' (New Delhi: OUP, 2010).

18. 'Annual Status of Education Report (Rural) 2012', January 2013, http://img.asercentre.org/docs/Publications/ASER%20Reports/ASER_2012/fullaser2012report.pdf .

19. UNESCO, 'EFA-GMR', 2015, p. 93.

the distance criteria followed in setting up of schools, and to withdraw the requirement of no objection certificate (NOC) for recognition. NOC is not issued for new schools set up in close proximity of an existing school. This is because there are adequate number of schools in urban areas which also have motorable roads and public transport facilities, unlike in rural areas. Thus, the argument of private schools filling gaps in access may not be valid in the Indian context. Equally so is the argument that public schools may fail to provide access to the disadvantaged population and hence private schools could cater to their educational needs. Most of the private schools are located in urban areas and they charge unaffordable fees. The acute problem of access is basically in rural and remote areas.

Apart from some of the systemic problems like the poor quality of education on account of, say, teacher absenteeism plaguing the government institutions, the accelerated growth of private schools seems to be mostly demand-driven. This is primarily on account of these institutions teaching English language at pre-Primary or Primary level itself, while some States were reluctant to start English at Class I or II level in publicly funded schools. This is yet another reason why States were not increasing support to private-aided institutions which widely provide English as a subject in Primary Schools. Since the language issue is a sensitive one, the Central Government often avoids confrontation with the States on this count and let them have a say on the medium of instruction and introduction of English language in schools. However, this often does not align with peoples' perception that learning English at early stages offers better 'life chances' for their children.

English in India has become a symbol of peoples' aspiration for quality in education and a fuller participation in national and international life. The pressure of admission in various States in the schools where English is taught from Nursery or Class I, or as a medium of instruction from class I itself, shows that English language has acquired an important and an inclusive place in the Indian psyche.[20] The National Knowledge Commission had stressed that an understanding or the command over English language is the most important determinant of access to Higher Education, employment possibilities and social opportunities. While

20. NCERT & EdCIL (India) Ltd, 'Teaching of English at Primary Level in Government Schools: Synthesis Report' 2012, http://www.ncert.nic.in/departments/nie/del/publication/pdf/English_Primary_level.pdf .

States like Tamil Nadu have solicited international cooperation in training teachers in English language involving development partners like the British Council, many other States insist on instructions and school texts in the mother tongue for Primary Education. There are umpteen tribal languages in the country for which very little progress has been made to develop even primers, and classroom transactions are in a language that is not the mother tongue of students.

Private unaided schools impart education in English right from the Kindergarten level. However, affordability is a major issue for the poor households. The average annual private expenditure for Primary Education is only Rs 473 per student in publicly-funded schools as against Rs 4,175 per student in private unaided school.[21] The NSS results of 1995-96 and 2007-08 rounds show that the private expenditure on education has increased substantially on account of escalation in the tuition fees. Studies also show that despite this, even the 'lower middle-class fractions and sections of working class' appear to have opted to enrol their wards in private schools. Possibly, the new brand of 'budget schools' fitted their bill and such schools,[22] both recognised and unrecognised, have mushroomed, often acting as feeders for big established private schools and most of the budget schools are in urban or suburban areas or close to service settlement areas (slums).[23]

In the Leh district of the Ladakh Union Territory, the Government of Jammu and Kashmir is contemplating closing down some of the publicly funded schools as there are not enough children left since private schools mop up enrolments. Chennai Corporation has closed down half a dozen schools with unviable enrolments, partly due to declining fertility rates and largely due to children enrolling in private unaided schools.

It may be noted, however, that the decline in income and poverty over time could have positively impacted the education of poor and to a lesser extent *very poor* households as compared to *very very poor* and destitute categories in the MPCE-based classification of poverty. With schemes such as the MGNREGA guaranteeing off-season employment in rural areas and thereby easing of income poverty, it has perhaps been possible for some

21. Ministry of Statistics & Programme Implementation, Government of India, 'Education in India: 2007-08 – Participation and Expenditure', 2010.

22. Ibid.

23. James Tooley, *The Beautiful Tree: A Personal Journey Into How the World's Poorest People are Educating Themselves,* (Washington, DC: Cato Institute, 2009).

BPL households in the first two categories to find resources for investment in English-medium schools for their children.

These possibilities could be brought out by case studies and micro-level studies. However, to test these with null hypotheses using State-level data of secondary sources and national surveys impose constraints due to acute inter-State and intra-State inequities in income and differential growth and poverty reduction. What is apparent, however, is that the poorest of the poor depend *entirely* on publicly funded schools. Therefore, it is imperative that access to marginalised sections should be ensured and the quality and standards of education in government schools substantially improved.

Research studies show that poor students often get poor teachers and students with good socio-economic status get better schools and teachers. There is hardly any accountability for government-run schools. School Management Committees (SMC) are ineffective as MHRD studies show over 60 per cent of the SMC members simply do not visit schools for more than three months.[24] Community ownerships of government schools remain a distant dream. On the other hand, teachers get fired for poor performance of children in private institutions.

Poor children getting poorer education is actually a *double jeopardy*. Without pre-School Education to the disadvantaged groups, inclusive education would be a far cry. A formal system of the Early Childhood Care and Education (ECCE) with qualified teachers needs to become an essential part of the Indian School Education System. Monitorable targets should be set to assess the delivery of quality educational services in the publicly funded schools.

It should be noted that it was not due to a lack of access to government schools that people were queuing up for private schools. People prefer to send children to schools where there are teachers, and where children learn English. Rising female literacy has built awareness among villagers and poor people in urban areas. In some large States, it has been observed that teacher absenteeism was worse than students' absenteeism in publicly funded schools. If the prevailing impediments (NOC, Essentiality Certificates, etc.) for setting up of private unaided institutions (PUIs) for Classes I to VIII are removed or even eased, competition among PUIs may possibly bring down the tuition fees in private schools. With increasing number of PUIs, exodus from publicly funded schools cannot be averted

24. MHRD, 'Some Inputs for Draft National Education Policy 2016'.

unless the government schools enhance quality, ensure availability of teachers and also meet peoples' aspirations. Pragmatic thinking calls for forging partnership with private providers in achieving the national and international goals on education.

RTE Act lends support for private institutions enrolling disadvantaged children and in fact there is a compulsion for earmarking 25 per cent of seats. Several States are yet to meet their obligation of compensating these schools as per the provision of the RTE Act, 2009. Many States are yet to take effective action on 25 per cent RTE-earmarked seats for the disadvantaged groups. Recently, Tamil Nadu Government took effective steps for filling up 25 per cent RTE quota for disadvantaged children in private schools. The schools were unwilling to enrol these children and parents of such children were reportedly harassed by the management. Therefore, the government decided to carry out Centralised admission under the RTE Act quota and directly secured applications. Other States could also apply this Centralised admission model.

On the basis of our empirical analysis and evidence gathered from other studies, it is clear that despite high inter-State and intra-State inequalities in income and differential growth performance, the falling HCR during the reference period of 2004-05 to 2009-10 appears to have impacted education positively in conjunction with other variables such as the provision of free education, increased investment in school education, nutritional support through MDMS. Declining HCR has impacted the NER and supported school attendance accompanied by a reduction in the child labour. There is some evidence to also show the withdrawal of children from the workforce to send them to school by households (as per NSS data), which augurs very well for the future.

There is a view that the accelerated growth and wealth creation in the States since 2004-05 has not been broad-based and equitable to reduce poverty of the marginalised groups to raise household demand for education.[25] Perhaps, the marginalised households require a Brazilian 'Bolsa Escola' type programme incentivising school attendance to reduce 'capability poverty' and to open up 'opportunities and choices' for the most disadvantaged.[26] This may be possible with Aadhar-seeded direct

25. UNESCO, 'EFA-GMR', 2015, p.23.

26. 'Bolsa Escola' is a social assistance programme introduced in Brazil to eradicate child labour and reduce school dropout rates by providing poor families with cash grants for their school-age children between 7 and 14 years of age.

benefits transfer (DBT) consistent with small family norms and other desirable social practices (such as raising the age-threshold for marriage).

EFA-GMR (2015) reiterates that poverty is perhaps the foremost constraint on education access. Comparing changes in Primary School completion rates between 2000 and 2010 for children from poorest quintile with those for the second-poorest quintile shows the enduring nature of marginalisation based on poverty.[27] Addressing this inequity must be central to the education policy for future.

(B) Gender and Social Inequities in School Education

The NSS data provides socio-economic status of households by employment and household assets, including land holdings and other assets. The Socio-Economic and Caste Census (SECC) provides details on household assets including the status of housing and access to facilities and other amenities. All these national statistics reveal that the Scheduled Tribes households are uniformly at the bottom of the heap, above them are the Scheduled Castes, Other Backward Castes and 'Others' in that order.

The NSS provides category-wise estimates on many aspects on socio-economic status for various social groups. The difference between the national average and the social group estimates would give one measure of inequity. The second would be the differences across the social groups, which give a relatively sharper focus on inequity. However, it may be noted that NSS estimates do not segregate Minorities and, apparently, they are clubbed with 'Others'. Several studies, including that of Sachar Committee, have shown poor educational attainments of Muslim Minorities which account for a large proportion of 'Others'. This obfuscates the acuteness of social inequity between the so-called forward communities and those in the bottom rungs. Even with camouflaging, sharp inequity between the Tribal estimates and those of 'Others' in regular and salaried jobs is evident from the results of the NSS 68th Round (2011-12).

27. United Nations, 'The Right to Education with Equity: Access and Quality Education for All in India', Global Education First Initiative, UN-INDIA, 2015.

(i) Enrolments

To analyse the gender and social inequities in enrolments, the GERs for various stages of education are presented in Table 4.2. It can be seen therefrom that at the Primary level the GERs for girls is marginally higher as compared to that of boys. This is also true for SCs though not for STs. With the stage of education, the GERs decline for both boys and girls, yet the GER for girls remain better than that for boys till the Senior Secondary level where parity is reached. As the sex ratio turns adverse for girls from 914 at Primary age groups to 901 at Secondary and further down to 879 at Senior Secondary age group, perhaps, the GERs should have been actually higher for girls at Senior Secondary level but they are not. The decline in GERs for Tribal girls is faster than that for SC girls. At the Tertiary Education level, girls' GERs are lower than that for boys of all categories, SCs and STs with a difference of around 2 percentage points.

Table 4.2: GERs in School and Higher Education by Social and Gender Classification

Stages of Education/ Gender	Gross Enrolment Ratio (GER)									Relevant Age Groups Sex Ratio
	All Categories			Scheduled Castes			Scheduled Tribes			
	Boys	Girls	Total	Boys	Girls	Total	Boys	Girls	Total	
Primary	98.1	100.6	99.3	110.8	112.2	111.5	111.5	108.8	110.2	914
Upper Primary	84.9	90.3	87.4	93.2	96.5	94.8	86.5	85.7	86.1	915
Secondary	73.5	73.7	73.6	76	76.2	76.1	67.5	66.7	67.1	901
Sr. Secondary	49.1	49.1	49.1	48.1	49.7	48.8	35.5	33.2	34.4	879
Higher Education	22.3	19.8	21.1	16	14.2	15.1	12.4	9.7	11	920

Source: Educational Statistics, 2013-14, MHRD.

Gender Parity Index (GPI)[28] derived from Table 4.2 shows that for 'all categories' and SCs, these were almost similar, but was lower for STs. At the Primary level, the GPI for 'all categories", SCs and STs were 1.03, 1.01

28. Gender Parity Index (GPI) is defined simply as the ratio of GER for Girls to GER for boys.

and 0.98, respectively. The same at the Higher Education level were 0.89, 0.89 and 0.79 for the three categories, respectively. Gender equity turns adverse at Higher Education level. Factors such as lack of access, poor transport facilities, lack of adequate hostel facilities, low proportion of female teachers and consideration of affordability seem to have adversely affected the female participation in Higher Education.

Measuring progress towards parity is necessary but is not sufficient to assess gender equality. Such assessment requires systematic analysis of whether countries have been able to address discriminatory social norms (for example, through legislation), remove gender bias from inputs such as textbooks, improve education processes and tackle unsafe learning environments.[29] The CABE Committee Report on Girls' Education noted a gross shortage of Secondary schools for girls (both co-educational and girls' schools combined). The dropout rate of girls is extremely high mainly in the Northern States, not only due to the low parental priority for the girls' education, but also due to poor accessibility of schools in rural areas. Opening of schools exclusively for girls appears to be necessary to overcome gender disparity in school education. States need to undertake school mapping for girls' education on a priority basis.

Addressing equity concerns for girls, the Government of India launched the Girls' Hostel Scheme in 2008 to provide for a girls' hostel (100-bedded) for each of about 3500 educationally backward blocks (EBBs) in the country to increase access to Secondary and Higher Secondary Education and increase the enrolment of girls. The aim is to ensure that the girls are not denied the opportunity to continue their study due to distance, non-affordability of fees and other societal factors. The Scheme provides for construction of girls' hostels in EBBs for girl students of Classes IX–XII. The location of the hostel should preferably be within the campus of KGBV or within a Government Secondary School campus.

(ii) School Retention and Dropout Rates

One serious factor which hampered school retention in the country is the heavy casualty in early classes of Primary Education (Classes I and II). It accounted for 21-22 per cent for almost a decade and still continues to be high around 14-15 per cent. Primary Education, although considerably improved with the implementation of DPEP and SSA, with many grants

29. UNESCO, 'EFA-GMR', 2015.

and pre-service and in-service training of teachers, and formidable support institutions like the Cluster Resource Coordinators and Block Resource Coordinators in several thousands, cannot still be said to have joyful learning conditions. There is a considerable distance between the teacher and the student. It is not uncommon in the government schools to find teachers not remembering the name of a child in his/her class. Teacher absenteeism adds to the problem in the Tribal belt as most of the teachers are not locals. Often a single teacher manages the school and his or her attention gets concentrated on the exit class, i.e., Class V, as the children are to move out of the school to Upper Primary or High Schools with Upper Primary classes. Least-cared children simply drop out and the agencies undertaking the survey of OoSC report 'child not interested in education'.[30]

Children dropping out of school early or failing to acquire basic literacy and numeracy skills partially reflect the poor quality of education.[31] High dropouts virtually nullified the successive enrolment drives in the special focus districts targeting SCs, STs, OBCs and Minority children and often called for re-enrolments. The Joint Review Mission of SSA has found the attendance of children falling much below the enrolment figures of the schools visited by the teams. The Reports of the Monitoring Institutions of SSA showed that in the States of Madhya Pradesh, Uttar Pradesh and Bihar, the average attendance rates of children in Primary schools were low at 72 per cent, 57 per cent and 42 per cent, respectively. Besides, repetition rates were also very high resulting in sheer wastage of human and material resources.

There are reasons to believe that most of the early dropouts are those children who have been detained. This menace has been stemmed with RTE Act provisions providing for no detention policy. It is increasingly realised that retaining the disadvantaged children enrolled in schools is more challenging than bringing them to schools. Providing them with soft skills and cognitive skills is even more challenging.

Delayed access in Tribal areas generally tended to enrol overage children. Several children of illiterate parents drop out as they struggle to cope with studies. The inverse relationship between their conceptual

30. A Social and Rural Research Institute (SRI) Report submitted to Ministry of Human Resource Development in 2014.

31. UNESCO, EFA-GMR, 2007.

knowledge and factual information loaded in school seem to put them at a high risk of dropping out. Except a few, like Santhalis, primers have not yet been developed for many Tribal languages. The Hindi textbooks and instructions require good amount of translation in classroom transactions by trained teachers in Tribal languages.

Remedial coaching at school is not common for government school teachers. Young learners from socially marginalised sections experience education in a distinctly different form from those who occupy mainstream positions of power and privilege.[32] Children of the disadvantaged group also face overt and covert forms of rejection in schooling.[33] Most of the disadvantaged group children lack school preparedness. In several countries, including 10 Latin American and Caribbean nations, Myanmar, Denmark, Israel and Netherlands, one year of pre-Primary Education is compulsory. Planning Commission had recommended it as early as in 2005 and had suggested at least one-year ECCE which can be universalised in a phased manner.[34]

Econometric studies carried out by the Planning Commission showed that female teachers contributed significantly to students' attendance and retention in Primary schools. The explanatory variables such as PTR and the proportion of female teachers explained nearly three-fourth of inter-State variation in Primary dropouts and the results were statistically significant. Planning Commission, therefore, recommended significant increase in the proportion of female teachers, particularly in educationally fragile States like Bihar, Rajasthan, Odisha, Jharkhand, Chhattisgarh and Uttar Pradesh. While SSA provided for one-third of additional teachers recruited to be females, no action was taken on school preparedness for the disadvantaged children.

Apparently, the equity issue in dropouts basically pertains to the differential rates for the social groups. The data presented in Table 4.3 captures social inequity only partially as all *categories* include SCs and STs. Nevertheless, the data brings out higher dropout rates for SCs and it is worse for STs. About one half of the SC children enrolled in schools are

---

32. Sunil Batra, 'Equity in Education in India: A Distant Dream or an Elusive Reality?', National Seminar on Universalising Elementary Education in India, IHD, New Delhi, 2006.

33. Krishna Kumar, 'Educational Experience of Scheduled Castes and Tribes', EPW, vol. 18, issue no. 36-37, 3 September 1983, pp. 328–47.

34. Planning Commission, 'Mid-Term Appraisal of the Tenth Five-Year Plan', 2005.

Table 4.3: Dropout Rates in School Education by Social and Gender Classification

Stages	All Categories			Scheduled Castes			Scheduled Tribes		
	Boys	Girls	ALL	Boys	Girls	ALL	Boys	Girls	ALL
Primary	21.2	18.3	19.8	17.7	15.4	16.6	31.9	30.7	31.3
Elementary	39.2	32.9	36.3	42.4	34.4	38.8	49.8	46.4	48.2
Secondary	48.1	46.7	47.4	51.8	48.0	50.1	63.2	61.4	62.4

Source: Educational Statistics, 2013-14, MHRD

not able to complete the Secondary level of education. Similar proportion for STs is as high as 62.4 per cent. The widely held view that more girls tend to drop out as compared to boys is not borne out by facts. In all stages of school education, the dropout rates for girls are much lower than that for boys. Perhaps, girls engaged in domestic work and sibling care never get enrolled at all.

(iii) Attendance Rates

At the outset, the point to be noted is the fact that 'Others' category in Table 4.4 on attendance rates should not be taken as general category persons or forward communities in India, as it includes Muslim Minorities as well. This softens the social group's actual status in the attendance rates. Only a couple of States have classified some Muslims in low-paid occupations in the OBC categories.

As can be seen from Table 4.4, the NSS data (68th Round) shows that in rural areas, the current attendance rate among persons of age 5–14 years was the highest at 92.4 per cent for 'Others', 89.2 per cent for OBCs, 88.7 per cent for SCs and 88 per cent among STs; while in urban areas, the current attendance rate in the same age-group was the highest at 94.5 per cent for 'Others', 93.6 per cent for OBCs, 92.3 per cent for STs and at 91.8 per cent among SCs.

In rural areas, among males in the age group 5–14 years, the rate was the highest for 'Others' category (93.3 per cent) and the lowest for ST (88.5 per cent), while among females it was the highest among 'Others' category (91.5 per cent) followed by OBCs (88.1 per cent), SCs (87.9 per cent) and STs (87.5 per cent).

In urban India, among males, current attendance rates in the age group

Table 4.4: Current Attendance Rates in Educational Institutions of Different Age/Social Groups (per 1,000 persons)

Social Classification	61st round 2004-05			66th Round 2009-10			68th Round 2011-12		
RURAL MALE	**05–14**	**15–19**	**20–24**	**05–14**	**15–19**	**20–24**	**05–14**	**15–19**	**20–24**
STs	767	390	86	814	478	132	885	563	142
SCs	809	396	97	861	522	129	895	582	167
OBCs	843	480	108	878	619	188	902	683	213
Others	876	548	149	902	641	249	933	712	315
All	835	471	114	872	587	186	905	656	220
RURAL FEMALE									
STs	678	249	52	814	373	58	875	460	60
SCs	737	288	35	821	435	57	879	502	86
OBCs	763	315	41	845	479	80	881	551	100
Others	842	427	59	874	545	121	915	631	156
All	767	333	45	842	473	82	887	550	106
RURAL PERSONS									
STs	726	322	68	814	430	91	880	515	99
SCs	775	348	65	842	483	92	887	546	126
OBCs	805	403	73	863	557	133	892	623	157
Others	860	491	105	889	600	186	924	675	235
All	803	407	79	859	537	133	896	608	163
URBAN MALE	**05-14**	**15-19**	**20-24**	**05-14**	**15-19**	**20-24**	**05-14**	**15-19**	**20-24**
STs	871	533	321	849	708	406	923	742	288
SCs	850	495	170	885	598	232	927	662	248
OBCs	881	529	197	907	647	306	942	709	314
Others	915	694	278	931	763	367	941	764	385
All	890	593	232	912	688	325	939	724	333
URBAN FEMALE									

Social Classification	61st round 2004-05			66th Round 2009-10			68th Round 2011-12		
STs	859	656	212	849	681	211	922	672	274
SCs	793	412	102	903	608	154	908	643	184
OBCs	878	504	116	902	622	177	930	678	213
Others	914	676	216	926	734	334	951	751	323
All	879	571	164	909	669	240	934	700	254
URBAN PERSONS									
STs	865	588	263	849	696	311	923	713	281
SCs	822	458	139	894	602	194	918	653	216
OBCs	880	518	159	905	636	243	936	695	265
Others	914	686	249	929	750	352	945	758	355
All	885	583	200	911	680	284	936	714	295

Source: NSS 68th Round, Report No 563, pp 36-37 (2015).

5–14 years were lower among STs (92.3 per cent) and SCs (92.7 per cent) than those for OBCs (94.2 per cent) and 'Others' (94.1 per cent); while among females, the rate was the lowest for SCs (90.8 per cent) and the highest for 'Others' category (95.1 per cent).

For the age group 15–19 years, in rural areas, current attendance rate was the highest (67.5 per cent) for 'Others', followed by OBCs (62.3 per cent), SCs (54.6 per cent) and STs (51.5 per cent); while in urban areas, apparently it was the highest at 75.8 per cent for 'Others' category of persons, followed by STs (71.3 per cent), OBCs (69.5 per cent) and SCs (65.3 per cent).

In Higher Education, in the age group of 20–24 years, the current attendance rates in rural areas was the highest among 'Others' (23.5 per cent), followed by OBCs (15.7 per cent) and SCs (12.6 per cent), and it was the lowest for STs at 9.9 per cent; while in urban areas, it was the highest at 35.5 per cent for 'Others' followed by STs (28.1 per cent), OBCs (26.5 per cent) and SCs (21.6 per cent).

Table 4.5 presents details of the current attendance rates in educational institutions for all India (rural + urban) in respect of different age/social groups, again drawing from the NSS data (61st, 66th and 68th Rounds).

Table 4.5: Current Attendance Rates in Educational Institutions of Different Age/Social Groups: 2004-05, 2009-10 & 2011-12 - All India. (per 1,000 persons)

Social Classification	61st round 2004-05			66th Round 2009-10			68th Round 2011-12		
ALL INDIA MALE	05–14	15–19	20–24	05–14	15–19	20–24	05–14	15–19	20–24
STs	775	410	111	816	505	165	889	588	164
SCs	815	418	116	865	538	154	901	600	188
OBCs	850	492	133	884	626	225	911	690	244
Others	889	603	204	912	687	300	936	733	347
All	847	504	151	882	615	231	913	675	258
ALL INDIA FEMALE									
STs	695	298	70	817	409	72	880	485	90
SCs	747	316	49	836	468	79	885	533	112
OBCs	786	358	58	858	518	108	893	585	134
Others	867	521	124	892	621	208	928	677	228
All	792	396	77	858	528	129	899	592	153
STs	738	356	89	817	461	114	885	541	126
SCs	783	373	82	852	507	116	893	570	150
OBCs	820	431	95	872	578	166	903	642	190
Others	878	564	165	903	658	256	932	708	289
All	821	454	114	871	576	180	906	637	206

Source: NSS 68th Round, Report No 563 (2015), pp. 36-37.

Comparing the results of NSS 61st Round (2004-05) and 68th Round (2011-12), it is observed that the attendance of 5–14 age group children in educational institutions had increased by 8.5 percentage points at the national level. The attendance rate for STs and SCs had increased at faster rates of 14.7 and 11 percentage points, respectively, for the corresponding period. While the attendance rate for OBCs improved by 8.3 percentage points that for 'Others' increased by only 5.4 percentage points. There are reasons to believe that even this increase could reflect mostly the attendance of Minority children who are clubbed with 'Others' as per the NSS classification.

The child population in the 5–14 years age group was 259.6 million (2011-12). The current attendance rate reveals that about 9.4 per cent of the children are not attending educational institutions. In absolute terms, about 21.8 million children in the age group of 5–14 years were not attending schools. This number was 29.3 million in 2009-10 as per an earlier survey of the NSS. In other words, the incremental addition to school attending children during the period, was 7.5 million, which is impressive. In this age group, children not attending schools are of higher proportion in rural (10.4 per cent) as compared to urban areas (6.4 per cent).

There are many explanations for the rural-urban differences. Three proximate reasons are: (i) access to pre-Primary classes in urban areas, (ii) higher earnings, and (iii) higher female literacy. As expected, the proportion of children belonging to STs (11.5 per cent) and SCs (10.7 per cent) not attending schools are higher as compared to that of 'Others' category (6.8 per cent).

A detailed analysis of NSS data of various Rounds reveal that the bulk of the children not attending schools are the children in utter destitution (street children, rag pickers, children in difficult circumstances including trafficked), working children (economically gainful and domestic unpaid work like sibling care/fetching water, firewood/dung collection, etc.) and the differently abled children. Some of these children may be attending unrecognised institutions and other religious institutions (UN recognised *Madrasas/Maktabs*), not transacting State curriculum and syllabi. Socio-economic inequities deprive schooling of the children belonging to the disadvantaged social groups. The NSS data show that the class/caste differences in children not attending schools are narrower in urban areas as compared to rural areas.

A comparative analysis of NSS 61st and 68th Round data also reveals the universal (i.e., all social categories) double-digit growth of attendance rates in 15–19 age group persons. This could broadly be compared to Secondary and Higher Secondary school-going age groups though not precisely. At the national level, the increase is 18.3 percentage points. While the attendance rate for STs increased by 18.5 per cent, that for SCs and OBC it increased by 19.7 per cent and 21.1 per cent, respectively. The lowest increase was for 'Others' category at 14.4 percentage points.

The unmistakable observation is that the decade-long implementation of SSA and promulgation of RTE Act has accelerated the demand for Secondary Education in the country. About 19 to 20 per cent increase in the attendance rate for STs, SCs and OBCs clearly shows that SSA pass-outs get to enrol in Secondary schools. However, in spite of a remarkable increase in the overall attendance rate for 15–19 age group, the level in 2011-12 was not more than 64 per cent. This indicates that the country still has a long way to go in achieving universalisation of Secondary Education.

With reference to the national average, the social gaps in the current attendance rates were higher at 9.6 per cent for STs and 6.7 per cent for SCs. The current attendance rates for OBCs and 'Others' were apparently above the national average.

(C) Gender and Social Inequities in Higher Education

The current attendance rate for Higher Education age group of 20–24 years was only 21 per cent at the national level. This proportion for 'Others' category is higher at 29 per cent. The OBC attendance rate comes next with 19 per cent. The SCs and STs lagged behind with attendance rates of 15 per cent and 12.6 per cent, respectively.

As can be seen from Table 4.5, those with higher socio-economic status —'Others' and OBCs—have recorded not only higher current attendance rates but have also managed an impressive growth performance in 2011-12 over that in 2004-05. While the growth of attendance for 'Others' category was 12.4 per cent and that for OBCs it was 9.5 per cent in 2011-12 over 2004-05, the corresponding increase in attendance rate for SCs was 6.8 per cent and for STs, it was no more than 3.7 per cent.

With countless numbers of Central and State scholarship regimes and Constitutional mandate for reservation for SCs and STs, actually the growth of attendance should have been much higher for SCs and STs given their very low base. It is not so because of the acute problems of accessibility and affordability. As can be seen from Table 4.4, the overall rural attendance rate for the 20–24 age group was only 16.3 per cent suggesting an acute problem in the access for Higher Education, particularly for girls (10.6 per cent). Not surprisingly, therefore, we find the rural attendance rates for girls belonging to SCs (8.6 per cent) and STs (6.0 per cent) much lower as compared to urban and other community girls who could afford transport and other costs for pursuing Higher Education.

The UGC Committee for Expansion of Higher Education had identified as many as 374 districts in the country, which lacked adequate access as their GERs were lower than the national average of 6 per cent at that time. Another scheme was also launched in the Eleventh Plan to set up 374 Model colleges in the low GER districts. The Scheme had teething problems. Moreover, States were underprepared for meeting counterpart funding. The UGC also lacked experience in handling a Centrally Sponsored Scheme of this nature. The UGC has been hitherto handling grants for individual institutions, case by case, based on proposals as and when they received it. In view of these problems, ultimately, the Scheme was brought under Rashtriya Uchchatar Shiksha Abhiyan (RUSA); and RUSA seems to have made some progress in the willing States. However, educationally advanced States with a few low GER districts were reluctant to take advantage of the Scheme as these States had private providers queuing for setting up or expanding their institutions, and all that they required was only permission and affiliation. The problem of access in these rural districts continues.

The affordability issue poses a formidable challenge in accelerating attendance rates for disadvantaged social groups. The OBCs could manage to take advantage of 27 per cent reservation in Higher Education and have done reasonably well in accelerating their attendance rate above the national average. On the other hand, widespread income poverty for SCs and STs subdued their accelaration in attendance rate despite reservation of seats. The underlying reasons are not far to seek.

The quantum of scholarship has never been indexed and has been grossly inadequate. Further, the scholarships are rarely released at the beginning of the academic year even in better administered States. Adequate boarding and lodging facilities are hardly there except in the Southern States. Moreover, the private expenditure on Higher Education is a deterrent as it is simply unaffordable for students belonging to low socio-economic status. Adding to the woes, a bulk of higher, professional and technical institutions in the country are with private providers of education whose fee structure and quantum is many folds higher than that of publicly funded institutions. The observation that educational disparities between the rich and the poor get exacerbated at higher levels of education, where affordability issues become more acute, is entirely valid.

Further, selectivity or restrictive reforms, usually implemented with an appeal to quality standards in Higher Education, often tend to enhance inequity. It has been argued that the Indian Higher Education System, actually promotes inequity as the Left-wing-oriented laudable policies actually get slaughtered with Right-wing rules and regulations on the so-called altar of merit.[35]

Admission rules are invariably restrictive and selective, and they lead to socially undesirable consequences. It is well known that publicly funded Higher Education institutions, both at the Centre and States, are highly subsidised and hence have a relatively lower fee structure compared to private institutions, including those charging capitation fees. In the unequal competition at common entrance test, typically, the rural students belonging to low socio-economic status who lack pre-School Education and come up despite poor quality education in government schools with inadequate library and laboratory facilities and devoid of any coaching facilities, are pitted against urban private school children from affluent sections who invariably take coaching for admission. A combined merit list is prepared and high-ranking children get admission in government institutions (low fee) in the first allotment and the low-ranking children in the merit list are allotted to private institutions (high fee, no transparency) in the second, third and at times even fourth counselling. Thus, those who can afford, get subsidised admission into Higher Education and those who do not, are forced to bear the higher debt burden in Professional Education. Non-Professional institutions have cut-off marks announced and the story is no different. This has been going on for long. However, some States have of late come out with fee regulations and set the maximum that could be charged by private institutions except for management seats.

Recently released Census 2011 Cultural Tables provide educational attainments of 15+ populations by gender. The details are presented in Table 4.6.

The total number of non-technical graduates in the country is estimated at 38.7 million of which females account for only 15.0 million giving an educational sex ratio (i.e., male–female) of 0.633. The ratio is even higher at non-technical postgraduate levels around 0.807. Women

35. Braga, Checchi and Meschi, 'Institutional Reforms and Educational Attainment in Europe', 2011.

Table 4.6: Higher Educational Attainments for Population in 15+ Age Group by Gender

Higher Educational Attainment	Persons	Male	Female	Females (%)	Gender Ratio
Graduates (non-technical)	38,742,338	23,723,290	15,019,048	38.8	0.633
Postgraduates (Non-technical)	13,607,951	7,531,225	6,076,726	44.7	0.807
Engineering and Technology	6,925,177	4,910,994	2,014,183	29.1	0.410
Medicine	1,399,696	829,253	570,443	40.8	0.688
Agri and Dairy	137,436	117,392	20,044	14.6	0.171
Veterinary	36,862	28,758	8,104	22.0	0.282
Teaching	2,742,346	1,363,406	1,378,940	50.3	1.011
Others	21,891	10,917	10,974	50.1	1.005

Source: Census 2011, Cultural Tables.

graduates in engineering and technology account for only 29.1 per cent and in medicine they constitute about 41 per cent. Although a large proportion of women are engaged in agriculture and animal husbandry activities in the country, female agricultural graduates accounted for less than 15 per cent and showed lowest educational sex ratio of 0.171 in Higher Educational attainments. However, in teaching profession and 'other' degrees, women graduates were able to establish parity as they account for a little more than half of the total graduates.

Current enrolments at various levels as revealed by All India Survey on Higher Education (AISHE) data presented in Table 4.7, show that females outnumber males in MPhil and Certificate Courses only. At PG level, the enrolments are close to parity. Female enrolments in Diploma courses are very low. Overall, females account for 45 per cent of Higher Education enrolments. Even in Distance Education, girls' enrolment accounted for only 1.5 million, lower than that for boys at 2.0 million.

The GER in Higher Education as per AISHE data was 21.1 per cent in 2012-13. The GERs for STs and SCs were much lower at 11 per cent and

Table 4.7: Level-wise Enrolment in Higher Education 2012-13

Level	Enrolments in Higher Education (in thousands)			Percentage of Girls to Total	Parity Ratio (female to male)
	Male	Female	All		
PhD	50	34	84	40.5	.680
MPhil	16	19	35	54.3	1.188
Postgraduate	1744	1631	3374	48.3	.935
Undergraduate	12723	10815	23538	45.9	.850
PG Diploma	164	51	215	23.7	.311
Diploma	1500	624	2124	29.4	.416
Certificate	81	95	176	54.0	1.173
Integrated	51	32	83	38.6	.627
Total Higher Education	16329	13301	29629	44.9	.815

Source: AISHE, 2012-13 (Provisional).

15 per cent, respectively. Despite reservation of seats for STs and SCs in Higher, Technical and Professional Education, their actual enrolments are much lower than their proportion to population and that provided under the Constitutional provisions.

Table 4.8 presents data on Higher Education enrolment by social and gender classification. These AISHE data clearly bring out relatively low participation of STs and SCs in Higher Education. Of the total enrolments, the share of ST students is only 4.4 per cent and that for SCs is 12.3 per cent. The share of 'Others' account for 83.3 per cent. The low enrolment gets reflected in low knowledge base and, consequently, poor employment opportunities in the organised sector, which most educated persons look for.

The Socio-Economic and Caste Census (Rural) shows that the proportion of households in salaried employment with government was only 0.73 per cent for SCs and 0.45 percent for STs. In the Public Sector Undertakings (PSUs), it is further low at 0.17 per cent and 0.06 per cent, respectively.[36] These are much lower than the constitutionally mandated

36. Socio-Economic and Caste Census 2011, Summary Tables, 2015.

Table 4.8: Higher Education Enrolments by Social and Gender Classification

Category	Enrolments (in thousands)			Percentage distribution		
	Boys	Girls	Total	Boys	Girls	Total
Scheduled Tribes	729	586	1315	4.5	4.4	4.4
Scheduled Castes	2005	1632	3637	12.3	12.3	12.3
Other Communities	13595	11083	24678	83.3	83.3	83.3
All	16329	13301	29629	100.0	100.0	100.0

Source: AISHE, 2012-13 (Provisional)

quota in public sector jobs. There is no reason to believe that urban ratio would be higher to compensate.

The low enrolment of SCs and STs and consequently low educational attainments are on account of numerous factors including lack of access, poverty, poor educational environment at home and devastating erosion of base at School Education due to exceptionally high dropout rates of 50 per cent for SCs and 62.4 per cent for STs. Both pull factors (socio-economic status) and push factors (discrimination, neglect of slow learners, lack of remedial teaching, adverse PTRs, single teacher schools, poor quality of education and class repetition, etc.) seem to have contributed to this phenomenon.

What is appalling is the failure of the effect of full reservation for the disadvantaged communities as per the Central Educational Institutions (Reservation in Admission) Act 2006, even in Government of India institutions where admissions are made on the basis of entrance examinations and merit lists invariably have waitlisted candidates. None of the premier institutions like IITs and IIMs have provided for 15 per cent reservation for SCs and 7.5 percent for STs, as revealed by All India Survey on Higher Education.

The data on the share of SCs and STs regarding admission in Government of India institutions are given in Table 4.9.

The Survey results show that admission to the Central Universities was no more than 5 per cent for SCs and 4 per cent for STs.[37] The

37. MHRD, Government of India, 'Annual Report 2013-14', p.153, https://mhrd.gov.in/sites/upload_files/mhrd/files/document-reports/AR2013-14.pdf

Table 4.9: Share of SCs and STs in Admissions in Centrally Funded Higher Education Institutions (2010-11)

Sr. No.	Centrally Funded Higher Education Institutions	SCs (%)	STs (%)
	Central Educational Institutions (Reservation in Admission) Act, 2006 mandate	**15%**	**7.5%**
i.	Central Universities	4.64	3.36
ii.	IGNOU	7.09	5.72
iii.	IIT	12.87	4.95
iv.	NIT	13.08	6.12
v.	IIM	7.83	3.46
vi.	IISER/IIIT	11.07	3.56

Source: AISHE, 2010-11

problem is, unlike reservations in jobs which are carried forward, courts do not allow any such carry forward in educational admissions and the admission process is invariably treated as closed for that academic year, even if the institution is found to be at fault. The affected party gets damages or compensation as decided by the Court but not admission for that year. The UGC and AICTE are supposed to monitor and ensure that the Government of India policies are implemented in letter and spirit. This puts the Government of India in difficulties in ensuring the implementation of proper reservation policy for SCs and STs in the State educational institutions where the private sector has a dominant share. If the Central institutions do not follow the Government of India policies, how does one expect States and the private sector to follow?

(D) Regional Inequities in Education

We have already noted that there are sharp rural-urban variations in educational attainments due to income differential and disparities in educational infrastructure facilities. The level of general awareness is higher thanks to the contribution of print and electronic media in urban and semi-urban areas. Even slums have electricity and transport facilities that enable access to all stages of education. In a vast majority of cities and towns, migrant growth appears to be higher than autonomous growth. While cities are growing vertically the slums are spreading to semi-urban areas often without adequate facilities for health and education. These are then the green pastures for private providers for health and education services, often with links with already established institutions in the main city/towns. Notably, educational and health services are minimal and so is the quality. Even these minimal services in semi-urban areas are far better than those available in rural areas and there is always access to alternatives with additional costs and within reachable distance.

Inter-State variations in educational indicators of access, equity and quality are very acute at all the stages of education. An analysis of GER at the Primary level from DISE data shows that most of the States/UTs achieved over 100 per cent enrolment and the national average was 105.98 in 2013-14. The GERs are over 100 per cent due to underage/overage enrolments. Enrolments in Primary Education (Grades I–V) of official Primary age group (6+ to 10+ years) expressed as a percentage of corresponding population is NER which is apparently lower than GER, at 88.08 per cent. As many as 19 States/UTs show lower NER than the national average, the lowest being that of Jharkhand (68.99 per cent). The GER at Upper Primary level is 89.33 per cent. This shows that despite underage/overage enrolments, the country is short of the universal enrolment by about 11 per cent. The net enrolment is poorer at 70 per cent. The NER for major States like Jammu and Kashmir (55.32 per cent), Uttar Pradesh (57.26 per cent), Rajasthan (61.97 per cent), Andhra Pradesh (62.25 per cent) and Uttarakhand (63.41 per cent) are much lower than the national average.

Although at the national level, the Secondary Education GER has been steadily increasing, the growth has been uneven across the States (Table 4.10). Among the major States, the GER at the Secondary level is as low as 60 per cent (Bihar) and around 66 per cent (Uttar Pradesh) which compare poorly with that of Himachal Pradesh (120 per cent) and Kerala (103 per cent). At Higher Secondary level, the GER at the lower end ranged between 24 per cent (Bihar) and 33 per cent (Assam) while that of Kerala and Himachal Pradesh were 88 per cent and 96 per cent, respectively. In about 15 States/UTs, the Secondary and Higher Secondary combined GER is less than the national average, and in some States like Rajasthan and Madhya Pradesh, the gender gap in enrolment at the Secondary level is very wide.

Table 4.10: Gross and Net Enrolment Ratios in Secondary and Higher Secondary Education

	STATES/UTs	Secondary		Sr. Secondary		GER Gaps
		GER	NER	GER	NER	(iii–v)
(i)	(ii)	(iii)	(iv)	(v)	(vi)	(vii)
1	Andhra Pradesh	75.2	43.56	60.3	37.58	14.9
2	Assam	71.21	50.32	32.94	22.14	38.27
3	Bihar	60.08	35.98	23.70	13.98	36.38
4	Chhattisgarh	97.99	51.89	57.23	28.54	40.76
5	Delhi	102.40	64.35	100.42	57.42	1.98
6	Goa	106.66	72.91	70.24	47.73	36.42
7	Gujarat	74.50	44.88	48.51	28.42	25.99
8	Haryana	86.21	46.20	69.55	36.37	16.66
9	Himachal Pradesh	120.31	68.07	96.13	52.21	24.18
10	Jammu and Kashmir	65.97	39.56	51.33	29.50	14.64
11	Jharkhand	70.14	44.38	43.96	26.97	26.18
12	Kerala	102.51	73.79	87.58	57.51	14.93
13	Madhya Pradesh	83.35	44.76	44.76	23.85	38.59
14	Maharashtra	85.58	56.27	58.77	35.61	26.81
15	Odisha	74.79	47.23	NA	NA	NA
16	Punjab	86.39	47.48	71.79	37.86	14.60
17	Rajasthan	78.68	41.04	53.03	27.34	25.65
18	Tamil Nadu	92.50	61.59	75.87	51.35	16.63
19	Tripura	117.01	87.95	40.99	29.16	76.02
20	Uttar Pradesh	66.18	36.67	61.27	34.18	4.91
21	Uttarakhand	88.18	46.37	76.31	37.70	11.87
22	West Bengal	74.82	41.66	48.13	29.06	26.69
	All India	**76.64**	**45.63**	**52.21**	**30.43**	**24.43**

Source: NUEPA (2013-14), Flash Statistics, Secondary Education in India, Progress towards Universalisation of Secondary Education.

The population in the age group 18–23 for Higher Education is 141 million (2012-13). The narrow base at Secondary Education could allow only 29.6 million in Higher Education reflecting a GER around 21 per cent. Nearly three-fourths of colleges are privately managed, and about 60 per cent are unaided and only 14 per cent are aided by the government. This makes access to Tertiary Education tougher for Grade XII pass-outs belonging to poor families. In some States like Andhra Pradesh, the private sector controls 80 per cent of the institutions. The highest number of government institutions is in Maharashtra (721) and even in that State two-thirds of the total Tertiary Education institutions are with the private sector.

The Eleventh Plan (2007–12) had given the impetus to propel an accelerated growth of Higher Education GER. Regrettably, the easy options won the first round. New technical institutions were set up along with Central Universities although their impact on boosting the GER was extremely limited. As noted before, these institutions do not even ensure proper implementation of the Government of India policies on reservation of seats in admission. The more difficult task of expansion and inclusion with quality education in uncovered and under-covered State universities and colleges was simply phased out to the Twelfth Plan (2012–17). The Model Colleges Scheme had strong teething troubles in low GER districts and the progress is very slow under RUSA. Therefore, the new Schemes of the Eleventh and Twelfth Plans have had a limited impact in correcting inter-State inequity. As a consequence, populous States like Bihar and Jharkhand had only six-seven institutions per 100,000 population; while Andhra Pradesh have 48, Himachal Pradesh 38, Karnataka 44, Maharashtra 35 and Tamil Nadu had 33 institutions per 100,000 population, and the national average is at 25 colleges per 100,000 population. A bulk of the Higher Education institutions are only in seven States — Andhra Pradesh, Tamil Nadu, Karnataka, Maharashtra, Rajasthan, Madhya Pradesh and Uttar Pradesh.

The Higher Education GERs across the States vary widely. At the bottom of the heap are four major States—Assam, Bihar, Chhattisgarh and Jharkhand—with their GERs trailing around 10-12 per cent. West Bengal's GER is only 13 per cent. It should be surprising that a State ruled for many years by a Left-oriented government did not invest in schools or colleges. States with strong semi-feudal features like Madhya Pradesh (468) and Bihar (480) had more number of Tertiary institutions in the government sector than in West Bengal (381).

The GER for females in Tertiary Education is at 19.8 per cent. The

GERs for SC and ST girls are still lower at 14.2 per cent and 9.7 per cent, respectively. The GERs for SC girls in Bihar are 5.5 per cent and ST girls in Chhattisgarh are 5 per cent. The overall GER for Muslim Minority is 4.9 per cent. Thus, Higher Education in the country is highly iniquitous. Unless the Governments — Central and States — invest in Higher Education for expanding access, and move to a strong scholarship regime as was recommended by Kothari Commission, the existing 'class education' cannot be changed in 'mass education', which is an imperative for establishing a knowledge society.

III. Inclusive Education for Persons with Disabilities

The Constitution of India enshrines equality, freedom, justice and dignity of all individuals and mandates an inclusive society for all, including persons with disabilities (PwDs) now also called Divyanga. PwDs have often been looked down upon in the past. However, there is a distinct change in peoples' perception in the recent years towards persons with disabilities. It is increasingly realised that with equal opportunities and proper rehabilitation, a majority of PwDs could be enabled to lead a better quality of life.

The Census 2001 placed the number of PwDs at 22 million accounting for a little over 2 per cent of the total population. This includes persons with visual, hearing, speech, loco motor and mental disabilities. The latest data in this regard are presented in Table 4.11.

As per Census 2011, the number of PwDs has increased to 27 million (15 million males and 12 million females) accounting for 2.21 per cent of the total population.[38] A majority of them live in rural areas and nearly half of them are illiterates. The Census 2011 places the number of PwDs at 5.6 million (4.0 million rural and 1.6 million urban) in the younger age group of 0–14 years. The current emphasis accordingly is more on social rehabilitation rather than purely medical rehabilitation.

Government policies prescribe action towards mainstreaming them in the society, based on their capabilities and these are backed by legislations enacted in the 1990s. Besides, the government has set up seven institutions and five Composite Rehabilitation Centres, four Regional Rehabilitation Centres and 120 District Disability Rehabilitation Centres (DDRCs)

38. Census of India 2011, Social and Cultural Tables, c21.

Table 4.11: Numbers of Persons with Disabilities (0–14 Age Group)

Sl. No	Types of disability	No. of children
1.	Seeing	1,044,348
2.	Hearing	1,177,204
3.	Speech	476,789
4.	Movement	627,488
5.	Mental Retardation	395,634
6.	Mental Illness	800,62
7.	Any Other Disability	1,288,044
8.	Multiple Disability	482,767

Source: Census of India 2011.

offering different rehabilitation services to the PwDs.

In keeping with the spirit of Article 21A of the Constitution, guaranteeing Education as a Fundamental Right (RTE Act 2009) read with Section 26 of the Persons with Disabilities Act, 1995, it is mandatory to provide free and compulsory education for all children with disabilities up to the minimum age of 18 years.[39] While SSA has the goal of eight years of Elementary schooling for all children including children with disabilities in the age group of 6–14 years, children with disabilities in the age group of 15–18 years are supported through Inclusive Education of the Disabled at Secondary Stage (IEDSS) which is now a part of RMSA.

SSA provides for a continuum of educational options, learning aids and tools, mobility assistance, support services etc. to students with disabilities. This also applies to education through an Open Learning System and Open Schools, Distance Education, Special Schools, wherever necessary home-based education, itinerant teacher model, remedial teaching, part-time classes, community-based rehabilitation (CBR) and Vocational Education. Under IEDSS, financial assistance for various facilities like special teachers, books and stationery, uniform, transport, readers allowance for the visually challenged, hostel allowance, equipment cost, removal/modification of architectural barriers, financial

39. Ministry of Social Justice and Empowerment, Government of India, 'Annual Report, 2013-14', http://socialjustice.nic.in/writereaddata/UploadFile/2013-14eng.pdf

assistance for purchase/production of instructional material, training of general teachers and equipment for resource rooms are made available.

Within the SSA, there are several major interventions for the benefit of Children with Special Needs (CWSN). These include identification of the disability, functional and formal assessment, appropriate placement for purpose of education, preparation of a customised educational plan focussing on needs of the individual, provision of free aids and appliances, transport and escort support, appropriate training of teachers, appointment of resource teachers, besides therapeutical support and barrier-free access. SSA provides Rs 3,000 per child per annum for the interventions related to education. The number of such children enrolled in schools is 2.5 million and about 1,30,000 CWSN are supported through home-based education. About 2,60,000 CWSN were provided with assistive devices through various modes, and inclusive education was organised for them with the involvement of about 760 NGOs. It is reported that about 82.3 per cent schools have been made barrier-free and about 15 per cent are provided with disabled-friendly toilets. Over 21,000 resource persons are deployed in the services of PwDs.

There are some issues which need to be addressed. The implementing agencies feel that the funding per child at a flat rate has a problem with regard to some type of kits including braille books, the cost of which tends to be higher than the norms prescribed under SSA. Flexibility is required when unit cost is fixed, which at present is being managed with some informal arrangements. The educational statistics show low enrolment of children with disabilities. At the Secondary level, it was 8.1 per cent and at Higher Secondary it was still lower at 2.2 per cent of the total disabled children.[40]

As is with all NGO-implemented programmes, the funding for schemes operated by the Ministry of Social Justice and Empowerment (MSJE) is often delayed. The Ministry's Annual Reports show only a few NGOs could take the second instalment of funds in time. Funds are delayed because Utilisation Certificates (UCs) are delayed and chasing UCs to avoid audit objection has regrettably become one of the main activities of the Central Ministries while monitoring and evaluation gets basically

40. NUEPA, 'Secondary Education in India, Flash Statistics: 2013-14,'. July 2014, http://dise.in/Downloads/Publications/Documents/SecondaryFlash%20 Statistics-2013-14.pdf

confined to financial expenditure. This is the problem with direct central hooking of NGOs bypassing the States. States are not involved in the screening and selection process of NGOs. There is no problem with good institutions whether these are State-sponsored or are directly entertained by the Central Government. In fact, delays could be compounding as most of the social sector funds are released only at the far end of the financial year in several States. There has to be a proper accreditation system for the quality of services rendered by the NGOs so that the problematic ones are weeded out at the earliest. Not all NGOs have high reputation and some of them handle as low as 50 children with a single project. It does pose problems for effective monitoring. The coverage reported by some of the institutions is also suspect.

On quantitative issues, as noted earlier, the number of persons with disability had increased from 22 million in 2001 to 27 million in 2011. The number of Disability Certificates issued however, continue to remain static at 10.5 million only. Census 2011 shows that in some of the States like Maharashtra, the number of PwDs has nearly doubled from 1.57 million to 2.964 million but the number of Disability Certificates issued remains unchanged at 0.71 million. This denies opportunities for the disabled persons and hence urgent steps are needed for identification and certification.

The issues relating to educational scholarships for the PwDs are threefold. First, the quantum of assistance needs to be indexed given the increases in tuition fees and escalation in the private expenditure on education. Second, although the eligibility income criteria has been revised from family income of Rs 6,500 to Rs 15,000 per month, it should be standardised and made comparable with other scholarship schemes. The number of scholarships should be increased. The number of scholarships under Rajiv Gandhi Scheme implemented by the UGC for the disabled should be increased. A total of 42 scholarships at the national level are too meagre.

To inculcate and bolster Skill Development suited to various types of productive activities, facilities for Technical and Vocational Education should be designed for PwDs by adapting the existing institutes or accelerating the setting up of institutes in un-served/under-served areas. NGOs should also consult the Sector Skill Councils so that the skills and training are made marketable. The Government, both at the Centre and States, should also persuade the private sector to employ PwDs for jobs where they could be inducted without any difficulties.

Barrier-free environment enables people with disabilities to move about safely and freely, and use the facilities within the built environment. The goal of barrier-free design is to provide an environment that supports independent functioning of individuals so that they can participate in everyday activities without assistance. Therefore, to the maximum extent possible, buildings/places/transportation systems for public use should be made barrier-free.

The Government has announced an Action Plan 2020 for the education of PwDs. Its progress is summarised in Table 4.12.

Table 4.12: Government Action Plan to Educate Children with Disabilities

S. N.	Action Plan	Progress So Far
i.	Make schools (building, approaches, toilets, playgrounds, laboratories, libraries, etc.) barrier-free and accessible for all types of disability.	Considerable progress has been made under SSA/RMSA. Over 80% schools are barrier-free.
ii	Medium and method of teaching will be suitably adapted to the requirements of most disability conditions.	Special schools have the necessary facilities but children mainstreamed do face problems.
iii	Technical/supplementary/specialised system of teaching/learning will be made available within the school or at a common centre easily accessible to a cluster of schools.	Districts with *CDC are better equipped but rest of the districts lag. Some training to teachers is provided through *BRCs and *CRCs not effective.
iv	Teaching / learning tools and aids such as educational toys, Braille / talking books, appropriate software, etc. will be made available. Incentives will be given to expand facilities for setting up of general libraries, e-libraries, Braille-libraries and talking books libraries, resource rooms, etc.	SSA has provided play way kits and has assisted through *TLM grants and facilities for library supported under RMSA/SSA. Braille books are provided. Nothing on the ground on e-library and braille library.
v	National open schools/distance learning promoted.	Good progress.

S. N.	Action Plan	Progress So Far
vi	Sign language, Alternative and Augmentative Communications (AAC) and other modes as a viable medium in interpersonal communication will be recognised, standardised and popularised.	Very little action on the field.
vii	Parent-Teacher counselling and grievance redressal system will be set up in the schools.	*PTA/SMC established in almost all the schools with very little outcomes.

Source: MSJ&E Annual Report 2013-14; Progress assessed on the basis of various Reports of MHRD including NIOS.

*CDC: Community Development Cell, BRC: Block Resource Centre, CRC: Cluster Resource Centre, TLM: Teaching-Learning Material, PTA: Parent Teacher Association, SMC: School Management Committee

IV. Inclusive Education and Muslim Minority

The Sachar Committee Report has brought out very sharply the relative deprivation of Muslims in the field of education. It noted that the literacy rate among Muslims in 2001 (59 per cent) was far below the national average (65.1 per cent); growth in literacy rates for Muslim has been lower than even that for SCs/STs. One-fourth of Muslim children in the age group of 6–14 years have either never attended school or are dropouts. Primary Education and Higher Secondary attainment levels were among the lowest for Muslims. For children in the age group 17+ years, the education attainment of Muslims at matriculation is 17 per cent as against the national average of 26 per cent; dropout rates were the highest among Muslims and seemed to go up significantly after middle school; only 50 per cent of Muslims who complete middle school were likely to complete Secondary Education compared to 62 per cent at the national level. Availability of Urdu schools was very limited; *Madrasas'* reach was very limited and less than 4 per cent school-going Muslim children go to *Madrasas*. School enrolment rates among Muslims are the lowest compared to all the socio-religious communities (SRCs) including SCs/STs. The level of educational attainment among Muslim women is quite low. Post Sachar Committee Report, some activities were witnessed in terms of an Action Plan, 15 Points Programme (15PP) and Multi-sectoral Development Programme (MsDP), and Scholarship Schemes.

The Government of India has taken several initiatives for educational empowerment of Muslims in flagships programmes of the Central Departments. In the Elementary Education sub-sector, SSA has identified 88 Minority-concentrated districts and inducted these in the special focus districts. SSA has been concurrently extended to volunteering *Madrasas/Maktabs*. Not all these are registered or recognised. The enrolment of Muslim girls in KGBVs is only around 7 per cent at the national level. However, in Special Focus Districts, their enrolment is about 25 per cent.

The Twelfth Plan (2012–17) had noted high intra-district variations even in Minority Concentrated Districts (MCD) and called for ranking of Blocks for special focus. MHRD had identified 1,228 Minority Concentrated Blocks (MCBs)—672 of these are in EBBs and covered under the Model School Scheme in the public sector and 271 schools have already been approved. Some of the MCBs will also get Block Institute of Teacher Education (BITE).

Table 4.13 provides details of school enrolment of Muslim Minority students at various stages of school education.

A comparison of the proportion of Muslim population with their enrolment share in various stages of education can provide a fair idea regarding their educational status and the disability faced, if any. The details for this exercise presented in Table 4.13 have been culled out from the latest U-DISE,[41] 2015-16, for selected major States with a relatively large share of Muslim population. The exercise would also facilitate a comparison of the educational enrolment of Muslims in Southern States vis-à-vis the Northern States.

The data reveal that in the States of Jammu and Kashmir and Delhi, the proportion of enrolments is either higher or around the same as the proportion of Muslim population. Tamil Nadu and Kerala also fall in this category. The proportion of Muslim enrolment being higher at the Primary level is not surprising given both underage and overage enrolments.

Most of the States have the share of enrolments higher than the population share at the Primary level. Muslim students' share in enrolment, however, tends to gradually fall short of their proportion to the total population from Upper Primary level onwards.

At the Secondary level, the enrolment proportion of Uttar Pradesh is

41. U-DISE.(Unified District Information System for Education) is a database on schools in India.

Table 4.13: Muslim Population and their Share in School Enrolments

States	Percentage of Population	Percentage of Muslims in Total Enrolments			
		Class I–V	Class VI–VIII	Class IX–X	Class XI–XII
Jammu and Kashmir	66.97	67.53	64.46	61.63	60.4
Assam	30.92	38.77	33.5	25.21	19.14
Uttar Pradesh	18.5	13.33	10.87	6.46	6.36
Bihar	16.53	16.71	13.74	11.69	11.69
Jharkhand	13.85	12.48	12.22	8.44	5.33
Delhi	11.71	15.96	15.42	13.67	11.15
Maharashtra	10.6	13.73	12.87	10.94	7.79
Rajasthan	8.47	8.85	6.67	4.93	3.78
Haryana	5.78	8.67	6.04	3.15	2.03
West Bengal	25.25	35.05	31.44	27.34	22.41
Kerala	24.7	34.51	33.26	31.93	23.69
Karnataka	12.23	15.11	14.63	12.84	8.22
Andhra Pradesh	9.17	8.11	7.21	6.71	Na
Tamil Nadu	5.56	5.89	5.73	5.41	5.18

Source: U-DISE, 2015-16.

only 6.46 per cent as against the population share of Muslims at 18.5 per cent. A big gap indeed! Jharkhand also has a large gap of about 8 percentage points between the two ratios. The State of Maharashtra maintains a good balance and impressive ratios up to the Secondary level but at the Higher Secondary level, enrolment percentage of Muslims is lower by around three percentage points as compared to their population share. At Secondary stage, the share of Muslim enrolment tends to be much lower than their share of population in the States of Rajasthan and Haryana. In the Coastal States of Kerala, Tamil Nadu, Karnataka and West Bengal, the Muslims' share in enrolment is close or higher than their share of population. The North-South divide is seen with reference to UP, Jharkhand, Rajasthan and Haryana where the enrolment share at Senior Secondary levels is much lower than their Muslim population share.

Interestingly, the U-DISE data show that the Muslim Minority maintains a better gender parity in favour of girls in almost all the States and there is no North-South divide either. In other words, the percentage of Muslim girls enrolled at the Senior Secondary level of education is higher than the percentage of Muslim boys enrolled at the same stage of education. This is a bit surprising but augurs well for educational empowerment of Muslim girls if it turns out to be true. This could perhaps be cross-checked as and when the Cultural Tables by religious groups are released by the Registrar General of India for Census 2011. U-DISE had utilised Census 2001 data and State reports on enrolment.

In order to provide an access to education in modern subjects to the children of educationally backward Muslim Minorities who attend *Maktabs* and *Madrasas*, the Central Government has been implementing the Area Intensive and Madrasas Modernisation Scheme.

(i) Scheme for Providing Quality Education in Madrasas

The Scheme for Providing Quality Education in Madrasas (SPQEM) was launched with the objective of encouraging *Madrasas* and *Maktabs* by offering financial assistance for introducing Science, Mathematics, Social Studies, Hindi and English in their curriculum. This is expected to promote academic proficiency for Classes I–XII for children studying in these institutions. A voluntary approach is adopted. It encourages linkages of *Madrasas* with NIOS as accredited centres for providing formal education that enable children studying in *Madrasas* to get certification for Classes V, VIII, X and XII.

(ii) Scheme for Infrastructure Development in Minority Institutions

The Scheme for Infrastructure Development in Minority Institutions (IDMI) of private aided/unaided facilitates the education of Minorities by augmenting and strengthening the school infrastructure at Elementary/Secondary/Higher Secondary Minority schools and expanding facilities for formal education. The Scheme, inter alia, encourages educational facilities for girls, children with special needs, and those who are most educationally deprived amongst the Minorities.

In Higher Education, as against the identified 374 low GER districts, Minority Concentrated Districts (MCDs) accounted for 64 and for them 27 Model colleges have been approved under RUSA. In addition, 55 polytechnics have been approved as against eligible 57 MCDs.

The scale of interventions in Multi-sectoral Development Programme (MsDP) has increased and a large number of schemes including educational scholarships are now accommodated under the 15 Point Programme. The Twelfth Plan 2012–17 had recommended a revision in the identification criteria for Minority Concentrated Blocks (MCBs) from 25 per cent to 15 per cent so that a large number of pockets of Minority Concentrated Districts (MCDs) that were left out earlier could be included.

An exercise undertaken by the World Bank on the basis of NSS 64th Round data shows that the MYS of Muslims (3.9 years) is much lower than the national average (5.1 years). The educational attainment gap between the top and lowest quartiles of expenditure classes is more than 7 years. It is well known that a bulk of Muslim Minorities, both in rural and urban areas, is in the 'very very poor' or 'destitute' categories.

The national MYS for Muslims, in fact, conceals acute regional variations. While the Muslims in the Southern States were able to improve their educational attainments on account of greater access to basic education, a vast majority of Muslim population in the Northern and Eastern States suffered benign neglect due to inadequate access to education and also acute poverty. The educational scenario has remained very unsatisfactory in most of the MCDs. In Mewat district, the largest MCD in Haryana, it has been utterly dismal for decades together. The large-scale backwardness of Muslims can be largely attributed to poor education which breeds an endless cycle of low-level sustenance.[42]

A World Bank Study (2009) observed that 'unlike traditional *Madrasas* in Pakistan and India, traditional *Madrasas* in Bangladesh seem to have undergone some structural changes even in the absence of any State intervention. Some have started to admit girls in recent years in addition to undertaking some modernisation of the curriculum'. The Government of Bangladesh has taken a series of steps to promote female education with very simplified scholarship regime whereby 40 per cent of girls in the class are supported by scholarships. Identification of the beneficiaries is left to the local school management committee. No wonder the MYS for females in Bangladesh has been accelerating at a faster rate than that

42. PMO, 'Sachar Committee Report on the Social, Economic and Educational Status of the Muslim Community of India', 2006, http://www.minorityaffairs.gov.in/sites/default/files/sachar_comm.pdf

for India and Pakistan.

The Government of India aims to modernise and mainstream *Madrasa* education as an expressed policy objective. This is reflected in the Government's schemes like SPQEM and IDMI as *Madrasas* mainly serve the country's poor and rural Muslim children. Also, they often lag behind in terms of quality in formal general education, in teaching and learning. Major steps are being taken for modernising the *Madrasa* education, including introducing modern subjects such as Mathematics, English, Social Science, etc. and hiring professionally qualified teachers for this purpose. The Government has extended SSA to *Madrasas*. MDMS has been extended to all the *Madrasas/Maktabs* supported under SSA.

The overall progress of the Muslim Minority development programmes appears to be inadequate, as many activities lacked proper planning and suffered at the implementation levels. At the State and sub-State levels, there was lack of coordination. Also, there is no parallel set up in the States, as in the Centre, to take up serious implementation of the Action Plan. NGOs could lend some support but the government has a vital role to play in achieving a credible progress.

Part Two

5

Draft National Education Policy, 2019: A Comprehensive Overview

For quite some time, it was felt that the National Policy on Education (NPE 1986), together with the modifications in Programme of Action (PoA, 1992), was grossly inadequate to meet the challenges of the 21st century education with fast changing educational scenario across the world. The advancements in information technology have revolutionised the teaching-learning process, knowledge creation and transmission. While the virtual classrooms have become a reality, internet services through mobile phones and other electronic gadgets have accelerated the learning process so much that the learning curve itself has shifted towards the right.

The earlier Education Policy (i.e., NPE 1986) was certainly not in tune with the time. It could neither anticipate the explosive growth of private sector in education, especially Higher, Technical and Professional Education, nor did the old Policy have wherewithal to energise the massive youth population of the nation with employable skills in the limited window of opportunity of Demographic Dividend. The NPE 1986

Policy had no mechanism to direct and channelise investments in the neediest regions which suffered acute socio-economic disparities.

During the last two decades the emphasis on education across the world, particularly on Tertiary Education, is increasingly tuned to economic imperatives. Accordingly, the focus is on the development of human capital in support of economic growth. This trend is likely to continue as more and more new generation of learners take to Tertiary Education, with inclusive policies pursued by governments in both developed and developing countries. Basically, the earlier Education Policy had largely extrapolated the education scenario of the 1970s and early 1980s into the future that was hardly aligned with liberalisation policies pursued in India in the aftermath of macroeconomic crisis of 1991. Needless to say, the earlier Education Policy was inconsistent with the aspirational goals of the 21st century education.

Adding to the woes, as explained in Chapter Two, cumbersome procedures, outdated rules and regulations (distance norms between schools), 'one-size-fits-all' kind of policy programmes did not help accelerating India's educational attainments in terms of Mean Years of Schooling (MYS). In fact, unwittingly it deepened corruption and widened the systemic issues plaguing all the stages of education—Elementary, Secondary, Higher, Technical and Professional.

With the massive growth of Higher Education Institutions (HEIs), the apex institutional arrangements that used to handle about 20 Universities and 500 odd colleges across the country at the time of India's independence, simply crumbled when their number shot up to 800+ Universities and over 40,000 colleges. This naturally led to over-regulation and under-governance of Universities and colleges.

At the School level, the OECD-PISA (2010) placed India at the bottom of the heap just above Kyrgyzstan and in respect of Higher Education, none of the Indian Universities could feature in the top 300 global institutions (Times Higher Education Ranking, 2019). India's Mean Years of Schooling (MYS) has been very low not only compared to the world average but also that of developing countries, with acute disparities by social, regional, religion and gender classifications.

Till the turn of the 21st century, Government of India played a very limited role in the education sector. Its prime activities included running Kendriya Vidyalayas (KVs) and Jawahar Navodaya Vidyalayas (JNVs), setting up and funding premier institutions in Higher and Technical

Education, providing grants to the Universities through University Grants Commission (UGC), announcing a host of regulations and approving Deemed-to-be Universities. A bulk of the national funding has been going to these institutions whose contribution to the total Tertiary Education enrolments is highly insignificant. The State Universities and colleges are really the mainstay of India's Educational System, which determine the national GER, but suffer from acute funding shortages.

The Constitutional Amendment in 1976 brought 'Education' from the State List to the Concurrent List and scheme-based funding to the states began. The Constitution (Eighty-sixth Amendment) Act, 2002, inserted Article 21A in the Constitution of India to provide 'free, and compulsory education for all children in the age group of 6–14 years as a Fundamental Right and implementation of Sarva Shiksha Abhiyan was modified to meet the Constitutional mandate.

Against this backdrop, it became imperative that the Constitutional provisions form an integral part of the National Education Policy, since the rights-based approach to education could no longer remain simply as an add-on to the extant Education Policy.

The Draft National Education Policy (NEP) 2019, was thus, long overdue. The urgency called for shorter temporal framework with intensive activities for achieving the goals, mostly over the medium term and a few with a long-term perspective of not exceeding 10 to 15 years. The Draft National Education Policy 2019 attempts precisely this while simultaneously overhauling the entire gamut of India's Educational System.

As explained in Chapter 1, the Government of India initiated a consultative process as early as in 2015 for a new National Education Policy. Several Consultative Groups/Committees were set up by the Ministry of Human Resource Development (HRD). Also set up was T.S.R. Subramanian 'Committee for Evolution of the New Education Policy', which submitted its report in May 2016. Thereafter, the HRD Ministry formulated and circulated 'Some Inputs for the Draft National Education Policy 2016'. A new Committee was set up thereafter under the Chairmanship of K. Kasturirangan to prepare a draft National Education Policy which profitably utilised the work done by T.S.R. Subramanian Committee and undertook detailed consultations with new groups formed for the purpose. The Committee came out with 477-page document entitled 'Draft National Education Policy 2019' and it was placed in the public domain on 1 June 2019 for suggestions and comments. There was an overwhelming response from the public. The HRD Ministry has reportedly received over two lakh suggestions.

The 477-page document titled, 'Draft National Education Policy 2019,' strangely, does not provide any executive summary highlighting salient features and key recommendations. Before offering a critique of the Draft National Education Policy (NEP) 2019, it is necessary to present its comprehensive overview, which is attempted in this chapter.

In the nine sections that follow, a detailed overview of the Draft NEP 2019 is provided, based on a taxonomy as under:

- Early Childhood Care and Education
- School Education (including Foundational Literacy and Numeracy)
- Higher Education (including Professional Education)
- Skill Development, Vocational Education and Adult Education
- Teacher Education and Development
- Equitable and Inclusive Education
- Technology in Education
- Financing Education
- Reforms in Education System

This would serve as a useful point of departure for a constructive critique that is offered in the next chapter i.e., Chapter 6.

I. Early Childhood Care and Education (ECCE)

Objective: Every child in the age range of 3-6 years has access to free, safe, high quality, developmentally appropriate care and education by 2025

During the ages prior to 3 years, quality Early Childhood Care and Education (ECCE) not only covers the health and nutrition of both the mother and the child, but also crucially includes cognitive and emotional stimulation of the infant through talking, playing, moving, listening to music and sounds. Exposure to languages, numbers, and simple problem-solving is also considered important during this period.

From 3 to 6 years of age, ECCE includes self-help skills (such as 'getting ready on one's own'), motor skills, cleanliness, the handling of separation anxiety, being comfortable around one's peers, moral development (such as knowing the difference between 'right' and 'wrong'), physical development through movement and exercise, expressing and communicating thoughts and feelings.

It is important that children of ages 3-8 have access to a flexible, multifaceted, multi-level, play-based, activity-based, and discovery-based education. It is essential to view years of pre-school (ages 3-6) to the end of Grade II (age 8), as a single pedagogical unit and it is necessary to develop and establish such an integrated foundational curricular and pedagogical framework.

In India, most early childhood education is delivered in the form of *Anganwadis* and private pre-Schools, with a very small proportion coming from pre-Schools run by NGOs and other organisations. Where well supported, the *Anganwadi* system of pre-primary Education, under the aegis of the Integrated Child Development Services (ICDS), has worked with great success in many parts of India. However, *Anganwadis* have remained relatively weak on the educational aspects of ECCE. They are quite often deficient in supplies and infrastructure for education, and have few teachers trained in early childhood education. On the other hand, private and other pre-schools have largely functioned as downward extensions of Primary School. They, too, have teachers untrained in early childhood education. They are generally very limited on the health aspects and do not usually cater to younger children in the age range of 0-4 years.

In order to reinforce the public system's commitment to provide quality early childhood care and education to all children before the age of 6, the Draft NEP 2019 suggests that ECCE be included as an integral part of the RTE Act.

Specific policy initiatives proposed in the Draft NEP 2019 are:

P1.1. The mandate of the National Council for Educational Research and Training (NCERT) will be expanded to include the development of a Curricular and Pedagogical Framework for Early Childhood Education. The Framework will consist of two parts:

- The first part will be guidelines for 0-3-year olds, and
- The second part will be an educational framework for 3-8-year olds.

P1.2. The new Curricular and Pedagogical Framework for Early Childhood Education will be delivered to children up to the age of 6 via:

- Strengthening and expansion of the *Anganwadi* system to include a robust education component. *Anganwadis* will aim to become outstanding educational centres that also contain a strong health and nutrition component.
- When possible, co-locating *Anganwadis* with existing Primary Schools will provide further benefits to parents and children,
- Co-locating pre-Schools with Primary Schools where possible, and
- High quality stand-alone pre-Schools will be built in areas where existing *Anganwadis* and Primary Schools are not able to take on the educational requirements of children.

P1.3. Oversight of Early Childhood Education by the HRD Ministry will be ensured. A detailed plan outlining the operational and financial implications of the integration of Early Childhood Education with the School Education system will be developed in consultation with the Ministry of Women and Child Development (MWCD) and the Ministry of Health and Family Welfare (MHFW).

P1.4. Learning-friendly environments will be designed for *Anganwadis*, pre-Schools, and Primary Schools

P1.5. State Governments will prepare cadres of professionally qualified educators for Early Childhood Education, through stage-specific professional training, mentoring mechanisms, and career mapping.

P1.6. Instituting an effective and quality regulatory system for ECCE in order to ensure compliance with essential quality standards.

P1.7. Generating demand from stakeholders for Early Childhood Education by means of large-scale advocacy such as public service messages and media campaigns, direct communication between pre-Primary Education programmes and parents.

P1.8. RTE Act will be extended to include Early Childhood Education. The availability of free and compulsory quality pre-Primary Education for all 3-6-year olds will be included as an integral part of the RTE Act.

II. School Education

(A) Foundational Literacy and Numeracy

Objective: To ensure that by 2025, every student in Grade V and beyond achieves foundational literacy and numeracy

Specific policy initiatives proposed in the Draft NEP 2019 are:

P2.1. Expansion of Mid-day Meal Scheme with inclusion of a nutritious breakfast.

P2.2. The school and classroom curriculum and schedules for Grades I–V will be re-designed to focus on foundational literacy and numeracy and to build a love for reading and mathematics among students.

P2.3. Workbooks provided would supplement the textbooks, build on lessons with a variety of exercises/examples.

P2.4. National repository of language and mathematics resources will be maintained.

P2.5. A National Tutors Programme (NTP) will be instituted, where the best performers in each school will be drawn in the programme.

P2.6. A Remedial Instructional Aides Programme (RIAP) will be instituted initially as a temporary 10-year project to draw instructors, especially women, from local communities to formally help students who have fallen behind and bring them back into the fold.

P2.7. Large-scale community volunteer involvement will be encouraged.

P2.8. Teachers will manage and continually work with tutors and Instructional Assistants (IAs) to monitor each child's progress and ensure that each child catches up with the average class level at the earliest.

P2.9. Regular adaptive assessment will be developed and implemented.

P2.10. Piloting other technological interventions as aids to teachers including apps and games on smartphones and tablets in various regional languages that teach literacy, numeracy and other foundational and curriculum material.

P2.11. School preparation module for all Grade I students will be implemented to reduce dropouts.

P2.12. Parents will be encouraged to meet with their children's teachers at least twice every year.

P2.13. Teacher education will be redesigned for foundational literacy and numeracy for teachers of Grades I–II.

P2.14. A Pupil Teacher Ratio under 30:1 at every school will be maintained.

P2.15. Expansion of public and school libraries and building a culture of reading and communication.

P2.16. Social workers and counsellors will be hired to school complexes to work with students—and their parents, teachers, tutors, IAs, and community members—to help ensure the retention in school and the mental health of all children.

P2.17. Mobilisation of local community and of volunteers with a view to 'end the learning crisis'.

(B) Reintegrating Dropouts and Ensuring Universal Access to Education

Objective: Achieve access and participation in free and compulsory quality School Education for all children in the age group of 3-18 years by 2030.

An estimated 62 million children of school age (between 6 and 18 years) were out of school in 2015. One key reason is that many students find themselves falling increasingly behind in school as time passes by—many not even attaining foundational literacy and numeracy by Grade V or even by Grade VIII—that it becomes a waste of their time to attend school. The problem of access to schools also remains a major concern. In 2016-17, for every 100 Primary Schools/sections in India, there were about 50 Upper Primary Schools/sections, 20 Secondary schools/sections and only about 9 Higher Secondary Schools/sections.

Socio-cultural and economic issues like child marriage, perceived roles of gender or caste, or child labour also play a significant role in dropout rates. Many children, especially girls, drop out due to lack of working toilet facilities; others—particularly girls and children from various other Underrepresented Groups (URGs)—drop out due to problems with harassment and safety or simply because they do not find school interesting or useful.

In this regard, two basic incentives are necessary:

- To provide effective and efficient infrastructure so that all students have access to safe and engaging School Education at all levels from pre-Primary School through Grade XII.
- Universal participation should be achieved in school by carefully tracking students, as well as their learning levels in school, in order to continually work towards ensuring that they are enrolled in and attending school, and have suitable opportunities for remediation and re-entry to catch up in case they have fallen behind or dropped out.

Once infrastructure and participation are in place, ensuring quality across the board is indeed key in retaining students.

(i) Creating Effective School Infrastructure

Specific policy initiatives proposed include:

P3.1. The number and coverage of schools/sections will be increased at all levels, especially Grades IX-XII, in order to work towards achieving 100 per cent GER through building new schools plus consolidation.

P3.2. Supporting transport facilities will be provided and school rationalisation will take place. Bicycles, school buses, organised walking groups, will also be provided as appropriate.

P3.3. Free room and board facilities in the form of hostels will be built—matching the standard of Navodaya Vidyalayas—in school locations where students may have to come from particularly far and/or for students who come from disadvantaged economic backgrounds.

P3.4. Appropriate measures will be taken at all schools at all levels to ensure the safety of students (particularly girls and other URGs). The local police will work with the social workers to instruct parents and students on identifying and reporting incidents of harassment, both within and outside the school.

(ii) Ensuring Participation and Learning

In this regard, specific initiatives proposed include:

P3.5. Transparent and reliable systems for tracking attendance of all students will be set up at the local level in collaboration with teachers and School Management Committees (SMCs).

P3.6. Teachers will consistently monitor learning outcomes of students through adaptive assessments in order to identify students who may be falling behind.

P3.7. An appropriate area-specific and locally relevant mechanism will be put in place to track out-of-school children.

P3.8. Social workers and counsellors will interact with students in cases of lengthy absences, enrolled students falling vastly behind, children who have never enrolled or who have dropped out.

P3.9. Schools, social workers, counsellors and/or health workers will help instruct parents, students and the community-at-large on good health, hygiene, cleanliness and timely vaccination practices.

P3.10. In cases of children or adolescents who have been out of school for multiple years, sustained programmatic initiatives will be undertaken to provide them meaningful education and training opportunities.

P3.11. Education and skills development opportunities (e.g. market-driven courses to make them rapidly employable) will be provided to dropouts aged 15 and above.

P3.12. To facilitate learning for all students, including Children with Special Needs (CWSN), the scope of School Education will be broadened to facilitate multiple pathways to learning involving formal and non-formal education modes. These include use of technology, such as the development and sharing of e-resources and promotion of e-learning, besides Open and Distance Learning (ODL) Programmes offered by the National Institute of Open Schooling (NIOS).

P3.13. Allowing multiple models for schools and loosening the input restrictions of the RTE Act to make it easier for both governments as well as non- governmental philanthropic organisations to build schools, to encourage local variations on account of culture, geography, and demographics and to allow alternative models of education such as *Gurukuls, Pathshalas, Madrasas,* and homeschooling.

P3.14. The availability of free and compulsory quality Secondary Education (Grades IX-XII; typically ages 14-18) will be included as an integral part of the RTE Act.

(C) Curriculum and Pedagogy in Schools

Objective: Transform curriculum and pedagogy by 2022 in order to minimise rote learning and instead encourage holistic development and 21st century skills such as critical thinking, creativity, scientific temper, communication, collaboration, multilingualism, problem solving, ethics, social responsibility and digital literacy.

In this regard, specific policy initiatives proposed include:

P4.1. The curricular and pedagogical structure of School Education will be reconfigured to make them responsive and relevant to the developmental needs and interests of learners at different stages of their development, corresponding to the age ranges of 3–8, 8–11, 11–14 and

14–18 years, respectively. It will thus be guided by a 5+3+3+4 design i.e., 5 years of the Foundational Stage, 3 years of Preparatory Stage, 3 years of the Middle Stage and 4 years of the High Stage.

P4.2. Holistic development of learners by moving away from rote learning to 'learning how to learn'. The curriculum would be reoriented towards higher order skills of critical thinking, creativity, logical deduction, collaboration/teamwork, social responsibility, multilingualism, quantitative reasoning and digital literacy.

P4.3. Reduce curriculum load in each subject to its essential core content to make space for more holistic, experimental, discussion-based and analysis-based learning.

P4.4. Empower students through flexibility in course choices and reducing the curriculum content load. All school subjects will be considered curricular rather than extra-curricular or co-curricular, including sports, yoga, dance, music, drawing, painting, sculpting, pottery making, wood craft, gardening, and electrical work. All students will have the opportunity to engage deeply in the arts and humanities as well as in the study of the sciences and social sciences. There will be no hard separation between 'arts' and 'vocational' steams.

(i) Education in local language/mother tongue; multilingualism and power of language

P4.5. It is important that local languages, including tribal languages, are respected and that excellent textbooks are developed in local languages, whenever possible and outstanding teachers are deployed to teach in these languages. Home language/mother tongue should be the medium of instruction when possible. Teachers will be encouraged to use a bilingual approach, including bilingual teaching-learning materials.

To leverage the enhanced language-learning abilities of young children, all students from pre-school and Grade I onwards will be exposed to three or more languages. Indian Sign Language (ISL) will be standardised across the country.

A choice of foreign language(s) (e.g., French, German, Spanish, Chinese, Japanese) would be offered and be available to interested students to choose as elective(s) dusring Secondary School. Such an elective would not be in lieu of the three-language formula.

Incorporation of relevant excerpts from great works of Indian literature throughout the curriculum will be done as well. In addition to Sanskrit, the teaching of other classical languages and literatures of India, including Tamil, Telugu, Kannada, Malayalam, Odia, Pali, Persian and Prakrit, will also be widely available in schools to ensure that these languages and literatures stay alive and vibrant.

(ii) Curricular integration of essential subjects and skills

P4.6. While students must have a large amount of flexibility in choosing their individual curricula, at the same time the Draft NEP 2019 envisions that certain subjects and skills should be learned by all students in order to become good, successful, innovative, adaptable and productive human beings in today's rapidly-evolving world. In addition to proficiency in languages, these skills include: scientific temper; sense of aesthetics and art; languages; communication; ethical reasoning; digital literacy; knowledge of India; and knowledge of critical issues facing local communities, States, the country, and the world.

Music and art experiences in the early years will be ensured for every student. They will have exposure to both vocal and instrumental music. Arts experiences will also include theatre, poetry, painting, drawing, and sculpture, and vocational arts such as carpentry and embroidery/ sewing/clothes-making. These initiatives for music and art would also help preserve local artistic traditions and cultural heritage.

Physical education, mind-and-body wellness and sports into the curriculum starting at the Foundational Stage will also be incorporated.

Introducing an 'ethics' component to the curriculum early on and throughout the years of school is also considered extremely important in helping students to build character, grow up into moral and good human beings, lead productive and happy lives, and contribute positively to society.

The process and the content of education at all levels will also aim to develop Constitutional values in all students. This will inform the curriculum as well as the overall culture and environment of every school. At the same time, ideas of personal freedom and responsibility will be important to develop as well. Students will be taught not to cave in to peer or societal pressure but to pursue what they are most passionate about. Basic training in health, including preventative health, mental health, nutrition, personal and public hygiene and first-aid will also be included in the curriculum.

(iii) The National Curriculum Framework (NCF) 2005

P4.7. The NCF outlines many excellent strategies that are still relevant for accomplishing a more constructivist type of learning. This document will be revisited and updated by the end of 2020, considering the changing context of education today as outlined above and, will be made available in all regional languages.

(iv) National textbooks with local content and flavour

P4.8. All textbooks shall aim to contain the essential core material (together with discussion, analysis, examples, and applications) deemed important on a national level, but at the same time contain any desired nuances and supplementary material in accordance with local contexts and needs.

An Indian Institute of Translation and Interpretation (IITI) will be established as a constituent unit of one of the existing national-level institutions or in a Central University, in collaboration with States, to carry out high quality translations of materials of importance between various Indian languages as well between foreign languages and Indian languages.

(v) Transforming Assessment for Student Development

P4.9. The changes in curriculum must be accompanied by parallel changes in assessment procedures and mechanisms. Learning assessment must shift towards testing only the understanding of core concepts and knowledge, along with higher-order capacities such as critical thinking, analysis, and application.

(vi) Board Examinations

In order to break the harmful effects of Board and Entrance Examinations during Secondary School, it is necessary that Board and Entrance Examinations be restructured. The Draft NEP 2019 recommends:

- Board Examinations should be given in a range of subjects to encourage holistic development;
- Students should be able to choose from many subjects in which they take Board Examinations, depending on their individualised interests;
- Board Examinations must test primarily core capacities rather than

months of coaching and memorisation.

The principles for University Entrance Examinations must be similar; the National Testing Agency (NTA) will work to offer high quality common modular entrance examinations multiple times each year in various subjects. The advantage of such a system is that students will be able to choose the range of subjects that they are interested in and each University will be able to see each student's individual subject portfolio and admit students into their programmes based on individual interests and talents.

P4.10. Every student has innate talents, which must be discovered, nurtured, fostered, and developed. Establishing a system of Centrally-funded topic-based residential summer programmes across the country in various subjects for students with singular interests and talents will be helpful.

(D) Efficient Resourcing and Effective Governance through School Complexes

Objective: To group schools into school complexes to facilitate the sharing of resources and render school governance more local, effective, and efficient

According to U-DISE 2016-17 data, nearly 28 per cent of India's Public Primary Schools and 14.8 per cent of Upper Primary Schools have less than 30 students. The average number of students per grade in the Elementary Schooling System (Primary and Upper Primary, i.e., Grades I-VIII) is about 14, with a notable proportion even below 6; during the year 2016–17, there were 119,303 single-teacher schools.

The strategy of school expansion has delivered access but has resulted in the development of schools with small number of students. Small size of schools makes it economically suboptimal and operationally complex, to allocate and deploy all the resources necessary to run a good school. The structural situation has led to 80 per cent of Elementary Schools having three or fewer teachers.

P7.1. The Draft NEP 2019 recommends schools to be organised into School Complexes which will be the basic unit of governance and administration. The complex will consist of one Secondary School together with all other schools offering lower grades in its neighbourhood.

The Principal of the Secondary School will be the head of the School Complex endowed with administrative, financial and academic powers to oversee the coordinated development of all the schools within the Complex.

P7.2. Better resources and sharing in schools through School Complexes such as subject teachers, sports, music and art teachers, counsellors will be possible. Adequate numbers of social workers will be appointed to the school complexes depending on the student population and the population of adult learners in that geography.

P7.3. The aim will be to create a coherent set of educational facilities including pre-Schools/*Anganwadis*, institutions offering Vocational Education and Adult Education, teacher support institutions and support for CWSN that are located within a well-connected geographical area and can support each other in their work.

P7.4. School complexes will be organised in such a way that they will have 80- 100 teachers each, so that a strong community of teachers can be formed to work together and support each other.

P7.5. Administration and management of individual school will be facilitated by creation of School Complex, through enabling peer interaction and support, and creating a single point of contact with government.

P7.6. Effective governance through school complexes will be ensured as decision making devolves downwards, towards Principals, teachers and other stakeholders within the school complex who are better placed to make these decisions and work towards improved learning outcomes.

P7.7. Effective governance and management of individual schools within School Complexes would be achieved through School Management Committees (SMCs) operating as the mechanism for community support and supervision.

Functioning of all schools (government/public, private-aided and private-unaided) will be supervised by the SMC, the constitution of which is mandatory since the enactment of the RTE Act.

Capacity development programs for SMCs will be run on a continuing basis, by the DSE and its institutions such as the Cluster and Block Resource Centres and civil society organisations with relevant capabilities.

(E) Regulation and Accreditation of School Education

Objective: India's School Education System is invigorated through effective regulation and accreditation mechanisms that ensure integrity and transparency and foster quality and innovation for continually improving educational outcomes

Regulation should invigorate India's school education system and work continually to improve its educational outcomes. The 'inspectorial' approach generally focused more on the appearances and procedural aspects of the school, rather than educational matters. There has been far too much asymmetry between the regulatory approaches to public and private schools, even though the goals of both types of schools should be the same: to provide a quality education.

P8.1. In this regard, the Draft NEP 2019 propose that the three distinct roles i.e., policymaking, the provision/operation of education and the regulation of the education system will be conducted by separate independent bodies, in order to avoid conflicts of interest and concentrations of power and to ensure due and quality focus on each role.

An independent, State-wide, regulatory body called the State School Regulatory Authority (SSRA) will be created for each State. All regulations will be carried out by the SSRA, based on very few basic parameters (i.e., safety, security, basic infrastructure, the number of teachers across subjects and grades, probity and sound processes of governance) to bring down significantly the heavy load of regulatory mandates currently borne by schools.

Public and private schools will be regulated on the same criteria, benchmarks, and processes, emphasising public disclosure and transparency rather than mandates, to ensure that public spirited private schools are encouraged and not stifled in any way.

For a periodic 'health check-up' of the overall system, a sample-based National Achievement Survey (NAS) of student learning levels will continue to be carried out by the NCERT. States will also be encouraged to conduct their own Census-based State Assessment Survey (SAS).

P 8.2. Accreditation will be the method used to ensure that schools are meeting the standards of the School Quality Assessment and Accreditation Framework (SQAAF) and Licence to Start a School (LSS).

The system and structure for accreditation of schools will consider the wide variability of local conditions, the flexibility that is required when dealing with younger students and with small institutions and the operational reality of dealing with the huge number of schools across the country.

A framework and mechanism for self-accreditation will be created. A mechanism of audit of accreditation will also be created. This will be done using peer schools and other organisations with capacity and credibility; all schools (government/public, private-aided and private-unaided schools) will be covered by this audit once in five years.

P8.3. Private school will not use the word 'public' in their names. 'Public' school will only be those that are funded publicly, i.e., government schools and government-aided school.

Private schools may be free to set their fees, but they shall not increase school fees (taken under any head) arbitrarily. Reasonable increases that can stand public scrutiny due to increase in costs can be made (e.g., inflation related).

P8.4. The Draft NEP 2019 envisages a comprehensive and detailed review of the RTE Act to ensure its enablement. Subsequently, the RTE Act may be suitably amended and/or the Government may consider a comprehensive legislative enablement of the NEP 2019, since the overall policy has many legislative dimensions, in addition to RTE Act.

Assessment of functioning of the school education system

P8.5. National Achievement Surveys and State Assessment Surveys will be carried out periodically. The cycle of assessment will be a minimum of three years, and will cover the entire range of curricular and learning domains, including knowledge and skills that are specific to disciplines. This survey should be based on a sample and should not venture into a full-scale census assessment.

States may conduct a census-based assessment of student learning at the class and school level similar to the NAS periodically—called the State Assessment Survey (SAS). This may be considered for Grades III, V and VIII. The SAS results should be made available transparently to teachers, students and their parents, the SMC, and the community. The data from SAS may also be used to guide Policy.

P8.6. Protection of the rights of the child and adolescent education will be ensured by prevention of corporal punishment; absence of emotional and physical harassment or abuse; precautions against injury during school activities; safe infrastructure; use of child friendly language and actions; non-discrimination; etc. It calls for creating the right environment for children that is sensitive to child rights. A zero-tolerance approach for any breach of child rights will be adopted to ensure physical and emotional safety of children.

III. Higher Education

(A) Quality Universities and Colleges: A New and Forward Looking Vision

Objective: To revamp the higher education system, create world-class multidisciplinary Higher Education Institutions (HEIs) across the country and increase GER to at least 50 per cent by 2035

India has over 800 universities and approximately 40,000 colleges, reflecting severe fragmentation and small size of HEIs. Remarkably, over 40 per cent of all colleges in the country run only a single programme, far from the multidisciplinary style of Higher Education that will be required in the 21st century. Moreover, more than 20 per cent colleges have enrolment below 100, while only 4 per cent of colleges have enrolment over 3,000 (AISHE 2016-17). To make matters worse, thousands of the smaller colleges hardly have any teaching faculty at all and there is little or no education taking place—thus affecting severely the integrity of the Indian Higher Education System.

This fragmentation of the system leads directly to severe suboptimality on various fronts: resource utilisation, the range and number of programmes and disciplines, as well as faculty and importantly, the ability to carry out high-quality multidisciplinary research.

Access to Higher Education has significantly improved in the past few decades but is still not sufficient to reach all our young citizens; equity in and quality of education still remain a big challenge. While the GER of Higher Education has risen over the last several years, to around 25 per cent and notable progress has been made, it still has a long way to go reaching the target GER of at least 50 per cent by 2035.

The lack of teacher autonomy has led to a severe lack of faculty motivation and scope for innovation. In particular, the system of affiliated colleges which are required to follow a central syllabus, curriculum, pedagogy, and textbook makes it very difficult to provide teachers with such autonomy.

Yet another reason for lack of novel initiatives from faculty and institutional leaders, is the lack of a suitable structure for career management of faculty and of institutional leaders. The system of selection, tenure, promotion, salary increases, and other recognition and vertical mobility of faculty and institutional leaders is, presently, not based on merit but tends to be either seniority based on arbitrary.

The lack of research at most Universities and colleges, and the lack of transparent and competitive peer reviewed research funding across disciplines is a major challenge going forward.

Governance and leadership of HEIs are, at the current time, deeply influenced and controlled by external bodies and individuals that have vested political and/or commercial interests in the HEIs. Public institutions are often operated as extensions of government departments. There are many fake colleges in existence that run with impunity, while excellent colleges and Universities feel constrained academically, administratively, and financially.

In this regard, the Vision presented in Draft NEP 2019 includes the following key changes to the current system:

P9.1. Moving towards a Higher Education System consisting of large, multi-disciplinary Universities and colleges- each of which will aim to have upwards of 5,000 or more students, by consolidating and restructuring existing institutions and building new ones including establishing new world-class model institutions across the country, and also establishing at least one large high quality multidisciplinary HEI in (or close to) every district.

P9.2. Moving towards a more liberal undergraduate education will help develop well-rounded individuals that possess critical 21st century capacities in fields across the arts, humanities, sciences, social sciences, and professional, technical, and vocational crafts, an ethic of social engagement, and rigorous specialisation in a chosen field or fields.

P9.3. Faculty will be enabled and motivated to innovate in their teaching and pedagogical approaches, student assessment, community service initiatives, and research, and share best practices and ideas with each other in University wide and larger forums in order to continually improve.

P9.4. Curriculum, pedagogy, assessment, and student support will be revamped. Curriculum, pedagogy, and assessment will move away from solely rote learning of facts and mechanical procedures. Open and Distance Learning (ODL) programmes will be reimagined to ensure that their quality is equivalent to the best in class programmes.

P9.5 All faculty positions will be filled, based on rigorous recruitment evaluations (including evaluation by students), and the practice of contract employment will be stopped.

P9.6 A National Research Foundation (NRF) will be established to grant competitive funding for outstanding research proposals across all disciplines, as determined by peer review and success of proposals. Most importantly, it will aim to seed, grow, and facilitate research at academic institutions.

P9.7. Higher Education Institutions will be governed by Independent Boards, with complete academic and administrative autonomy. Clear merit-based procedures for appointments of the Board of Governors, the Chancellor, and the Vice-Chancellor/Director/Chief Executive of HEI will ensure elimination of external interference, including from the government.

P9.8. The regulatory system will be transformed to have only one regulator for entire Higher Education, including Professional Education. Accreditation on basic parameters (such as financial probity) will form the basis for all regulation—these parameters will be minimalistic but rigorously enforced. Private and Public institutions will be treated on par by the regulatory regime.

(B) Institutional Restructuring and Consolidation

Objective: To create vibrant multidisciplinary institutions of high quality that increase capacity of Higher Education in India (HEI) and ensure equitable access

The vision presented above calls for a new concept of what constitutes HEI. All HEIs will aim to become large and multidisciplinary. Access to high quality institutions in disadvantaged geographies will be a priority. This consolidation, expansion and improvement shall ensure equitable and high-quality Higher Education across the country.

P10.1. HEIs will be developed into vibrant communities of high-quality teaching, research, and service, and these will form a national ecosystem of learning and knowledge generation, with special measures to provide equitable access to all citizens.

P10.2. Public institutions will be developed and improved, strongly reaffirming a commitment to the national importance of public education.

P10.3. To make quality Higher Education accessible to all who desire to pursue it and to foster high quality research, a new institutional architecture with three kinds (or Type) of institutions shall be developed —Research Universities (Type 1), Teaching Universities (Type 2) and Colleges (Type 3).

P10.4. A liberal education approach will be the basis of Undergraduate Education in all fields and disciplines at the undergraduate level, including Professional Education. All HEIs, including all Universities, shall be required to offer liberal education undergraduate programmes.

P10.5. The development of this new institutional architecture across the country will be energised by the autonomy of the institutions, substantial increased public financial support, and encouragement of private philanthropic efforts.

P10.6. There will be a fair and transparent system for determining (increased) levels of public funding support for public HEIs. This system will give equitable opportunity for public institutions to grow and develop.

P10.7. The existing Central Universities (CUs), Centrally-Funded Technical Institutions (CFTIs), Institutions of National Importance (INIs) and other institutions substantially (around 50 per cent or more) supported by the Central government (e.g., National Institutes of Technology), and Research Institutions (RIs) will all be supported to become Type 1 institutions.

P10.8. All State governments should prepare and execute a comprehensive 10-year plan for the development of this institutional architecture in their States.

P10.9. All HEIs will have the opportunity to access and raise funds for support for their development, including for development as Type 1 and 2 HEIs. These mechanisms are in addition to the public funding that may be committed through the IDP.

P10.10. Private HEIs will be encouraged to develop into Type 1 and 2 institutions and must develop to become Type 3 institutions. The private HIEs will have equal access to NRF funding for research support as public institutions.

P10.11. All types of institutions may run ODL programmes, provided they are specifically accredited to do so. Disadvantaged geographies will be a priority—there will be at least one Type 1-3 institution for every district within 5 years.

P10.12. Institutional categories, and University nomenclature will be simplified. Nomenclatures such as 'Deemed to be University', Affiliating University 'Unitary University' will be phased out. Universities will be characterised only as public, private, private-aided: and as multidisciplinary Research Universities (Type 1) or comprehensive Teaching Universities (Type 2).

P10.13. Degree-granting powers are, at present, vested only with Universities. This will change, as Autonomous Colleges will also gain the freedom to grant their own degrees.

P10.14. All affiliating Universities shall completely transform their institutional structure. They will transition to a Type 1 or 2 institutions, with one or more campuses. Universities will have no affiliated colleges. There will either be Universities or degree granting Autonomous Colleges.

P10.15. In order to kick-start the efforts and to ensure that a significant number of high-quality Type 1, 2 and 3 institutions are in place by 2030, Mission Nalanda (MN) and Mission Takshashila (MT) will be launched in tandem. A few new model institutions may also be set up and developed as a part of this mission, e.g., the Multidisciplinary Education and Research Universities (MERUs) which will be pace-setting institutions for multidisciplinary undergraduate education and research.

(C) Towards a More Liberal Education

Objective: Move towards a more imaginative and broad-based liberal education as a foundation for holistic development of all students, with rigorous specialisation in chosen disciplines and fields.

A broad-based liberal education will in fact help in attaining better expertise and creativity in one's field due to better overall development of a range of capacities and the ability to think in a cross- and interdisciplinary manner. Thus, Undergraduate Education will consist of great flexibility in choosing courses to satisfy core subject distribution requirements, together with a selection of courses to establish expertise in a chosen field or fields, including community service.

In order to facilitate the attainment of all the ideal attributes of liberal education, a four-year Bachelor of Liberal Arts (BLA) or Bachelor of Liberal Education (BLE) degree (or BLA/BLE with Research) will be offered by those institutions which are ready to run such programmes consisting of a broad-based liberal education together with rigorous specialisation in a field or fields.

In this regard, policy initiatives proposed include:

P11.1. Redesigning Undergraduate Programmes for liberal education to ensure that it has a common core curriculum/subject distribution requirement for all students and one or two area(s) of specialisation.

All Undergraduate liberal education programmes shall have a robust element of skills and professional competence, along with practical engagement. Curriculum and pedagogy shall have a strong connection with the world of work.

Professional and vocational areas of study (eg., engineering, medicine, law, and teacher education) will be an integral part of, and will work towards, this liberal education approach and curriculum.

There shall be at least one high quality HEI offering four-year undergraduate BLA programme in or near every district in the country. The design of these programmes could also offer an exit option for the student after three years with a BA, BSc, **Bachelor of Vocational Studies** (BVoc), or other relevant undergraduate degree if a student so desires.

P11.2. All Masters, Doctoral, Professional and Vocational programmes will also be significantly enhanced by being in vibrant multi-disciplinary institutions, by the breaking of silos and via the overall liberal approach.

One of the goals of the liberal education approach will be to better connect research and education at all levels. To enhance their own connection with education, Doctoral students at HEIs will engage in teaching as a substantial part of their learning experiences.

P11.3. The large number of Professional Education (including Technical Education) and single-field programmes across the country should over time morph into full-fledged liberal education programmes, offering the entire range of majors and minors.

P11.4. The injection of a liberal education ethos into research culture will truly enhance research, improve its quality, and make it more interdisciplinary, and more relevant. This would include, inter alia, promoting Inter-University Centres for collaborative research and teaching.

Access to high quality multidisciplinary libraries and online journals play a key role in liberal education and also in the performance of high-quality research. The Government of India will set up a mechanism, e.g., becoming a single buyer, for online access to journals for all public institutions in the country, to save on costs and improve access.

P11.5. The awarding of specific degrees, diplomas, and other certificates at each HEI will require specific combinations and numbers of courses to be completed successfully.

(D) Optimal Learning Environments and Support for Students

Objective: Ensure a joyful, rigorous, and responsive curriculum, engaging and effective pedagogy and caring support to optimise learning and the overall development of students.

Effective learning requires a comprehensive approach, beginning with a curriculum that is engaging, relevant and clearly articulates a vision for the desired outcomes and how to attain them. Moreover, it would require effective pedagogy to successfully impart the curricular material to students, thus directly influencing learning outcomes.

The current challenges to effective learning environments include:

- Curricula remain rigid, narrow, and archaic.
- Faculty too often lack the autonomy to design curricula, and this lack of autonomy also negatively impacts pedagogy.
- Student support is currently almost non-existent at most institutions.

Curriculum and pedagogy must be designed by institutions and motivated faculty to ensure a stimulating and engaging learning environment for all students, and assessment must be used to further the goals of each programme.

Students from socio-economically disadvantaged backgrounds require encouragement and support to make the transition to Higher Education successfully. Providing access is only the first step; continuous support must also be provided. Universities and colleges must be required to set up high quality academic support for educationally disadvantaged groups and must be given adequate funds and academic resources to carry this out effectively.

In this regard the Draft NEP 2019 proposes inter alia the following policy initiatives:

P12.1. A National Higher Education Qualifications Framework (NHEQF) outlining the learning outcomes associated with degree/ diploma/certification shall be the guiding document for curricula across all disciplines and fields.

P12.2. Academic, financial and emotional support will be available for students to help them attain better outcomes.

P12.3. The full potential of ODL as a curricular and pedagogical approach that can substantially expand access to Higher Education will be fully leveraged by ensuring that ODL programmes are of the highest quality.

An online digital repository with all content developed for ODL will be included in an online digital repository with adequate funding to continually improve the quality.

Internationalisation of Higher Education

P12.4. The approaches to promoting internationalisation of Higher Education will involve facilitating student and faculty mobility, establishing international partnerships for research and cross-border delivery of Higher Education programmes, easing the processes through which institutions can enrol students from around the world, as well as the feasibility of carrying credits across institutions in multiple countries, and other such measures.

Opportunities for Research collaborations, student exchanges, offshore campuses, will be explored. Select foreign universities may be invited to India and there will be increased focus on outreach and branding for Indian Institutions.

(E) Energised, Engaged and Capable Faculty

Objective: Empowered faculty with high competence and deep commitment, energised for excellence in teaching and research.

P13.1. Higher education faculty must be valued and supported with excellent preparation and conducive working environments.

Motivating and energising faculty to achieve high quality in Higher Education will be the priority. For this service conditions conducive to excellent teaching and research will be maintained and excellence will be incentivised through merit-based career management.

Permanent (tenure) employment track for University staff including faculty will be introduced. The probation period will typically be five years, which may be reduced or increased upon evaluation. Confirmation will be based on a rigorous and comprehensive assessment process and could include 360-degree feedback (supervisor, peer and student review) over a period of time and assessment of a portfolio of work.

Faculty development plan should be put in place and include capacity development in the field/discipline, pedagogical capacities, research and contribution to practice. Institutions could consider putting in place a mentorship programme for young faculty members and a self- assessment tracking system that would encourage faculty to assess their own progress and learning.

(F) Professional Education

Objective: Build a holistic approach to the preparation of professionals, by ensuring broad-based competencies and 21st century skills; an understanding of the social-human context and a strong ethical compass; in addition to the highest-quality professional capacities.

Professional Education in India—in Agriculture, Law, Healthcare and Technical Education—is offered largely in silos of individual subjects and separate from general Higher Education. Professional Education will be an integral part of the overall Higher Education System.

P16.1. Reintegrating Professional Education into Higher Education must involve: (i) an education in the ethic and importance of public purpose; (ii) an education in the specific profession and its role in realising that purpose; and (iii) an education for professional practice.

All Universities and autonomous colleges offering Professional Education will be empowered to offer Vocational Education in their related disciplines at the undergraduate level through Diploma, Advanced Diploma and BVoc degrees that are aligned with NSQF Levels 5, 6 and 7.

In order to facilitate the free exchange of ideas across disciplines, pathways for multiple entry points into various disciplines of Professional Education programmes will be created, including integration of learners with demonstrated competence or work experience in relevant areas.

P16.2. Capacity planning for professionals will be done and the Rashtriya Shiksha Aayog (RSA) will commission a comprehensive perspective plan for Professional Education in India, which will be based on comprehensive data gathering and analysis.

P16.3. Postgraduate education curriculum and pedagogical approach will be revamped to ensure strong exposure to professional practice in the context of each specialisation. This may require tight collaboration between HEIs and different professional institutions (e.g., the healthcare system) in the country.

P16.4. Departments of Education for preparing faculty for Professional Education will be setup and the shortage of faculty across disciplines will be mitigated. A professional council for faculty in each discipline of Professional Education is necessary, to take responsibility for ensuring that every faculty member receives refresher courses at regular intervals.

P16.5. Fees for Professional Education courses will be left to the management of educational institutions, both public and private. Up to 50 per cent of students qualifying for admission must receive some degree of scholarships and a minimum 20 per cent of these must receive full scholarships.

P16.6. Undergraduate Education in Agriculture is currently unable to cope with the demand from industry and particularly from agri-business, for trained graduates. It is imperative to present the opportunities that exist in Agriculture to both students and parents, to help them make informed choices.

Every Agricultural university must engage with local groups of farmers and provide them with extension services, — e.g., with knowhow to help mitigate their risks (deal with pests, etc.); ways to increase their income through access to knowhow in agri-processing and other areas by way of short-term courses.

P16.7. Professional Education in Law must be globally competitive, adopting best practices and embracing new technologies for wider access to justice and timely delivery of justice. A new Legal Education Policy is, therefore, found imperative for assigning direction for future change.

P16.8. All MBBS graduates must necessarily possess: (i) medical skills; (ii) diagnostic skills; (iii) surgical skills; and (iv) emergency skills. The revamped education of medical students must ensure this. Curriculum, pedagogy, assessment and opportunities for gaining work experience during the studies must all be improved. The compulsory rotating internship, which has become virtually non-existent, will be reintroduced and made more robust and effective.

A national accreditation body for Nursing Education and other sub-streams will be created. Nurse Practitioners courses will be introduced and recognised throughout India so that nurses can compensate in part for the non-availability of doctors. Further, a certificate skills-based training programme (minimum 1 to 2 years with significant on-the-job training) for General Duty Assistants (GDA), Emergency Medical Technicians-Basic (EMT-B) and Laboratory Technicians who can be employed in Primary Health Centres (PHCs) and other government set-ups will be introduced to strengthen delivery of healthcare.

P16.9. As to the Technical Education, curricula must be renewed with a focus on opportunities to engage deeply with the field and be more inclusive of other disciplines. India must take the lead in preparing professionals in cutting-edge areas that are fast gaining prominence such as Artificial Intelligence, 3-D Machining, Big Data Analytics and Machine Learning among others aspects in Technical Education, besides Genomic Studies, Bio-technology, Nanotechnology, Neuroscience and so on in the Sciences.

Interactions leading to innovation and research need to be strengthened considerably between industry and institutions offering Technical Education. There will be multiple initiatives to increase the enrolment of students from URGs in Technical Education. These efforts will include ensuring that each district has at least one government-supported accredited institution that offers programmes in Technical Education; providing merit-based scholarships for students from URGs who are preparing for technical education and those who are studying in high quality Technical Education institution.

IV. Skill Development, Vocational Education and Adult Education

(A) Vocational Education

Objective: Integrate Vocational Education into all educational institutions - schools, colleges and Universities. Provide access to Vocational Education to at least 50 per cent of all learners by 2025.

Vocational Education must become an attractive option for students to choose from. The Draft NEP 2019 suggests decisive actions—both in the immediate and long term—to address this matter. The Policy stipulates that Vocational Education will be an integral post of School and Higher Education.

Many aspects of the integration of Vocational Education will require more detailed study and the creation of mechanisms for coordination with all stakeholders, to envision and implement. A separate National Committee for the Integration of Vocational Education (NCIVE) will need to be set up, consisting of members from across Ministries, to review the long-term goals outlined here and to work out the steps that need to be taken towards achieving them.

Educational institutions will need to develop capacity among the management, administration and teachers to do the following:

- Collaborate with ITIs, Polytechnics, local industries and businesses, farms, hospitals, NGOs and all other such facilities where students can receive practical skills training.
- Work with NCERT through the Pandit Sunderlal Sharma Central Institute of Vocational Education (PSSCIVE) and with the State Council for Education Research and Training (SCERT) to create curriculum and supplementary educational materials for Vocational Education that are adapted to local needs.
- Induct many external experts in different vocations, either part time or full time, as faculty and provide them with the necessary orientation for training students. Appropriate training modules for faculty to teach students of different age groups will need to be created.

P20.1 A concerted effort will be needed by all the stakeholders in the system: (i) Ministry of Skill Development and Entrepreneurship (MSDE), MHRD, and all other Ministries of the Central and State governments engaged in Vocational Education; (ii) enablers of Vocational Education such as the National Skills Development Agency (NSDA), now National Council for Vocational Education and Training (NCVET), State Skill Development Missions (SSDMs), SSCs, financial institutions and others; (iii) implementing bodies such as ITIs, Polytechnics, industries, businesses; other training providers along with schools, colleges and Universities; and (iv) the beneficiaries themselves, youth and adults.

State governments will create more fine-grained mappings of training requirements in different regions of their States and must also set aside a separate fund for the integration of Vocational Education into educational institutions.

It is imperative that MHRD and MSDE, including all Ministries involved in the provision of skills training, work in close cooperation to facilitate the interaction of academic institutions. A considerable amount of data gathering, and analysis will need to be done on a continuous basis to ensure that the rollout of Vocational Education at educational institutions remains on track.

Frameworks and Standards

P20.2. The National Skills Qualifications Framework (NSQF) was notified in 2013 with ten levels of competency. It was also mandated in the NSQF that the eligibility criteria for all jobs and for admissions to educational institutions would be defined in terms of the NSQF competency levels.

The generic competencies defined at each of the 10 levels by the umbrella framework of the NSQF will be translated into specifics for each of the disciplines/vocations/professions in different sectors. Course content and assessment criteria, and appropriate curricular and assessment frameworks will be standardised.

P20.3. As far as Secondary Schools are concerned, the integration of Vocational Education into educational institutions will ensure that every student receives training in at least one vocation. The reimagination envisaged for the last four years of schooling, Grades IX–XII, by introducing the liberal approach and a semester system in which students can take courses of their choice from subject groups such as Languages, Mathematics, Vocational Education etc. and the easing of norms for Board examinations will facilitate the introduction of Vocational Education.

P20.4. In respect of Higher Education, Vocational Education at the Undergraduate level will be expanded and targeted to offer enrolment to all interested learners (up to 50 per cent of the total enrolment) by 2025, up from the present level of enrolment of well below 10 per cent.

P20.5. In respect of Vocational education for adults and youth, expertise must be built in creating a curriculum that is aligned with NSQF and Qualification Packs–National Occupational Standards (QPs-NOS) at the earliest, and combining this with the recognition of prior learning (RPL) assessment mechanism so that all youth and adults can get access to Tertiary Education irrespective of their prior educational experience.

State governments that have not already done so will be encouraged to open State Institutes of Open Schooling (SIOS) to deliver on the goal of educating every child till Grade XII.

(B) Adult Education

Objective: Achieve 100 per cent youth and adult literacy rates by 2030, and significantly expand adult and continuing education programmes.

P21.1. Developing a curriculum framework for Adult Education is crucial. In this regard an autonomous Central Institute of Adult Education (CIAE) will be established as a constituent unit of NCERT, consisting of experts in Adult Education, tasked to develop a National Curriculum Framework for Adult Education (NCFAE), prepare effective teaching-learning materials for Adult Education, and support planning, implementation, and monitoring of adult education programmes. The National Curriculum Framework for Adult Education will be in at least five broad areas: (i) foundational literacy and numeracy; (ii) critical life skills; (iii) vocational skills; (iv) basic education, and (v) continuing education.

P21.2. In order to ensure access to Adult Education programmes (of all five varieties) for all adults, and to attain 100 per cent literacy in the country at the earliest, support will be provided to create appropriate institutional structures and infrastructure across the country for adult education. Adult Education Centres (AECs) will be included within school complexes to facilitate a beneficial sharing of material and human resources.

P21.4. Locating and inviting persons in the community to join Adult Education programmes as both learners and instructors will be done regularly. Convergence and partnerships will be forged with States and with various agencies and community organisations for establishing adult literacy and education programmes.

V. Teacher Education and Development

Objective: To ensure that all students at all levels of education are taught by passionate, motivated, highly qualified, professionally trained and well equipped teacher, who have received highest quality training in content, pedagogy, and practice.

Teachers form the very heart of education process due to their role in shaping the future generations of the society and are, therefore, indispensable in the transition towards a progressive and educated society. Accordingly, Teacher Education is vital to improve the education system of the country.

Studies from across the world show the best practices regarding teachers and Teacher Education are: qualified and trained teachers, teachers invested in communities they serve, teacher satisfaction with the teaching environment, well-resourced infrastructure, teachers role limited to engaging in only teaching in their subjects, autonomy to innovate in teaching, regular teacher trainings and growth opportunities, professional development, career management and performance based economic incentives.

At this time, however, most of these practices are not followed in India due to a variety of reasons, which include: lack of incentives to attract best people to teaching profession, shortcomings and suboptimal practices in deployment of teachers, insufficient infrastructure and resources to support teachers, engagement in non-teaching activities, paucity of professional development opportunities, and absence of incentive based salaries, promotions and career growth.

Another critical factor is inadequate recruitment methods and lack of Teacher Education. The qualifications, training and education required for teachers is inadequate and lacking the essential skills required to impart education. To recognise and ensure the best teachers' training in content and pedagogy is vital. This will require a gradual shift in Teacher Education towards multidisciplinary colleges and Universities with Education Departments offering Bachelor's and Master's degrees in Education while restoring integrity and credibility in the Teacher Education system.

(A) Teacher Development

For Teacher Development, specific policy initiatives proposed in the Draft NEP 2019 are as under:

P5.1. Merit based scholarships to encourage outstanding students to enter the teaching profession: offering scholarships for high-performing high school students upon graduating from Secondary School to study at outstanding four-year integrated B.Ed. programmes at colleges and Universities across the country. Partnerships between governments, colleges and Universities, and philanthropic organisations to be established to fund and establish such scholarships. These scholarships will be especially targeted at outstanding students from underprivileged backgrounds; scholarship offers would be based on school performance, NTA test scores and geographic and socio-economic background.

In hiring school teachers, at all stages but particularly at the Foundational, Elementary, and Middle stages, strong preference will be given to local teachers and to teachers fluent in the local language, so that teachers may communicate easily with students, and with their parents and community members.

Suitable incentives will be developed for excellent teachers to desire teaching jobs in schools in rural, tribal, and remote areas, where they are especially needed. These incentives will include quality housing on or near the school premises.

Research and understanding of the development of teachers draws attention to the initial post-employment period as being crucial and requiring support and mentoring to integrate into a community of their peers.

Recruitment of teachers will be carried out through a robust process based on projections for the number of teachers needed, taking into consideration the requirements for subject teachers as well as special teachers at all schools within a school complex.

P5.2. Teachers must be given constant opportunities for self-improvement and to learn the latest innovations and advances in their profession.

P5.3. Teachers must have access to more short courses that are certified, for modular approaches that allow them to accumulate credits and earn certificates and diplomas, even leading to professional degrees (including an MA in Education or MEd degrees).

P5.3. All Continuous Professional Development (CPD) will be redesigned, keeping in mind the following considerations:

- A well-integrated CPD curriculum will be developed for all stages and subjects including subject content, pedagogical content knowledge, development of school culture and classroom practice.
- Teachers must be able to choose what they want to learn, the content as well as the delivery methods.
- Teachers will complete, at minimum, 50 hours of CPD training per year, across all platforms, as per their choosing.

All States should adopt a technology-based system for enabling choice-based CPD and to track the professional trajectory of each teacher. ICT (Information and Communications Technology) will also be utilised extensively for CPD. Teachers will be given access to the internet and to technology platforms both at school and from their homes.

Every Head Teacher and/or school Principal will be responsible for building strong in-school teacher development processes and a supportive school culture that enhances the capabilities of all the teachers in the school.

P5.4. A tenure track system for hiring teachers across all levels of education will be established. Under the tenure track systems, teachers will be on a three-year probationary/tenure track period followed by a performance-based confirmation.

Independent of the stage of School Education they are currently engaged with, teachers will be able to progress within that stage via merit-based promotions and salary increases.

In addition to moving across ranks within their own stage or stages of teaching, teachers will also be able to move into either educational administration or Teacher Education as part of their career progressions.

(B) Teacher Education

For Teacher Education, specific policy initiatives proposed in the Draft NEP 2019 are:

P5.5. Teacher Education for all levels - Foundational, Preparatory, Middle, and Secondary - will take place within the University/Higher Education System as a stage-specific, four-year integrated B.Ed. programme, combining content, pedagogy and practical training. The four-year integrated B.Ed. will, by 2030, become the minimal degree qualification for school teachers (Ref: P15.2.1 of the Draft NEP 2019).

The two-year B.Ed. degree will be offered to Bachelor's degree holders in various disciplines for the preparation of teachers for various levels of schooling, e.g., as subject teachers for Middle and Secondary Education, and will again include a strong practical training component in schools.

P15.2. Admission to pre-service teacher preparation programmes, like all HEI admissions, will be carried out in large part through subject and aptitude tests as conducted by the NTA.

P15.3. Government funding for Teacher Education will be increased considerably on a priority basis. Departments of Education/Centres of Excellence in Teacher Education will be set up at interested Universities, based on predictive data analysis on the requirements for teachers in School and Higher Education, and the corresponding faculty for Teacher Education.

Departments of Education must include diverse faculty who represent the range of expertise required for teacher preparation: knowledge of and experience of teaching, multidisciplinary perspectives on society, aims of education, nature of knowledge and inclusion, and knowledge of pedagogy, curriculum, and evaluation.

P15.4. The large scope of the teaching programmes required for school teacher preparation across all levels and disciplines points to the need for faculty with a wide range of specific expertise. PhDs in Education and in many related disciplines such as Science Education, Mathematics Education, Psychology, Child Development, Sociology, Linguistics and so on, from reputed institutions that meet international standards, must be encouraged to enter the profession and contribute as faculty of Teacher Education programmes.

P15.5. All fresh PhD entrants, irrespective of discipline, will be required to have taken 8-credit courses in teaching/education/pedagogy related to their chosen PhD subject, during their doctoral training period.

Given that teachers will be expected to lead the reform and help transform the Education System, any concerns or difficulties that teachers have must be immediately addressed.

VI. Equitable and Inclusive Education

Objective: Achieve an inclusive and equitable education system so that all children have equal opportunity to learn and thrive and so that participation and learning outcomes are equalised across all social categories and genders by 2030.

URGs can be broadly categorised into those having given (a) gender identities (including women and transgender individuals); (b) socio-cultural identities (such as SC, ST, OBCs, Muslims, migrant communities); (c) special needs identities (such as learning disabilities), and identities based on socio-economic conditions (such as the urban poor).

While overall enrolments in schools decline steadily from Grades I–XII, this decline in enrolments is considerably more pronounced for many of those in the URG. According to U-DISE 2016-17 data, about 19.6 per cent of students belong to SC at the Primary School level, but this fraction falls to 17.3 per cent at the Higher Secondary level. The enrolment drop-offs are even more severe for ST students (10.6 per cent to 6.8 per cent), Muslim students (15 per cent to 7.9 per cent) and differently-abled children (1.1 per cent to 0.25 per cent), with even greater declines for female students within each of these URGs. The declines in URGs enrolment in Higher Education is even steeper.

Exclusion and discrimination in education happens due to lack of access to quality schools; discriminatory and exclusionary practices and realities, various economic, social, political and historical factors often leading to such barriers; poverty—poor families have to struggle to send their children to school (even when there is access) and to provide support for their schooling when they do; social mores and biases (e.g. differential classroom seating based on caste). Finally, school curriculum and textbooks also often play a role. For some communities, the connection between formal schooling and their own lives is unclear.

There has been various successful policies and schemes implemented over the years (e.g., targeted scholarships etc.) These successful policies and schemes of past years must be renewed and significantly strengthened for URGs across the country.

It will also be essential to take into account research that ascertains which measures are particularly effective for certain URGs. For example, providing bicycles and organising cycling and walking groups to provide access to school have been shown to be particularly powerful methods in increasing participation of female students.

Data shows that certain geographical areas contain significantly larger proportions of URG. Accordingly, the Draft NEP 2019 states that certain regions of the country with large populations from URGs should be declared Special Education Zones (SEdZs), where all the above schemes and policies are implemented to the maximum extent through additional concerted efforts and funding from the Centre and States in order to truly change the educational landscape of these Zones.

The exclusion and inequity that URGs face are only amplified in respect of women. The Draft NEP 2019, therefore, states that the policies and schemes designed to uplift students from URGs should be especially targeted towards the girls in these URGs.

(A) Upliftment of Underrepresented Groups in Education

P6.1. The New Draft NEP 2019 has intensified efforts for inclusion and equity in education. In particular, the following policy initiatives are proposed:

- Targeted attention and support for students from underrepresented groups.
- Special Education Zones will be set up in disadvantaged regions across the country. It is known that there is inequitable development across regions—even within States that are otherwise performing better than the national average on human development indicators. States can determine such zones and receive extra investment from the Central Government.

Taking care of availability and capacity development of teachers under three critical policy initiatives:

- To address the underrepresentation of teachers from URG, alternate pathways for the recruitment of high-quality teachers from URGs will be developed.
- Pupil-Teacher Ratio in schools with a high proportion of learners from URGs should not be more than 25:1. This ratio is arrived at keeping in mind the remedial measures and bridge activities that will be required at every such school on a continuous basis until such time that the gaps are bridged.

Establishing mechanisms to address discrimination, harassment and intimidation in administration, pupils, as well as in admissions processes by:

- Establishing a clear criterion on equity and inclusiveness that schools will be expected to follow to eliminate exclusionary practices.
- Developing sensitivity and appreciation of the diverse cultures and traditions to which we belong among students.
- Inclusivity to be exhibited in school curricula, syllabi and teaching learning materials (especially textbooks) by review and removal of overt or hidden bias and stereotyping.

Up-to-date information for each student will be maintained in the National Repository of Educational Data (NRED). While some education indicators will be common to all URGs, specific indicators may be tracked for particular groups.

Financial support to individual students:

- A special National Fund will be created specifically for providing scholarships and developing resources and facilities for students from URG.
- Besides scholarships, other means of support to be made available such as meal programmes and internships.

Targeted funding and support for inclusion and access to districts and institutions:

- Provision of district-wise financial assistance for initiatives related to inclusion and access.
- Institutions serving the educational needs of students from URGs will identify specific needs; initiatives to address these needs will be backed by adequate financial resources by the system.
- Funding will be made available to teacher development and impact evaluation for independent research on inclusive education.

There will be a focused approach and carefully planned synergy among all efforts towards increased participation of URGs in School Education.

(B) Education of Girls as a Cross-cutting Theme

P6.2. The Government will develop a 'Gender-Inclusion Fund' to build the nation's capacity to provide quality and equitable education for all girls.

The Fund will authorise two funding streams—formula and discretionary grants. Formula grants will be available to States to implement priorities determined by the Central Government critical for assisting women and girls in gaining access to education (such as the provision of sanitation and toilets, bicycles, conditional cash transfers, etc.). On the other hand, discretionary grants will enable States to support and scale effective community-based interventions that address localised and context-specific barriers to girls' access to and patriation in quality education.

In order to facilitate the hiring and retention of women in education, the amended Maternity Benefit Act will be implemented to provide crèche facilities for educators. To address the gender imbalance among school teachers (especially in some rural schools), alternate pathways for female teacher recruitment will be developed.

Acknowledging the special role that women play in society, all policy initiatives for the upliftment of underrepresented socio-economic and socio-cultural groups will be especially targeted towards the girls and women in these groups.

(C) Education of Children belonging to Scheduled Caste Communities and Other Backward Classes

P6.3. Special initiatives should be taken up by the concerned Ministries and Departments to up-skill these children and prepare them to be recruited as teachers in schools, especially in their home regions where they can become excellent role models.

Many students from SC and OBC communities have home languages that are different from the State/official language. Easy-read material translated into local spoken languages will be used in the early grades to initiate children into learning.

(D) Education of Children from Tribal Communities

P6.4. Tribal Communities and children from Scheduled Tribes also face severe disadvantages at multiple levels due to various historical and geographical factors. Contextualising curriculum and incorporating tribal knowledge traditions will be an immediate action, while encouraging students from the community to gain qualifications as teachers will be a longer-term one.

(E) Education of Children from Educationally URGs within Minority Communities

P6.5. Supply-side interventions to incentivise Muslims and other educationally underrepresented minorities to complete school education need to be made. *Madrasas, Maktabs* and other traditional or religious schools need to be strengthened and their curriculam modernised.

(F) Education of Children from Urban Poor Families

P6.6. Focused efforts on educational access for the urban poor, the new and existing schools to also invest in hiring excellent social workers and counsellors and curricula that takes into account the needs of the urban poor.

(G) Education of Transgender Children

P6.7. As a part of the initiative to promote education of transgender children, a reliable national database on transgender children will be crated. The creation of safe and supportive school environment which would not violate their Constitutional rights will be accorded priority.

(H) Education of Children with Special Needs (CWSN)

P6.8. One of the priority areas of action regarding education programmes for CWSN will continue to be mainstreaming them in neighbourhood schools and supporting their participation in the schooling process from the Foundational stage through Grade XII.

Clear and efficient avenues for obtaining financial support will be provided to schools or school complexes for integration of CWSN, as well as for the establishment of resource centres at the village/block level. Such centres would assist parents/guardians in part-time or full-time homeschooling and in skilling such learners.

Physical access to schools for children with special needs will be enabled through prioritising barrier-free structures, ramps, handrails, disabled-friendly toilets and suitable transportation for CWSN to comfortably attend schools. While in the long-term, the goal will be for all schools to have such facilities, in the interim schools and school complexes will be able to apply for funding to arrange and build such facilities as needed.

Assistive devices and appropriate technology-based tools, as well as adequate and language-appropriate teaching-learning materials (e.g., textbooks in accessible formats such as large print and Braille) will be made available to help CWSN integrate more easily into classrooms and engage with teachers and their peers.

Home-based education will be provided for children with severe and profound disabilities who are unable to go to schools. Orientation of parents/caregivers along with wide-scale dissemination of learning materials to enable parents/ caregivers to actively support their children's learning needs will be accorded priority.

Special educators and therapists with cross-disability training will assist teachers in catering to the needs of all learners more fully. As a part of the efforts to enhance participation of differently-abled children in school education scholarships for talented and meritorious students will be offered on a more liberal scale, especially at the Secondary Education, to facilitate their entry into Higher Education.

VII. Technology in Education

Objective: Appropriate integration of technology into all levels of education - to support teacher preparation and development; improve teaching, learning and evaluation processes; enhance educational access to disadvantaged groups; and streamline educational planning, administration and management.

The Draft NEP 2019 observes that technology plays an important role in four areas: (a) improving the classroom processes of teaching, learning and evaluation, (b) aiding in preparation of teachers and Continuous Professional Development (CPD) of teachers, (c) improving access to education in remote areas and for disadvantaged groups including differently—abled students, girls and women. and (d) improving the overall planning, administration and management of the entire education system.

The Draft NEP 2019 recommends focused electrification of all educational institutions since electricity is a pre-requisite for all technology-based interventions. Further, it recommends:

(i) The National Educational Technology Forum

P19.1. A National Education Technology Forum will be set up, as an autonomous body, to facilitate decision making on the induction, deployment and use of technology.

(ii) National Repository on Educational Data

National Repository on Education Data will be set up to maintain all records related to institutions, teachers, and students in digital form. Further, a single online digital repository will be created where copyright-free educational resources will be made available in multiple languages. (P19.6. in the Draft NEP 2019).

VIII. Financing Education

The Draft NEP 2019 highlights multiple issues and challenges faced by the Indian Education System and presents an approach to addressing them.

A1.2. Inadequate Investment and other Financial Issues

The Draft Policy reaffirmed the commitment of spending 6 per cent of GDP as public investment in education. Notably, the first NEP 1968 had recommended that public expenditure in education must be 6 per cent of GDP, which was reiterated by the second NEP in 1986. In 2017-18, public expenditure on education in India was barely 2.7 per cent of GDP. This was in a sharp contrast to the public expenditure as a ratio of GDP of 5 per cent (in the US, Malaysia, Kenya and Korea), 5.5 per cent (in the UK and the Netherlands), 6 per cent (in Brazil, South Africa and Kyrgyzstan), 7 per cent (in Finland and Costa Rica) and 7.5 per cent (in Sweden and Zimbabwe).

The Draft Policy seeks to double the public investment in education from the current 10 per cent of total public expenditure to 20 per cent in the next 10 years.

Operational Problems and Leakages

The Draft Policy observed operational problems and leakages in disbursement of funds. For instance, it observed that DIET have about 45 per cent vacancies which have led to their allocations not being used or being used ineffectively. It recommends optimal and timely utilisation of funds through relevant institutional development plans.

A1.3. Policy for Higher Investment to Improve Quality and Equity of Education

The overall public investment in education (by both Central and State governments) will be scaled up substantially in the coming years to realise the goals of education that the nation requires. Along with this, other sources of financing will also have to be scaled up.

While the Draft NEP 2019 reaffirms the national commitment of 6 per cent of GDP as public investment in education, it recognises that this would only be possible when India's tax-to-GDP ratio improves. It is hoped that with the recent decisive actions and encouraging outcomes in this regard, it would certainly be possible to reach the 6 per cent number in the mid-to-long term.

Efficient Disbursal and Use of Public Funds – Addressing Operational Issues

The structural, governance and regulatory mechanisms to enable efficient management of the public education system along with a high degree of probity will enable sound financial management and smooth funds flow by tackling the current hurdles, which will be eliminated systematically. These include ensuring utilisation of allocated funds, genuine utilisation of funds, capacity development for optimal utilisation of funds, systematic encouragement and opportunity for 'philanthropic' support to education, research and innovation from multiple sources will add to the funds required to finance Education.

IX. Reforms in Education System

The Draft NEP 2019 discusses reforms in the Indian Education System mainly in three categories:

A. Effective, Enabling and Responsive Regulation
B. National Research Foundation and,
C. Rashtriya Shiksha Aayog

(A) Effective, Enabling and Responsive Regulation

Objective: Effective, enabling and responsive regulation to encourage excellence and public-spiritedness in higher education.

India currently does not have a positive regulatory framework to support education reforms in a way which promotes the growth via Higher Education while addressing the challenges of such a large system.

Regulation in case of education must be responsive and minimalistic–light but tight, to ensure public spiritedness, equity, excellence, financial stability and probity, along with good governance.

An independent and empowered regulatory body is essential to create checks-and-balances in the system, minimise conflicts of interest and eliminate the concentration of power. Therefore, a common regulatory regime is needed for the entire Higher Education sector, eliminating isolation and disjunction.

In this regard, specific policy initiatives proposed in the Draft NEP 2019 are as under:

National Higher Education Regulatory Authority

P18.1. The fundamental design and operating principles of the regulatory system, structure, and culture of regulation must be delineated (and has been done under P18.1.1 of the Draft NEP 2019).

National Higher Education Regulatory Authority (NHERA) to be the sole regulator for Higher Education, including Professional Education. The responsibilities of each institution within the new regulatory architecture and framework shall be clearly delineated. NHERA shall regulate based on the following dimensions: good governance, financial probity and stability, and educational outcomes.

P18.2. National Assessment and Accreditation Council (NAAC) shall be reinvented and separated from the UGC into a completely independent, autonomous body and be given the responsibility of overseeing accreditation of all institutions of Higher Education, across all disciplines and field.

P18.3. Current regulatory bodies shall transform into Professional Standard Setting Bodies.

General Education Council (GEC) shall be constituted as an academic leadership institution, to define attributes and learning expected from students who graduate from the Higher Education System.

P18.4. The UGC shall transition into the Higher Education Grants Council, continuing with the responsibility for funding institutions and individuals.

The State Departments of Higher Education will play the role of relevant policy formulation, coordination and orchestration of the overall improvement of the Higher Education System in the State, including the development of the Higher Education Institutional architecture, as envisioned in Draft NEP 2019.

Sponsors of private institutions must ensure financial stability and probity, since without this, institutional governance will be compromised.

P18.5. Any new HEI will only be set up by the Parliament or a State Legislature or with an 'HEI Charter' from NHERA.

All new colleges starting from 2020 onwards must only be Autonomous Colleges (Type 3). After 2030 there shall be no affiliated colleges in existence – all colleges must develop to become autonomous degree granting colleges or a University.

P18.6. All HEIs—public and private—shall be treated on par within this regulatory regime.

The RSA will issue common national guidelines for all legislative Acts that will form private HEIs.

Private HEIs with philanthropic and public-spirited intent will be encouraged through a progressive regime of fees determination.

Institutions that are not classified as HEI in the Policy, may also be governed and regulated with principles enumerated in this Policy.

(B) National Research Foundation (NRF)

Objective: Catalyse and energise research and innovation across the country in all academic disciplines, with a special focus on seeding and growing research at universities and colleges—create a conducive ecosystem for research through competitive peer-reviewed funding, mentoring, and facilitation.

Knowledge creation and catalysing research are critical factors in creation of an educated, economically harmonious and socially uplifting society. Prospering societies have one important distinction from their counterparts — an encompassing education system.

Studies have shown that in this fast paced and changing world, it is important to incorporate and promote a multidisciplinary research ecosystem by creating and promoting a talent pool to create a knowledge society responsible for economic and intellectual progress of the nation. Data shows a positive correlation of economic growth with research and innovation, exhibiting the higher GDP per capita on higher Research and Innovation (R&I) investments.

While the correlation between economic growth and investment in R&I is apparent, India invests an exceedingly small portion of its GDP in Research and Innovation. Therefore, a culture to promote research and innovation is of vital importance in bringing about the change in India's Education System.

There are several challenges in conducting research in India now which need to be addressed. These challenges are:

- Lack of funding for research,
- Lack of a research culture and mindset, and
- Lack of research capability in most Universities

The Draft NEP 2019 envisions a comprehensive approach to transforming the quality and quantity of research in India and significantly expanding research and innovation in the country through a new NRF. Proposed NRF will fund, seed, facilitate research and act as a liaison between institutions, researchers, government and industry.

In this regard, specific policy initiatives proposed in the Draft NEP 2019 are:

P14.1. A new NRF will be set up through an Act of Parliament, as an autonomous body of the Government of India, to fund, mentor, incentivise, and build capacity for quality research across the country in all disciplines, primarily at Universities and colleges, both public and private.

The NRF will consist of four major divisions—Sciences; Technology; Social Sciences; and Arts and Humanities—with the provision to add additional divisions (e.g., health, agriculture, environmental issues), whenever it may be determined to be beneficial by the Governing Council of the NRF.

The NRF will be given an annual grant of Rs 20,000 crores (or 200 trillion—approximately 0.1 per cent of GDP) and will be conferred with the autonomy to set its own finances, governance rules, and statutes.

Researchers from all educational institutions, universities, colleges and schools, both public and private, as well as from research institutions, will be eligible to compete for funding from the NRF. Institutions that currently fund research at some level, as well as various private and philanthropic organisations, will continue to independently fund research according to their priorities and needs.

P14.2. Every year, each Divisional Council will make public calls for research proposals of various types.

P14.3. The NRF can fund larger national and international projects, those that help build research, teaching and other capacities at universities, or that has a direct impact on society or fundamental knowledge in other ways. International research collaborations will be encouraged and supported by the NRF, especially in areas where India does not yet have enough research strength on its own.

P14.4. Many government Ministries have research needs that are not being met at the present time. Several Ministries have research cells that are largely not functional. The NRF will offer its expertise to Ministries for their research needs.

P14.5. The NRF will institute a system of awards for truly successful research taking place in the nation, and for research funded by the NRF.

(C) Rashtriya Shiksha Aayog (RSA)

Objective: Synergistic functioning of India's education system to deliver equity and excellence at all levels, from vision to implementation, led by a new Rashtriya Shiksha Aayog.

A new apex body, the RSA or National Education Commission (NEC) will be constituted headed by the Prime Minister with the vision to meet the ambitious socio-economic development goals of new India.

Under this proposal, there are specific policy initiatives proposed in the Draft NEP 2019:

P23.1. A new apex body, designated as the RSA/NEC will be constituted, will be responsible for developing, articulating, implementing, evaluating and revising the vision of education in the country on a continuous and sustained basis.

P23.2. To focus on education and learning, the MHRD will be reorganised and renamed as the Ministry of Education (MoE).

P23.3. The PM of India will be the Chairperson of the RSA. The PM will convene a meeting of the RSA at least once a year, or as often as it is deemed necessary, to review the progress.

P23.4. The Union Minister for Education (UME) will be the Vice Chairperson of the RSA. The UME will provide leadership and chair key operating bodies of the RSA.

P23.5. The RSA will consist of approximately 20-30 members. Membership will include some of the Union Ministers, with portfolios impacting education directly, as well as a few Chief Ministers of States, in rotation, the Principal Secretary to the Prime Minister, the Cabinet Secretary, Vice-Chairperson of the NITI Aayog, the senior-most Secretary in the Ministry of Education, and other such senior bureaucrats/ administrators as the government may deem appropriate.

P23.6. RSA Appointment Committee (RSAAC), consisting of the PM, the Chief Justice of India, the Speaker of the Lok Sabha, the Leader of the Opposition in Parliament and the UME, will be constituted to enable the appointments to the RSA and to other key related roles and structures.

P23.7. RSA will have an Executive Council (EC) that will be chaired by the UME in his capacity as the Vice-Chairperson of the RSA. The EC will ensure proper functioning of the RSA.

P23.8. An Executive Director (ED) will be the executive head of the RSA, who will also be the Vice-Chairman of the EC and will be appointed by RSAAC.

P23.9. The EC will have 10-15 members who will be nominated by the RSA for five-year terms which will be renewable just once.

P23.11. The existing functions and roles within the present MHRD (and related Ministries) will be reviewed, mapped and harmonised with the RSA for complementarity, including the roles and responsibilities of its support structures and teams.

P23.12. The RSA will also be supported by an Advisory Council (AC) consisting of a diverse group of 20-30 people including some of the foremost national and international experts in education.

P23.13. The RSA will nominate the members of the AC and appoint its chair. The AC will consist of members from the following groups:

- Eminent educationists from India and from across the world, and
- Members from civil society and other fields related to education and research. All members will have five-year terms.

P23.15. The RSA will be supported by a strong Secretariat, consisting of several layers of bureaucrats and technocrats, who will work on efficiently and effectively progressing the various decisions of the RSA.

P23.16. The following National level apex bodies will report to the RSA, which will oversee their smooth and effective functioning. The RSA will appoint the chairpersons, chief executives, and members of the Board of all the bodies that report to it:

- (Proposed) National Higher Education Regulatory Authority (NHERA)
- National Accreditation and Assessment Council (NAAC)
- (Proposed) General Education Council (GEC)
- (Proposed) Higher Education Grants Council (HEGC)
- National Council of Educational Research and Training (NCERT)
- National Institute of Educational Planning and Administration (NIEPA)
- (Proposed) National Research Foundation (NRF)

P23.18. Budgets and their utilisation by all agencies of the Government of India related to education in any way will be reviewed and approved by the RSA.

P23.19. Similar to the RSA, a Rajya Shiksha Aayog (RjSA)/SEC may be constituted in each State, chaired by the Chief Minister with the Minister of Education, nominated by the chair, as Vice-Chair. The creation of the SECs in the States will facilitate better coordination with the Centre.

Part Three

6

Draft National Education Policy, 2019: Executive Summary and A Critique

The Committee under the Chairmanship of K. Kasturirangan came out with a 477-page document titled, 'Draft National Education Policy 2019' which was placed in the public domain on 1 June 2019 for suggestions and comments.

As indicated in Chapter 5, a National Policy on Education (NPE) was long overdue. The first NPE was formulated in 1968—18 years after India became a Republic. The second NPE appeared 18 years thereafter, in 1986. This was revised and adopted in 1992. Now, 27 years later and after nearly four years of extensive consultations, the 'Draft National Education Policy 2019' has finally come out. Not surprisingly, the response has been truly overwhelming.

As expected, formal response in print media and blogs has been mixed. On the positive side, the Draft NEP 2019 has been hailed as a commendable reform[1] and for demonstrating 'how liberal education

1. Venita Kaul, 'A commendable reform in the draft National Policy on Education,' *The Hindu,* 25 June 2019.

can be Indianised to produce pragmatic technocrats'.[2] On the negative side, the list is rather long. Some call the Draft NEP 2019 as 'a case of confused thinking',[3] while others say that it is 'not so "national" education policy'.[4] Some commentators thought that the Draft NEP 2019 offers 'poor remedies to learning crisis', and that it 'amounts to rearranging deck chairs on the *Titanic*',[5] yet others felt that it 'misses a critical chance to address inequalities'.[6] Some critics even went to the extreme of calling it 'an alarming attempt to redefine India'.[7]

More nuanced and balanced comments came from a former Vice-Chancellor, National University of Educational Planning and Administration (NUEPA), according to whom, some issues raised and recommendations made in the Draft NEP 2019 'are path-breaking, many deserve applause and quite a few require rethinking'.[8]

Against this backdrop, the present chapter offers a brief Executive Summary and a detailed constructive critique of the Draft NEP 2019.

2. Chaitanya Ravi, Juhi Sidharth and Shivakumar Jolad, 'National Education Policy: How liberal education can be Indianised to produce pragmatic technocrats,' *Business Today,* 9 October 2019, https://www.businesstoday.in/opinion/columns/national-education-policy-how-liberal-education-can-be-indianised-to-produce-pragmatic-technocrats/story/383660.html

3. Rohit Dhankar, 'A case of confused thinking: on draft National Education Policy', *The Hindu,* 13 July 2019, https://www.thehindu.com/opinion/lead/a-case-of-confused-thinking/article28415519.ece

4. Ravi Kaushal, 'A Not So "National" Education Policy', *Newsclick,* 2 November 2019, https://www.newsclick.in/not-so-national-education-policy

5. Geeta Kingdon, 'Poor remedies to learning crisis: Draft National Education Policy amounts to rearranging deck chairs on the Titanic', *The Times of India,* 24 June 2019, https://timesofindia.indiatimes.com/blogs/toi-edit-page/poor-remedies-to-learning-crisis-draft-national-education-policy-amounts-to-rearranging-deck-chairs-on-the-titanic/

6. Anjela Taneja, 'New education policy misses a critical chance to address inequalities in system', *Livemint*, 12 June 2019, https://www.livemint.com/opinion/online-views/new-education-policy-misses-a-critical-chance-to-address-inequalities-in-system-1560282262183.html

7. Ramit Singh Chimni, 'The National Education Policy 2019: An Alarming Attempt To Redefine India', *Business World,* 31 July 2019, http://www.businessworld.in/article/The-National-Education-Policy-2019-An-Alarming-Attempt-To-Redefine-India/31-07-2019-174188/

8. Jandhyala B.G. Tilak, 'Perennial Problems and Promising but Perplexing Solutions': A Commentary on the Report of the Committee on National Education Policy 2019'. I am grateful to Prof. Tilak for sending me an advance copy of his detailed paper before publishing in *Economic and Political Weekly.*

The chapter begins with the much needed Executive Summary of the voluminous Draft NEP 2019, for a ready reference (Section I). Then comes the critique. The critique has been organised into seven sections: Overall Comments (Section II); followed by specific comments on Early Childhood Care and Education (ECCE) (Section III); School Education (Section IV); Higher Education (Section V); Teacher Education (Section VI), Equitable and Inclusive Education (Section VII), and, finally Financing Issues (Section VIII).

I. Executive Summary

Key elements and major recommendations of the Draft NEP 2019 may be summarised as under:

ECCE, Elementary Education and RTE Act

- A major reconfiguration of curricular and pedagogical structure with Early Childhood Care and Education (ECCE) as an integral part of School Education.
- Instead of the existing 5+3+2+2 or 10+2 structure of School Education system, there will be a 5+3+3+4 curricular and pedagogical structure based on cognitive and socio-emotional developmental stages of children.

Sl.no	Stages of Education	Age in years	School Grades
1	Foundational	*3–8*	*3 years of pre-Primary plus Grades-I and II*
2	Preparatory	*8–11*	*Grades III–V*
3	Middle	11–14	Grades VI–VIII
4	Secondary	14–18	Grades IX–XII

- A timeline has been set that every child in the age range of 3-6 years will have access to free, safe, high quality and developmentally appropriate care and education by 2025.
- ECCE will be an integral part of the RTE Act. All *Anganwadi* Centres and pre-Primary Schools will be linked, physically or formally/ pedagogically to a Primary School and the Ministry of Human Resource Development (MHRD) will have the oversight of ECCE.

- The Foundational Stage of education will be a single pedagogical unit covering pre-School age (ages 3–6) and to the end of Grade II(age 8).
- The curricular and pedagogical framework will aim at instilling excellent multilingual skills in children as early as possible and developmentally appropriate.
- Pre-School and Grade I onwards children will be exposed to three or more languages since research shows that children pick up languages extremely quickly between 2–8 years.
- *All* children will take at least 2 years of a classical language of India in Grades VI–VIII with the option to continue through Secondary and University Education. For example, students in Hindi-speaking States that take Hindi, Sanskrit and English can take Tamil to meet language requirement.
- MDM Scheme will serve quality food and include a simple energising breakfast in the morning. The food cost will be indexed for inflation.
- *Every* student in Grade V and beyond will achieve Foundational Literacy and Numeracy by 2025. Parental participation for optimising learning is envisaged and a Pupil-Teacher Ratio (PTR) of 30:1 is prescribed for every school.
- Free and Compulsory Education from pre-School to Class XII covering the age groups of 3 to 18 years, i.e., extension of RTE Act 2009 to cover children of ages 3 to 18 years.
- The RTE Act requirements for schools are to be made substantially less restrictive so that alternative models of education such as *Gurukuls, Pathshalas, Madrasas* and homeschooling also find their space.
- The Draft NEP 2019 calls for a comprehensive review of the RTE Act itself, especially the mandates and obligations in accordance with ground realities, needs and local constraints giving importance to outcomes and not inputs.
- The recent amendments to the RTE Act on Continuous and Comprehensive Evaluation (CCE) and the no detention policy must be reviewed. There should be no detention of children in Grades up to VIII.
- The Draft NEP 2019 attempts to make a case for the repeal of clause 12(1)(c) of the RTE Act earmarking 25 per cent seats in private schools for disadvantaged children and argues that the provision is not in tune with the principle of autonomy of the institutions.

- A top priority has been assigned to bring 62 million (6–18 years) out-of-school children (OoSC) back into educational fold as early as possible and prevent further dropouts.
- The Draft NEP 2019 envisages a reduction in the content load of the School Education Curriculum. Co-curricular and extra-curricular are to be merged with curricular activities. All subjects, including Arts, Music, Crafts, Sports, Yoga, Community Service, etc. will be curricular. National Curricular Framework (NCF) 2005 will be revised by the end of 2020.

Secondary Education

- Secondary Education GER target set at 100 per cent by 2030.
- Schools will be reorganised into School Complexes so as to ensure that adequate enrolments, infrastructure facilities for laboratory, library etc. are provided.
- Introduction of a broad-based liberal education for four years of Secondary Education that will facilitate multidisciplinary studies with appropriate exit options.
- A Semester System is proposed to be introduced for the Secondary Education (8 Semesters@ 2 per annum and 40+ Semester courses@ 5-6 per Semester).
- The notions of Higher Secondary and Junior Colleges will be eliminated.
- Private schools will not have the nomenclature of public schools. They may be free to set their fee but the increases shall not be arbitrary.
- Private schools will also have SMCs and the financial statements should be vetted by them to be valid.
- Provision for improving scores in Board and Entrance Examination are allowed so that best of multiple attempts is reckoned with.
- It promotes active pedagogy that will focus on the development of core capacities and life skills, including 21st century skills.
- All students will take State Census examinations in Grades III, V and VIII in addition to the Board examinations in Grades X and XII.

Teacher Education

- Sub-standard Teacher Education Institutions will be shut down, moving all teacher preparation/education programmes into large multidisciplinary Universities/colleges.
- The 4-year integrated stage-specific B.Ed. programme will eventually be the minimum degree qualification for teachers. Teacher Eligibility Tests (TET) will be strengthened. NTA scores in relevant subjects, however, will be factored besides viva voce and teaching demonstration in teacher selection process.
- All para-teachers, *Shiksha karmis, Shiksha mitras* etc. will be wound up by 2022.
- The Draft NEP 2019 reposes faith in State Institute of Educational Management and Training (SIEMAT) and SCERT, the apex body at the State level on all academic matters including curriculum, textbooks and standards for teacher related process and learning standards. It will lead and lend support to Cluster Resource Centre (CRC), Block Resource Centre (BRC) and DIETs.

Higher Education

- The Higher Education GER target has been set at 50 per cent by 2035.
- The Higher Education System will be revamped to create world-class multidisciplinary HEIs across the country.

Restructuring of HEIs with three types of Higher Education Institutions

Types	Focus
Type 1	*World-class research and high-quality teaching;*
Type 2	*High-quality teaching across disciplines with significant contribution to research;*
Type 3	*High-quality teaching at undergraduate education.*

- These will be driven by two Missions: **Mission Nalanda** (will ensure at least 100 Type-1 and 500 Type-2 HEIs by 2030) and **Mission Takshashila** (will strive to establish at least one high quality HEI per district or in the vicinity and two or three for bigger districts).

- There will be a Mission Directorate and a few new model HEIs may be set up and developed, e.g., Multidisciplinary Education and Research Universities **(MERUs)**.
- Restructuring of Undergraduate programmes (e.g. BSc, BA, BCom, and BVoc) of 3 or 4 years duration, having multiple exits and entry options.

New Institutional Framework

- Setting up of a new apex body, **Rashtriya Shiksha Aayog** (RSA), to enable a holistic and integrated implementation of all educational initiatives and programmatic interventions and to coordinate efforts between the Centre and States.
- Creation of a new National Research Foundation (NRF), an apex body for creating a strong research culture and building research capacity across Higher Education.
- The four functions of Standard Setting, Funding, Accreditation and Regulation are to be separated and charged with independent bodies:
    1. National Higher Education Regulatory Authority as the only regulator for all Higher Education including Professional Education;
    2. Professional Standard Setting Bodies for each area of Professional Education;
    3. Creation of Accreditation Eco-system led by revamped National Assessment and Accreditation Council (NAAC);
    4. UGC to transform as Higher Education Grants Commission (HEGC).
- Private and public institutions will be treated on par and education will remain a 'not for profit' activity.
- In addition, several new policy initiatives have been proposed for promoting the internationalisation of Higher Education, strengthening quality, ODL, technology integration at all levels of education besides adult and lifelong learning. Moreover; initiatives to enhance participation of URGs, and to eliminate gender, social category and regional gaps in education have been stipulated in the Draft National Education Policy 2019.

II. Overall Comments

1. Monumental Document

Draft National Education Policy 2019 is a monumental document. The sheer enormity of the work and effort that has gone into preparation of this document is indeed awe-inspiring.

Kasturirangan, Chairman of the Committee, had thought that the job was 'doable in six months', building on the 'extensive work already done by the T.S.R. Subrahmanian Committee...'. The Committee soon realised that 'in order to do justice to the deep, multidimensional and practical knowledge and suggestions that we were receiving, we would have to do more than just tinker with the existing documents'. Building on the inputs that had come in from early 2015, the Committee further interacted with a large number of individuals, institutions, organisations and groups representing different regions, diverse cultural and social backgrounds representing different educational ideologies and ideas. The Committee received 'an avalanche' of inputs. All this went into the preparation of Draft NEP 2019 with a view to make it 'relevant and applicable for at least two decades, within the context of the dynamic and fast changing nature of the education space in India and the world'.[9]

2. Evolving an India-centric Education System

The Draft NEP 2019 aims at evolving an India-centric Education System emphasising India's rich cultural heritage and values such as liberty, equality, fraternity and social justice enshrined in the Constitution of India.

3. Building an Equitable and Vibrant Knowledge Society

The Draft NEP 2019 attempts to build a framework for universal and equitable access to broad-based high-quality education. This is sought to be done using an 'integrated, yet flexible approach', focussed on multidisciplinary liberal arts education. The underlying fundamental

9. All the quotes above are from the Preamble of the Draft National Education Policy 2019, MHRD, July 2019, pp. 23-24. The summary part of this review is drawn exclusively from the Draft NEP 2019, with only minor paraphrasing. As such, separate quotations have not been provided.

objective is to facilitate the much-needed complete transformation of the Indian Education System with a view to fostering India's economic growth and overall development in the 21st century. Hon'ble President of India Shri Ram Nath Kovind, in fact, said that the Draft NEP 2019 'will help establish the country as a "knowledge superpower" and get global recognition for talents of students'.[10]

4. Draft NEP 2019 is not a Policy Document

Notwithstanding the title, Draft National Education Policy 2019 is *not* a policy document. It is essentially a report of the Kasturirangan Committee.

Formulation of a National Policy on Education is, of course, the prerogative of the Government of India, with the necessary legislative approvals coming from the Parliament of India. The Kasturirangan Committee Report *may* form the basis of India's National Policy on Education, but all recommendations therein may not be acceptable to the Government of India, nor would the final policy document if issued, be confined to this Report alone.

5. No Analytical Foundation or Statistical Basis

While the Draft NEP 2019 is based on consultations with a large number of individuals, institutions, and groups, the Report does not have any structured analytical foundation nor does it put out a whole lot of statistical information buttressing its recommendations. This point becomes clear when one examines the experience of earlier efforts.

The National Commission on Education (1964-66), popularly known as Kothari Commission, had specific mandate to examine all aspects of education in India, evolve a standardised national pattern of education and to advise guidelines and policies for development of education in the country. It had set up 12 Task Forces, seven Working Groups and 21 Sub-Groups, besides a panel of 20 eminent consultants—national and international. The Commission went about its mandate meticulously with a detailed desk work analysing the facts and figures and evolved a 10+2

10. *PTI,* 'New Education Policy will establish India as knowledge superpower, get global recognition: Ram Nath Kovind', *Outlook,* 30 October 2019, https://www.outlookindia.com/newsscroll/new-education-policy-will-establish-india-as-knowledge-superpower-get-global-recognition-kovind/1651720.

national pattern of education that is still continuing in all the States and Union Territories.

The Policy was to be reviewed on a five-yearly basis to work out new policies and programmes. The NPE 1986 was the result of such detailed reviews. Subsequently, Acharaya Ramamurti Committee was set up to review NPE 1986 and to make recommendations for modifications. The Central Advisory Board of Education (CABE) Committee under the Chairmanship of N. Janardhana Reddy took into consideration the modifications suggested by Ramamurti Committee and other relevant developments. This led to formulation of National Programme of Action, 1992, aimed at promoting national progress, a sense of common citizenship and culture and strengthening national integration. Accordingly, universalisation remained the cornerstone of NPE 1986, modified in 1992 to correct acute social and gender imbalances across the country. It surely had clear cut priorities to alter class education to mass education with emphasis on inclusiveness, common curriculum and substantial improvement in quality of education.

In the context of Draft NEP 2019, although the Government of India had initiated the process of formulating a New Education Policy with exhaustive 'democratic' exercises over a period of 30 months, both T.S.R. Subramanian and Kasturirangan Committees did *not* have the kind of analytical support that the earlier Committees had. Except the time frame, the Kasturirangan Committee had no specific terms of reference or any mandate other than preparing the draft with help of details of the democratic process of consultations already undertaken.

As pointed out by Prof. J.B.G Tilak,[11] the Kasturirangan Report 'opens with a vision for the education system, drawing from human rights perspective on education (*a la* UN Declaration of Human Rights), India's rich heritage, previous education policies in Independent India, mainly 1986 policy and the global sustainable development goals, and proposes a series of reforms'. He laments, however, that the Report does not take cognizance of the Kothari Commission Report 'which was based on extensive research on a variety of issues in education', nor does it take on board 'a plethora of development schemes launched, not just RTE Act 2009 and the developments during the last three decades'.

Draft NEP lacks a basic background document justifying the sweeping

11. Tilak, 'Perennial Problems and Promising but Perplexing Solutions'.

changes proposed. No wonder, Draft NEP 2019, at times fumbles on basics due to lack of analytical support.

6. Targets without Action Programmes

The Draft NEP 2019 sets out several time-bound quantitative targets, such as, universal participation in School Education by 2030, GER of 50 per cent in Higher Education by 2035 and so on. However, there are no clear-cut objective roadmaps leading to the achievement of the stated targets.

The Draft NEP is also full of strong qualitative assertions regarding equity and inclusivity, besides those emphasising 'education as a public good', 'criticality of public education' and stating that 'education must be a not-for-activity'. However, here again, no clear-cut strategies have been laid out for meeting those laudable objectives.

In sum, in the absence of concrete programmes of action (i.e., roadmaps) to achieve the quantitative targets and strategic courses of action to meet the qualitative goals, the Draft NEP's claims 'seem to be more in the nature of lofty intentions'.[12]

7. Imperatives of Policy Planning Overlooked

Planning for a new educational policy should invariably be evolved on the basis of a detailed analysis of the current status, emerging trends in domestic and global educational scenario and with sound reasoning/ justification for the changes proposed and these should be placed in the context of national priorities. While doing so, the dysfunctionalities in the extant policy programmes, systems and procedures, rules and regulations and the bottlenecks that hamper the achievement of the goals, directly or indirectly, need to be identified so as to insulate the new policy from the potential pitfalls.

There should be a proper appraisal regarding the viability of any new proposal especially when it is a massive one. The collateral damage, consequences and risks that may be expected on account of imposing new policy replacing the extant one should also be assessed and the viability of proposals appraised. When sweeping changes are made, each policy statement should be backed by unassailable concrete evidence leading to

---

12. Ibid

the changes proposed. Regrettably nothing of the sort seems to have been carried out in evolving the Draft NEP 2019.

Without providing a proper up to date educational status report for the people to gauge the enormity of the changes proposed, the Draft NEP 2019, at one stroke, takes on Early Childhood Education, School, Higher and Technical and Professional Education with proposals for far-reaching changes in the entire educational structure, pedagogy, regulatory framework, assessment systems and training. The Draft NEP 2019 also makes a feeble attempt to secure more funds for Central institutions by working out and earmarking half of the incremental allocation for the Higher Education sub-sector and reiterates the ever-elusive, age-old, 6 per cent GDP goal for education and pins hope on improved tax-GDP ratio for enhanced funding.

The Draft NEP 2019 'lacks operational details and does not offer insights into how the policy will be funded'.[13] As another expert has pointed out 'the details about financing and institutional structures should be fleshed out at the earliest'.[14] In other words, 'the Draft NEP 2019 itself lacks the very abilities it emphasises, namely critical thinking and deeper understanding'.[15]

8. Education 4.0 Not Built-in Adequately

For the last three-four years, world is going through the Industrial Revolution 4.0[16] based on the so-called New-Age Technology (which includes Artificial Intelligence and Machine Learning, Data Analytics, Robotics, Blockchain Technology, Automated Technology, Additive

13. Prashant K. Nanda, 'Draft new education policy is robust, but has its limitations', *Livemint,* 12 June 2019, https://www.livemint.com/education/news/draft-new-education-policy-is-robust-but-has-its-limitations-1560282687888.htm

14. Amitabha Bhattacharya, 'Fine-tuning the education policy', *The Hindu,* 5 June 2019, https://www.thehindu.com/opinion/op-ed/a-brave-new-education-policy/article27473093.ece

15. Dhankar, 'A case of confused thinking', *The Hindu,* 13 July 2019.

16. First Industrial Revolution was spurred on by the invention of steam engines, the second one by electricity, the third one by the Internet whereas the prevailing fourth one i.e., Industrial Revolution 4.0 is emanating from the so-called New-Age Technology. See Narendra Jadhav, *New-Age Technology and Industrial Revolution 4.0: Global Public Policy Issues in Economy, Democracy, National Security and World Peace* (New Delhi: Konark Publishers, 2019).

Manufacturing, Internet of Things and Augmented Reality). This transformative technology is changing the world rapidly and irrevocably. As such, there is an imperative need to make a transition towards what may be called Education 4.0.

The Draft NEP does mention Artificial Intelligence and Data Analytics (misspelt as Data Analysis), but this supposedly visionary document hardly makes any conscious effort towards transition to Education 4.0—not much in curriculum and not even in the technology-based pedagogy. As noted by an expert, 'knowledge has already started flowing freely over the walls that academies... have built to keep it exclusive. The... emergence of Artificial Intelligence that is demanding a change in what humans need to learn and what is best left to machines. As a nation still stuck with MCQ based exams that check data-retrieval ability of brain to define learning-ability of humans, we are just being silly'.[17]

Even while appreciating the enormity of the work undertaken, it is difficult to accept the Draft NEP 2019 without serious amendments and fine-tuning. This would become clear in the discussion of specific reforms that follows.

III. Early Childhood Care and Education (ECCE)

The Draft NEP 2019 proposes that Early Childhood Care and Education (ECCE) be an integral part of the Right to Education (RTE) Act. A timeline has been set that every child in the age range of 3-6 years will have access to free, safe, high quality and developmentally appropriate care and education by 2025. For this purpose, all *Anganwadi* Centres and pre-Primary Schools will be linked, physically or formally/pedagogically to a Primary School. MHRD will have the oversight of ECCE. In addition to the mid-day meals, a nutritious breakfast will also be provided.

Actually, the evidence on the desirability of early child schooling is mixed. One view is that it 'disrupts the mother-child attachment relationship, reducing opportunities for interactions, and causing infants to lose confidence in the availability and responsiveness of their parents'. On the other hand, some other research shows at least 'modest

17. Samir Shukla, 'The world needs a new education policy that teaches interconnectedness', *Science Nomad, The Times of India,* 3 August 2019, https://timesofindia.indiatimes.com/blogs/science-nomad/the-world-needs-a-new-education-policy-that-teaches-interconnectedness/

cognitive and social benefits' from early childhood care and education programmes.[18]

Notably, experts in the erstwhile Planning Commission such as Chandramohan have consistently been arguing that one or two years of pre-School Education is absolutely necessary for school preparedness and to prevent high dropouts in Class I as well as for minimising underage enrolments in Primary Schools. It is also argued that in India, private school children often outperform the government school children for many reasons including pre-Schooling (Jr. KG and Sr. KG).

There is certainly a case for ECCE. The Draft NEP 2019, however, does not seem to recognise the role that is played by private pre-Primary education centres. 'This omission suggests that they favour the *status quo* of them being privately run as for-profit enterprises.... ...the new policy enforces a diktat for all children to enter into pre-Primary centres, without speaking of the current dichotomy. This is not only disturbing, but also bears a resemblance to the numerous times an industry has lobbied for its financial gain and policymakers have succumbed to their demands without an analysis of the consequences.'[19]

Another possibility may be that the Draft NEP 2019 is contemplating creating ECCE-pre-Primary integrated centres across the country. This would be beset with many practical problems. First of all, a massive investment would be needed. There are as many as 1.34 million ICDS–*Anganwadi* Centres in around 1.31 million habitations. Not many of them offer pre-School Education. Thousands of them are still operating in small one-room tenements on rental basis within the habitation. A bulk of these are not all-weather structures. Yet, if the Government is willing to undertake the massive investment, ECCE would certainly be worthwhile.

Providing mid-day meals and simple energising breakfast to ECCE (and other school children) is most welcome. Proposal to entrust the supervision of ECCE to MHRD is also a very good idea.

It may be useful to clarify some historical background here. During the review of the Tenth Five Year Plan, erstwhile Planning Commission had observed substantial enrolment of underage children in Class I and detention of these children by the end of the year. This was due to the lack

18. Both quotes are from Tilak, 'Perennial Problems and Promising but Perplexing Solutions'.

19. Chimni, 'An Alarming Attempt To Redefine India', *Business World,* 31 July 2019.

of ECCE/pre-Primary Education. In some States like Assam, the detention rate in Class I was as high as 20-22 per cent. School retention was dismal with high dropout rates.

Planning Commission had also observed that the education component of the Integrated Child Development Services (ICDS) was very weak and there was utter lack of school preparedness among the children. Therefore, it provided Rs 10,000 million for pre-Primary Education during the Eleventh Plan (2007-12) and made a financial provision in the budget for FY 2007-08 of the MHRD, since ECCE was within the business rules of MHRD. The Ministry took no action for formulation of the Plan scheme, got its business rules changed and the budget provisions were allowed to lapse. Thus, MHRD discarded the ECCE, which is no longer with MHRD but with MWCD. MHRD is where the supervision of ECCE really belongs. Restoring it back from MWCD to MHRD is, therefore, a good idea.

It is noteworthy that the 86th Amendment to the Constitution of India, 2002 has provided for universalisation of ECCE directing the States to provide for ECCE to all children until they complete the age of 6 years. The RTE Act categorically states that with a view to preparing children above the age of three years for Elementary Education and to provide ECCE for all children until they complete the age of six years, the appropriate Government may make necessary arrangements for providing free pre-School Education for such children.

In this regard, another issue that merits attention is the recommendation of introducing three languages to 3–8-year-old children. The Draft NEP 2019 quotes some research from neurosciences in support of the recommendation. Nevertheless, going by anecdotal evidence, one is less sanguine about exposing the young kids to three languages, before they become fully familiar with one.[20]

A sharper criticism comes from another expert: The Draft NEP 2019 mistakes 'language acquisition when children are immersed in more than one language' with a 'language teaching' situation where immersion is impossible in three languages. It then extends it unjustifiably to a learning of three scripts. It prescribes teaching script and reading in three languages to three-year-old children, but writing is supposed to be taught to six-year-old children. It also wants to introduce 'some textbook' only at age eight. One wonders why there is a three-year gap between teaching

20. Tilak, 'Perennial Problems and Promising but Perplexing Solutions'.

reading and writing. If script and reading are already taught, then why withhold text books till age eight? This is seen as a case of confused thinking.[21]

IV. School Education

1. Out-of-School Children (OoSC)

The Draft NEP 2019 uses the terms 'all' and 'every' interchangeably. The objective stated early on is to ensure that 'every' child has access to free, safe, high quality and developmentally appropriate education. In that spirit, a top priority has been assigned to bringing 62 million (6–18 years) out-of-school children (OoSC) back into educational fold as early as possible and prevent further dropouts. This number is actually 80 million as per Census estimates (C10-Cultural tables, 2011). Of these, 44 million children have never been enrolled in schools *at all* and the remaining 36 million were dropouts in 6–18 age group. In the RTE Act age group (i.e., 6–14 years), the number of OoSC was 43 million, of which 34 million had never been enrolled at all. This implies that in the age group of 15–18, there are in all 37 million OoSC of which 10 million have never been enrolled in school and 27 million are dropouts.

Where should we fix the priority? If, in the group 6-14 years, as many as 34 million children could *not* be enrolled in Primary Schools, how do we get older children of 15-18 years (10 million in number) back in the education fold? Who are these children and where are they languishing? The Registrar General's office has a handbook of Census information on CDs to provide even village wise data. The Draft NEP 2019 simply ignores this blatant violation of the Fundamental Right of the children and makes a cursory recommendation to get all OoSC back to the education fold.

2. Clubbing ECCE Pre-School with Grades I and II

The Draft NEP 2019 combines three years of ECCE pre-School (ages 3-6) with Grades I and II of Primary School and treats it as a single pedagogical unit and terms it as the 'Foundational Stage'.

The RTE Act, 2009, has prescribed five years of Primary Education

21. Dhankar, 'A case of confused thinking', *The Hindu,* 13 July 2019.

(Classes I-V). Some States like Karnataka and Maharashtra that had Primary Education from Classes I–IV were forced to bring Class V from Upper Primary to Primary Schools. These States progressively added Class V to the existing Primary Schools and complied with the provision of the RTE Act.

Private providers of education suffered a lot in these States to comply with the RTE Act norm of five years of Primary Education. Now, asking them to further modify and delink Classes I and II to be merged with ECCE pre-School would impose an additional burden on them. For publicly funded schools, the task is even more complicated as not all ECCE centres are located in Primary Schools and most of the *Anganwadis* are within the habitation. In densely populated villages as in Bihar there is only one Primary School but more than one *Anganwadi*. Moving the tiny tots to Primary schools would invariably involve many practical problems.

The structural changes proposed for combining ECCE pre-School and Grades 1 and II of Primary Schools involve mind boggling numbers. Decades of effort had brought in a massive 1.34 million *Anganwadi* Centres covering about 40 million children under the pre-School Education. It has been a challenge to persuade the States to provide access to education to all the 1.31 million habitations in the country with about 0.85 million Primary Schools. The *Anganwadi* Centres are based on population norms while for Primary Schools, the norm consists of access within 1 km radius of the habitation.

The process of physically integrating habitation-based ICDS pre-Schools with Primary Schools has been a very slow process in several States due to logistic problems of moving very small children to a one kilometer distance of the habitation and the problem gets accentuated further during the monsoon seasons.

The proposed Foundational Stage of education would involve around 95 million children (40 million from *Anganwadi* pre-Schools and 55 million from Grades I and II from 0.85 million Primary Schools in 1.31 million habitats). The magnitude of the change proposed here is clearly a colossal one.

The Draft NEP recommendation involving this massive structural change at the grass root level and pedagogical meshing does *not* appear to be necessary and has hardly any justification. Nowhere in the world does one find a part of Primary Education Grades merged with ECCE as a single pedagogical unit.

This recommendation of the Draft NEP 2019 clearly needs to be discarded.

3. New Pedagogical Structure

The Draft NEP 2019 proposes a complete overhaul of the pedagogical structure of School Education: First is Foundation Stage (3–8 years), Second is Preparatory Stage (8–11 years), Third is Middle Stage (11–14 years) and the final Fourth is Secondary Stage (14–18).

What does the evidence from developed countries suggest?

In France, 7-11 years cover Elementary Education and the pre-School does not form a part of it. In the United States of America pre-School or pre-KG is for children in the age group 3–5 (PK), children in the age group 5–6 are in kindergarten (KG) and those in 6–11 years are in Elementary Stage; 11–14 years in Middle Schools; and 14–18 years (up to K12) in the High Schools. In Finland, children's pre-School is in *'daycare'* and one year pre-School or KG for 6 year olds is mandated and thereafter, children move to formal stage of Primary Education (7–9 years). These are the countries best known for quality education. Nowhere in the world, a part (Grades I and II) of formal Primary Stage of general School Education is segregated and merged with ECCE to form a single pedagogical unit.

Where does the proposed truncated 'Foundational' pedagogical unit fit in the International Standard Classification of Education?

Table 6.1 offers a comparison of the Indian Standard Classification of Education (InSCED) and the International Standard Classification of Education (ISCED).

It is not clear whether the proposed 'Foundational Stage' is to be classified as Level 0 or Level 1 of the International Standard Classification of Education (ISCED).

There is no compelling reason to change the pedagogical structure of School Education in India. It makes sense to stick to the Indian Standard Classification of Education (InSCED) and stay aligned with the International Standard Classification of Education.

Table 6.1 : InSCED and ISCED – A Comparison

InSCED 2014		ISCED 2011	
First Digit code	**Description**	**ISCED First Digit code**	**Description**
A	Pre-Primary	Level 0	Early Childhood Education (ECE)
B	Primary	Level 1	Primary
C	Upper Primary	Level 2	Lower Secondary
D	Secondary	Level 3	Upper Secondary
E	Senior Secondary	Level 3	Upper Secondary
F	Undergraduate	Level 5 Level 6	Short cycle Tertiary Bachelor or Equivalent
G	Postgraduate	Level 7	Masters or Equivalent
H	M Phil	Level 7	Masters or Equivalent
I	PhD	Level 8	Doctoral or Equivalent

Source: MHRD.

4. Misdiagnosis of the Learning Crisis

The Draft NEP 2019, it has been argued,[22] 'offers feeble prescriptions for the gargantuan problems in school education'. There is 'no explicit focus on learning levels as the main thing to fix, and indeed, no citing of the staggering statistics on learning levels as the very cause of the perceived need for a new NEP'. In fact, there is a 'monumental misdiagnosis' of the situation regarding poor quality of education. It is *not* as if the paucity of resources alone is the root cause of poor-quality education. What lies at the core of poor-quality education is the "lack of school and teacher accountability."

The Draft NEP 2019 fails to 'recognise the elephant in the room—namely poor school and teacher accountability—with no mention of teacher absenteeism and low teacher effort as key problem....... As such, before asking for more resources, it is imperative to improve the appalling inefficiency'.

---

22. Kingdon, 'Draft National Education Policy amounts to rearranging deck chairs on the Titanic', *The Times of India,* 24 June 2019.

5. *Extension of the RTE Act up to Age 18*

The Draft NEP 2019 proposes to extend RTE Act from ECCE to Grade XII or from the age of 3–18 years for all as against the existing provision for 6–14 years. ECCE is already a part of RTE Act in so far as private schools are concerned, in respect of the 25 per cent earmarked seats; the Draft NEP proposes to extend it to all government, government-aided and local body schools. This is most welcome. The Draft NEP proposes to extend it to Secondary and Higher Secondary or Integrated Secondary Schools (i.e., Grades IX-XII), facilitating multidisciplinary studies with appropriate exit options as well.

The extension up to Grade XII (age 18 years) is fine. However, allowing for exit before the age of 16 seems to be inconsistent with the rights-based approach for compulsory School Education.

In the UK no child is allowed to leave school before the age of 16 since schooling is compulsory, although free education continues up to the completion of key stage V or (16-18 years of age). In the world of work, 10 years of schooling in general education ought to be the minimal bench mark. Thereafter, students could have the option to continue general education with electives on multiple exit basis or look for job-oriented courses including apprenticeships or take job.

In the proposed modified School Education structure, the Secondary Phase of four years of Grades IX–XII (Secondary and Senior Secondary combined), has been proposed so as to facilitate multidisciplinary studies, with appropriate exit options and going all the way into UG and PG and research. How does it fit with the proposal of extending RTE Act up to Grade XII or 18 years? Compulsory education will have a meaning only if the exit is sealed up at certain stage of general education. Thus, permitting exit before Grade X or 16 years of age would be inappropriate and consideration needs to be given to modify this recommendation.

6. *Review of the RTE Act*

The Draft NEP 2019 has recommended a comprehensive review of the RTE Act, especially the mandates and obligations in accordance with ground realities, local needs and constraints. According to the Draft NEP the RTE Act also calls for a comprehensive review in view of the fact that it gives importance to inputs rather than outcomes.

These recommendations are simply not acceptable. The Right to Education is a Fundamental Right. Providing a proper school environment and good quality education of nationally accepted standards, ought to be a national priority, whatever be the ground reality, local needs and constraints.

It is important to note that the RTE Act has not been implemented in full measure-certainly not in letter and spirit. The RTE harmonised SSA had an approved funding of Rs. 2410 billion, which was not provided. The 2 per cent cess money was supposed to be an additionality to the budget provision, which was expected to grow at least by 10 per cent per annum. A Prarambhik Shiksha Kosh was created for cess money so that it wouldn't get lapsed at the revised estimate (RE) stage. The UPA government altered the structure of education cess and used the fungibilibility clause to substitute budget provision and the so called additionality remained only on paper.

Sarva Shiksha Abhiyan (SSA) was short of nearly a million teachers. The intended policy programmes of RTE Act dealing with equity and social justice issues were sacrificed due to underfunding. Many interventions for quality improvement in Elementary School could not be launched at all, and only 10 per cent schools were compliant with its basic requirements. Over nine hundred thousand teachers are yet to be recruited. How can one expect meaningful learning without qualified teachers, good materials and nurturing learning environments?

Incidentally, a bulk of those left out activities are reprocessed in the Draft NEP 2019 to meet the equity goals without any commitment of funding. If half of the incremental allocations for the next 10 years would go for Tertiary Education, as proposed in the draft NEP 2019, which has a huge presence of private sector, what will be left to meet the eluding provisions of the RTE Act in Elementary Schools largely with the government sector?

Under these circumstances, there is no compelling need to amend the RTE Act.

7. 'Census' Examinations in Grades 3, 5 and 8

The Draft NEP 2019 propose 'Census' examinations in Grades III, V and VIII without linking performance in these examinations to promotions to the next class.

It may be noted that the original RTE Act envisaged 'No Detention

Policy'. There was a widespread criticism of this provision on the grounds that children virtually learn very little in school and yet, the RTE Act allows them to be promoted automatically. Recently there was an amendment to the RTE Act which prescribed examinations in Grades V and VIII and in a way 'restored' detention of the children failing in these examinations i.e., up to Grade VIII.

If the Draft NEP 2019 recommendation about the so-called 'Census' examinations is accepted, it would nullify the latest amendment to the RTE Act and would support the 'No Detention' policy again. Arguably, the Government should resist the tendency to rush an amendment to the Fundamental Right to education.

The 'Census' examinations are slated to "benefit students, parents, teachers, Principals and School Management Committees in planning improvements to schools and teaching-learning processes". The 'Census' examinations will test the pupils' understanding of core concepts and knowledge of matters relating to their national and local curricula. They will assess skill, not rote learning. The Grade III 'Census' examination will be a test of basic literacy, numeracy and other foundational skills. Apparently, these would be standardised tests. Perhaps, the Draft NEP Panel wanted to ward off the criticism of exposing the children to Board Examination at tender age and hence invented a term 'Census' examination.

Importantly, there is a risk here that first generation learners will find themselves in a constricting school environment. Children coming from poor socio-economic background will find the standardised tests difficult since they do not have educational environment at home. They will invariably get to know the results. The school may not fail them but it cannot prevent them from dropping out.

8. Enabling Multiple Pathways to Learning

The Draft NEP 2019 has advocated the idea of creating greater educational choices among students and competition among schools.

As rightly pointed out by some experts, this 'may not be a good idea in case of public goods like education. The western ethic of individual choice and the economic principle of ability to pay do not and should not have a place in case of education. School Education, and more particularly Elementary Education is considered as a pure public good and even in advanced countries individual choice is limited'.[23]

Notably, the RTE Act 'has not favoured alternative modes of schooling, non-formal education and open education etc. According to the RTE, universalisation has to be done through a recognised formal school system'.[24]

Enabling multiple pathway of learning especially in Elementary Education, is quite likely to take education farther away from a common school system. In all probability, the variety of alternate ways of learning and alternative models of school is likely to widen the inequalities between different socio-economic strata of the society in respect of both, the access to and quality of education. This, in turn, would tend to exacerbate the prevailing socio-economic inequalities.

The Draft NEP 2019 seems to have missed the opportunity of presenting National Education Policy with a long term vision of moving towards developing a common school education system.

9. Board Examinations

At the Secondary level, instead of taking one Board examination each at Grade X and Grade XII, the students would now have to appear for eight Board exams—one after each six-month Semester in Classes IX–XII. The Draft NEP explains as to how 24 subjects will be split: two Semester Board examinations in Mathematics, two in Science, one in Indian History, one in World History, one in Contemporary India, one in Ethics and Philosophy, one in Economics, one in Business/Commerce, one in Digital Literacy/ Computational Thinking, one in Art, one in Physical Education, two in Vocational subjects, one basic test each in the three languages they study, and at least one literature paper in one Indian language from among the three. Various other elective subjects will also be available. The Draft NEP indicates that National Testing Agency should conduct aptitude tests in various subjects from 2020, multiple times a year, with the Universities encouraged to use these scores to admit students instead of holding their own entrance exams.

How does an ideal Semester System work elsewhere in the world? Simplified core syllabi for each subject with not more than 15 core topics;

---

23. Tilak, 'Perennial Problems and Promising but Perplexing Solutions'.
24. Tilak, ibid.

about 20-25 essential reading materials photocopied and made available in the library; compulsory students' seminar and tutorial classes two each, per week under supervision and guidance; and at least two demonstration classes per week in the laboratory; a term paper for internal assessment and practicals for grading for the subject; a snap test and plenty of options in formal Semester examination papers; a very speedy assessment and appeal system that settles the issue within a week and full complement of faculty to run the Semester System. Are we prepared for this? Is the Draft NEP talking of Semester System in reality? Or it just meant half yearly Board/University examinations on multiple core and elective subjects, including for repeaters and call it a Semester System?

The universalisation at the Secondary level would mean a total strength of nearly 85 million children in Secondary Education. Can we run 40+ subject examinations on half yearly basis for such a huge number? What other activities the CBSE and State Boards could be performing if they are overburdened with Semester examinations? Apparently, the Draft NEP has neither analysed the numbers nor scaled the magnitude of their proposal. The Government will do well to discard this proposal or it could perhaps restrict it to the Grades 11 and 12, at least initially.

10. Relaxation of RTE Norms

The Draft NEP 2019 recommends making the RTE Act requirements on inputs to be substantially less restrictive.

This recommendation is unwarranted, for several reasons: first, in spite of nearly 10 years of implementation, only a small fraction of schools actually satisfy the RTE norms. As such, any relaxation in the RTI norms would only worsen the situation regarding the basic infrastructure in schools. Secondly, it would be highly undesirable to tinker, yet again, with the Fundamental Right to education provided under the RTE Act. Thirdly, a good basic infrastructure and appropriate learning environment is indeed a pre-requisite for addressing several persistent weaknesses in the School Education System, such as dropouts, non-enrolment, non-completion and poor levels of learning. Fourthly, while accent on outcome is important, one cannot overlook the fact that more often than not, desirable outcomes themselves are contingent on critical inputs.

11. Home-work Assignments for Parental Involvement

The Draft NEP 2019 recommendations regarding Foundational Literacy and Numeracy are also completely devoid of understanding the ground realities.

The Draft NEP urges the teachers to give take-home worksheets, activities or assignments to be completed in collaboration with parents so as to develop parental involvement in children's schoolwork, learning and progress. Arguably, studying in class gets superior results while extra schoolwork or home work is just extra work and that has adverse impact on the child. Non-academic priorities (good sleep, family relationships and active playtime) are vital for balance and well-being of the children. These also directly impact a child's memory, focus, behavior and learning potential. Foundational lessons are reinforced every day in school. After-school time is precious for the child.

There is no evidence that any amount of homework contributes to accelerate performance of Elementary School students. Homework is basically a `push factor' that puts the child away from schools. Everybody knows how bad India's School System works, traditionally. The child that could not do or complete homework stands segregated and punished verbally and often physically.

Imposing extra burden on children or partly shifting the burden of providing quality education on to parents is one of the routine intimidating methods adopted by private fee charging schools in our country. In India, there are still thousands of households that do not even have single point electricity. Children in the urban slums have no healthy home environment either. Nearly half of the rural households do not have single adult literate woman.

While reviewing the Draft NEP 2019 the Government should discard this recommendation as well.

12. Private Tuitions Not Recognised

It has been widely recognised that while progressing from Primary to Secondary schooling, across all economic strata, students are prompted to go through private tuitions. 'Often, these tuitions are imparted by their own school teachers. The internet conflict of interest is not just optical, but a harsh reality that has been ignored by the drafters of the NEP.'

13. Flexibility in Course Choice

The Draft NEP 2019 aims at empowering students by reducing the curriculum content load and by offering flexibility in course choices. There is no hard separation of Arts and Sciences and no hard separation of content in terms of curricular, extra-curricular or co-curricular areas. Even more importantly, there is no hard separation of 'vocational' and 'academic streams'. National Curricular Framework (NCF) would be revised by end of 2020.

All these recommendations are excellent, indeed most laudable. They are essential for all round development of body and mind. These recommendations of Draft NEP should be accepted wholeheartedly.

14. Universalisation of Secondary Education

The Draft NEP 2019 has set the GER target for Secondary Education at 100 per cent, to be achieved by 2030.

This is another commendable recommendation. The quantum leap envisaged from the present levels of GER—80 per cent for Secondary, and 56 per cent for Senior Secondary (as per U-DISE data)—is certainly most welcome.

It must be remembered, however, that achieving this ambitious target, a special focus on Scheduled Castes and Scheduled Tribe children and especially girls would be necessary, so as to check dropouts and improve retention at Elementary Stage.

15. Re-organising Schools into School Complexes

The Draft NEP states that schools will be re-organised into School Complexes so as to ensure adequate enrolments, infrastructure facilities for laboratory, library etc. The country has total of 1.52 million schools, of which, Primary and Upper Primary Schools account for 1.26 million, while Secondary and Senior Secondary Schools are 0.14 million and 0.12 million, respectively. Notably, 0.42 million out of 1.52 million (27.6 per cent) schools are with private management; private sector plays a dominant role especially in the Secondary Education in the country.

A pragmatic plan is needed for this massive exercise of reorganisation of schools since the bulk of the Secondary Schools are under private management. New schools established under Rashtriya Madhyamik Shiksha Abhiyan (RMSA) and Model Schools in the State sector and those in PPP mode could follow this approach straightaway. Some States have a policy to set up schools based on geographical units. The largest number of Secondary Schools in the government sector in the country is in Andhra Pradesh where every Mandal has a Secondary School. For decades, the UP Government did not open any Secondary School. The position was worse in West Bengal. Now that they are opening new schools, an Educational Complex idea should be insisted upon.

It may be noted, however, that there are many practical constraints in implementing this pathbreaking recommendation. For example, the Bihar government surrendered entire funding meant for toilets under RTE harmonised SSA since they could not find enough space for constructing them in the existing schools. There are other such constraints in implementing the recommendations.

16. Changing Nomenclature

The Draft NEP 2019 advocates renaming of MHRD as Ministry of Education (MoE) as it was known once upon a time when it comprised of many departments including Youth Affairs and Sports and Culture. Now, all these are independent Ministries and as such, much water has flown under the bridge. These Ministries have already spread their tap roots and set up countrywide network and parallel departments in the States. Perhaps, the change in nomenclature appears to be necessary as hardly any State had followed Government of India nomenclature of HRD. In fact, education continues to be handled by several independent departments including social welfare. Also the Skill Development which was being dealt by the Ministry of Labour earlier is now handled by a separate Ministry. Although this is not a vital recommendation, the Draft NEP 2019 appears to be quite right in restoring the MHRD's original nomenclature.

17. Private Schools Calling themselves Public Schools

The Draft NEP 2019 states that 'Private schools will not use the word "public" in their names. "Public" schools will only be those that are funded publicly, i.e., government schools and government-aided schools' (p.189).

The drafting panel for NEP 2019 has clearly got it wrong. A 'public meeting' does not mean a meeting funded by government, similarly a public school does not mean it is funded by the government. The Draft NEP 2019 has got adverse criticism in media for poor drafting and use of inappropriate grammar.

Needless to say, this recommendation should be discarded.

18. Regulation of Private Schools

The Draft NEP 2019 recommends that 'Private schools may be free to set their fees, but they shall not increase school fees arbitrarily. Reasonable increases that can stand public scrutiny can be made' (p.190).

As a matter of fact, the experience nation-wide clearly shows that, more often than not, this freedom of charging fees has been 'terribly misused, to such an extent that it is just impossible to effectively regulate fee levels in private institutions at school or higher level whatever be the regulating mechanism'.[25]

19. Regulatory Mechanism for School Education

With a view to regulating School Education, the Draft NEP 2019 proposes, at the State level, separation of policy making from operational and regulatory roles. This is sought to be achieved by creating three bodies:

- **Rajya Shiksha Aayog** (State Education Commission) for overall monitoring and policy formulation in education in the State;
- **Directorate of School Education** for handling all operations and provision of educational services in the public schooling system; and
- **State School Regulatory Authority** as the sole regulator for the entire School Education Sector at the State level.

While this regulatory framework is prima facie desirable, two major issues arise:

- Regulation of private schools, not only in respect of fees charged, but on *any* aspect has become an exceedingly difficult task. The Draft NEP 2019 does not take cognisance of this ground reality and therefore, does not suggest a strong and effective mechanism to regulate the operations of private schools. On the other hand, the

25. Tilak, ibid.

Draft NEP advocates treatment of private schools on par with public schools and recommends that private schools be 'empowered and freed of the regulatory overload' (p. 189 of the Draft NEP 2019). The Draft NEP confines itself to asking for 'using existing laws diligently' (p. 409 of the Draft NEP 2019) in order to arrest the growth of profiteering in education. The point to be noted here is that the existing laws are highly ineffective.[26]

- It is rather unfortunate that Draft NEP 2019 takes too soft a stance towards the private sector and does not recommend a tougher mechanism to effectively regulate and oversee the growth and operations of private schools in the country.
- It is not clear as to why the Draft NEP 2019 limits the scope of regulation of the proposed State School Regulatory Authority to 'a very few selected parameters such as safety, security, basic infrastructure, number of teachers, probity and sound processes of governance'. There is absolutely no justification for the regulatory mechanism to be confined to these aspects alone. Arguably, a comprehensive regulatory mechanism should cover almost every aspect of School Education. Such a mechanism would come in handy for preventing undesirable methods and unhealthy practices and in effect, promoting autonomy of School Education in an operationally meaningful manner.

V. Higher Education

1. Raising GER in Higher Education

The Draft NEP 2019 aims at raising the Gross Enrolment Ratio (GER) in Higher Education to 50 per cent level by 2035 from the prevailing level of around 24-25 per cent.

This objective is not overly ambitious. In fact, most developed countries and even some emerging market economies like China are way ahead of India. But even this moderately ambitious target will certainly cover at least a part of the large catching up that India needs. A higher GER of the order of 50 per cent will generate much larger supply of skilled and highly educated person-power and thus, would be a major step in harnessing the fortuitously available Demographic Dividend in India.

26. Tilak, ibid, has also made similar arguments.

2. *Creation of World-class Multi-disciplinary HEIs*

The Draft NEP 2019 envisions creation of world-class multidisciplinary Higher Educational Institutions (HEIs).

This recommendation is indeed, the order of the day. For a country that has consistently been the fastest or the second fastest growing economy in the world over the last few years, *not* having a single world-class university among the top 300, certainly does not augur well for its future. It also raises serious questions regarding the sustainability of India's long-term growth prospects.

While this recommendation of the Draft NEP is quite admirable, there is need for a reality check.

A world-class status for Higher Education Institution is not conferred like *Honoris Causa* of the Deemed to be Universities in the country. It is a status that is earned through international recognition and reputation for which, there is need to adopt a special framework that goes beyond the regulatory framework, training and State support. It hinges on such crucial factors such as concentration of talents, academic and administrative autonomy, high quality research assessed through citations, abundance of resources for research facilities and other infrastructure, besides a healthy and happy student life on the campus. India has abundance of talent in *crème de la crème* of students and well qualified faculty in the Institutes of National Importance. Campus life, however often, leaves much to be desired. There is not much scope for faculty-student interactions (e.g., regular weekly interactive seminar classes and tutorial systems). Our faculty in Higher, Technical and Professional Education is not trained for 21st century education. There is a strong case for sending them to Ivy League universities, Oxbridge and other world-class institutions simply for observation sabbaticals for a full term. This will change their common 12–14 hour a week mindset. Research doesn't flourish in HEIs in work culture with poor interaction with the students.

India has not been producing enough PhDs. Very few students continue on to research degrees compared to other countries: only around 1,40,000 (1 per cent) students are enrolled as post-Graduate researchers. The lack of enquiry-based learning and early researcher skills has been limiting the capacity of Indian institutions to engage in vital research and innovation activity. For example, despite having the world's largest cadre of agricultural scientists and nationwide network of institutions for research and education, India could not take forward the Green Revolution of 1970s to other parts of the country. The premier institutions (e.g., IITs) produce world-class scientists and engineers, but ironically, the national research system has rarely produced world-class results. It is also ironical that a nation that produces world-class CEOs for foreign companies and multinationals is starved of domestic talent!

One possible reason is the missing link between scientists in universities and the research institutes and practitioners in agriculture and industry. Another explanation possibly is that the non-teaching research institutes in India lack continuous in-flow of young talented research scholars. Dichotomy between research and teaching does not augur well for attaining educational excellence. (This point also has a bearing on the Draft NEP proposal of restructuring universities, as discussed below).

At another level, the quality of research produced in the Universities/ Technical Institutions is also not up to the mark when it comes to additions to the existing body of knowledge in the subject chosen. Most of the Supervisor/Guides seem to be satisfied with the output of the scholars in the course work and lack capabilities to facilitate 'stretching the mind' of the young scholars.

As a serious consequence of limited enrolments for Ph.D. and poor-quality outcomes in research, universities are facing acute shortage of quality faculty for guiding research work. Therefore, faculty shortage needs to be met with increased fellowships for PG/Research Degrees and also compulsory Undergraduate (UG) teaching assignments for Junior Research Fellows (JRF) so that Readers and Professors could devote more time to Postgraduate (PG) Research scholars and undertake some mandatory funded research. Most Universities in the UK and the USA engage PhD scholars for Undergraduate teaching and often involve them regularly in weekly Seminar/Tutorial classes for PG students and are paid for their services. In India, they are not even called scholars but only as students. In most developed countries, they are almost part of the faculty. India should learn how to nurture budding talent and adopt good international practices. In India, they engage superannuated faculty members on contract basis. However, this can only be a short-term measure.

It has been observed that except a few, many private universities operate in secrecy and seclusion. International institutions often avoid collaborative work with them and instead prefer Central Government funded Institutions. For example, most research collaborations between India and the UK formed through programmes or initiatives (of UK Research Councils and the UK-India Education and Research Initiative-UKIERI) are focused primarily on the Centrally-funded universities and Institutes of National Importance, where only 2.6 per cent of Indian students are enrolled. There remains very limited international research collaboration with State universities and private institutions, with a few notable exceptions such as Savitribai Phule Pune University in Maharashtra.

A positive student experience at Higher Education Institution has an impact on student retention and further study. This could go a long way in providing a regular stream of bright scholars for engaging in the teaching profession. Maintaining and improving the quality of teaching, learning and student experience are crucial factors in the success of Universities. While the Draft NEP overhauls the institutional arrangements by creating multiple authorities/agencies, it is not clear as to how the institutional arrangements will provide students with a stimulating and rewarding Higher Education experience and meet the goals of self-fulfilment, personal development and the pursuit of knowledge as an end in itself.

Nothing in the Draft NEP 2019 guarantees student satisfaction in the campus, nor is there any indication of efforts to provide a wide range of student services, facilities and quality amenities which are integral to student engagement and the experience. Moreover, in India students are not engaged in managing these services. There is very little interaction of students and the faculty outside the classrooms. Student Unions and Faculty Associations have their own agenda which are not related to making the student experience on the campus lively and rewarding.

If Indian universities aspire to be in the top ranking global institutions, it is imperative to make proper assessment of student life in the campus. Building a great complex by itself is, of course, no guarantee for earning a world-class status.

3. Creation of Multi-disciplinary Universities

The Draft NEP 2019 envisions a nationwide ecosystem of vibrant multidisciplinary universities and colleges. All single-field or single discipline universities including the Indian Institutes of Technology (IITs) will be converted into multi-disciplinary institutions for better knowledge development and dissemination, true to the basic notion of a university. Moreover, Professional Education, Vocational Education and all other areas of higher learning would be an integral part of Higher Education. In addition, the Draft NEP 2019, strongly favours liberal education and advocates four-year liberal Undergraduate programme (with multiple exit options). This would provide a wholesome range of liberal education with a wide variety of choice of majors and minors.

All these are commendable recommendations and should be accepted wholeheartedly.

A caveat may, however, be added here. The definition of multi-disciplinary HEI subsumed in the Draft NEP 2019 is a rather narrow one. It includes offering 'at least two programmes or majors in the arts and humanities, at least two in science and mathematics and at least one in the social sciences' (p. 212).

Why should multi-disciplinarity be confined to a *minimum* of five programmes stated above? If the past is any guide, the minimum number of disciplines would become practically, the optimal or 'operationally meaningful' one. Many universities could spring with just five departments with only one or two contractual teachers in each department, thus defeating the basic notion of the University.

4. Restructuring of Higher Education Institutions

The Draft NEP 2019 recommends a drastic restructuring of HEIs in to three categories:

- Type 1: World-class research and high-quality teaching;
- Type 2: High-quality teaching across disciplines with a significant contribution to research;
- Type 3: High-quality teaching at Undergraduate level.

For the purpose of accreditation, each type of institutions will invite different yardsticks. The three-tier system of HEIs may invariably also lead to discrimination in terms of resource allocation by the Government and even in terms of faculty recognition. This would mean building a hierarchical system which could adversely affect the Indian Education System over time.

Teaching and research are two sides of the same coin and cannot be segregated naturally. In an ideal Higher Education Institution (HEI), teaching and research operate in a mutually reinforcing manner. One of the major shortcomings of the prevailing education system is that teaching and research are unnecessarily separated from each other and that the inter-linkages between the two are largely ignored. The proposal by Draft NEP 2019 would strengthen such undesirable tendencies even further. Indeed, if the proposal is accepted, there would be a substantial risk of teaching receiving a low priority in Type 1 Universities whereas most Type 2 and Type 3 Universities would be inclined to undermine the research activities. A 'clear cut demarcation of teaching and research roles between the three types of institutions is neither tenable nor desirable'.[27]

There is no logical reason why Type 3 institutions, i.e., colleges should be confined to teaching alone and not be encouraged to undertake research. In fact, my own experience as Vice-Chancellor of University of Pune (now Savitribai Phule Pune University) shows that encouragement with financial incentives yields excellent research outcomes even from remotely located colleges, especially in social sciences.

HEIs ought to be rated and ranked on the basis of a set of objective criteria based on international standards and not on the basis of the artificial distinction proposed in the Draft NEP 2019.

5. All HEIs will be either Universities or Autonomous Colleges

The Draft NEP 2019 stipulates that all Higher Education Institutions (HEIs) will either be Universities or degree-granting autonomous colleges. There will be no Affiliated Colleges.

As far as Affiliated Colleges are concerned, one has to tread carefully. At present they are the ones which are holding the key to achieving the proposed GER target. They should not be dismantled in a tearing hurry.

Conversion of Affiliated Colleges into Autonomous colleges is an uphill task and could expected to be very slow unless the proposed Mission Directorate comes up with a detailed practical plan and does handholding, where necessary.

6. Ideal Size for Universities and Colleges

The Draft NEP 2019 proposes on-campus student enrolments between

27. Tilak, 'Perennial Problems and Promising but Perplexing Solutions'.

5,000-25,000 for universities and between 2,000-5,000 for colleges. Given the preponderance of small colleges (e.g., in 2017-18, 19 per cent colleges had an enrolment below 100), raising the lower limit for enrolment makes economic and managerial sense. But the same is not true for the upper limit for enrolment, where it is the choice of appropriate technology that really matters for pedagogy and governance.

Take the case of Savitribai Phule Pune University. The number of students (excluding those under Open Distance Learning or ODL) are currently around 7,50,000 and there are 700+ affiliated colleges. Going by the prescriptions from the Draft NEP 2019, should the University be divided into 30+ campuses? Jurisdiction of the University has been restricted to only three districts: Pune, Nashik and Ahmednagar. This could mean around 10 University campuses per district? A campus in each Tehsil? And after all, to what advantage?

Sure enough, there are small colleges affiliated to big State Universities such as Savitribai Phule Pune University. How would the authorities go about merging small colleges which belong to different private managements?

There are for too many practical problems involved here and one is not sure whether the Committee was able to debate and discuss them threadbare.

Take the case of confusion regarding the number of HEIs. The Draft NEP 2019 proposes one Type 1 University for every 5 million population, one Type 2 University per half-a-million population and one Type 3 University per 0.2 million population. This would mean that for the largest five districts in the country such as Thane, Pune and Suburban Mumbai, each of which has a population in excess of 10 million, there would be 2 Type 1 Universities, 20 Type 2 Universities and around 50 Type 3 Universities.

If there are far too many universities in one district, there is big danger of losing 'universality' in the universities. There is some merit in the fear that has been expressed: 'Every university will have students from within the district,' since students do not feel the need to go outside the district for Higher Education. 'Even teachers and administrators are recruited from within the district. As a result, universities become local and localised institutions and even parochial in nature. "Universe" in such universities will be confined to district boundaries.... This would cause the biggest damage to the very concept of a university'.[28]

28. Tilak, Ibid.

As the Draft NEP 2019 has observed elsewhere, what is needed is 'a thoughtful consolidation of existing HEIs into a fewer number of HEIs, considering issues of access, distribution, and the quality of existing and future outcomes' (p.217).

7. Denial of the Existence of a Shadow Economy

The Draft NEP 2019 categorically states: 'this Policy is unambiguous and explicit that education must be a not-for-profit activity and enterprise in society' (p.401).

The Draft NEP 2019 had the opportunity to explicitly provide for penalties to be imposed on profit-making higher educational institutions (HEIs). At the very least, the Draft NEP could have given a strong message that profit-making HEIs shall not be tolerated. However, the Draft NEP merely hints at the existence of for-profit HEIs and does not go any further. Unfortunately, the Draft NEP does not acknowledge 'the rampant shadow economy which fearlessly runs education as a for-profit business'. On the contrary, the Draft NEP seemingly makes 'suggestions which may possibly promote and legitimise this shadow economy'![29]

The Draft NEP proposes entrance tests through NTA for admission to universities. It is hoped that this would reduce the burden of Class XII Board Exams and various entrance tests for different universities, which in turn, could reduce dependency on coaching classes.

This is unlikely to happen because the students would now become dependent on coaching centres for *these* entrance tests. As has been pointed out, 'coaching centres are notoriously for-profit and thrive on the gigantic divergence between school and entrance exam curricula. Coaching centres will either have more services and products to add to their shelf or will continue to prosper unhindered.'[30]

8. New Institutional Framework

(a) Rashtriya Shiksha Aayog (RSA)

The Draft NEP 2019 proposes setting up of a new apex body titled,

29. Chimni, 'An Alarming Attempt To Redefine India', *Business World,* 31 July 2019.
30. Ibid

Rashtriya Shiksha Aayog (RSA) with Prime Minister as the Chairperson. The objective of RSA would be to enable a holistic and integrated implementation of all educational initiatives and programmatic interventions and to coordinate efforts between the Centre and States.

The RSA would be a standing National Education Commission. It would be the apex body, responsible for everything in education including, inter alia, developing, implementing, evaluating and revising the education policy.

This recommendation is most welcome. The Kothari Commission (1966) had recommended setting up a National Education Commission every five years. With a rapidly changing educational scenario in India and abroad, there is an imperative need for a National Education Commission that is continually functional. This is precisely what the Draft NEP 2019 has recommended.

Hon. Prime Minister as the ex-officio Chairman of the NSA would add the necessary gravitas to this much-needed authority.

Since education is *de jure*, on the Concurrent List of subjects in the Constitution of India, the States should be adequately represented in the RSA.

(b) National Research Foundation

National Research Foundation (NRF) as an apex body for creating a strong research culture and the time for building research capacity across Higher Education has come now.

NRF can play a very useful catalytic role. It would need corresponding units at the State level and/or institutional bureaus so as make an effective contribution. Distribution of fellowships should be a minor role. There should not be any parallel activities with the proposed reformed UGC.

(c) Separate Bodies for:

Standard Setting, Funding, Accreditation and Regulation

The four basic components of the regulatory architecture of Higher Education:

- Standard Setting
- Funding,

- Accreditation and
- Regulation

are to be segregated and entrusted to different bodies.

In respect of Professional Education, there would be separate Standard Setting Bodies, one for each one of the areas of Professional Education.

As to the funding, UGC will be transformed into Higher Education Grants Commission.

As far as accreditation is concerned, according to the Draft NEP 2019 proposes that NAAC will be revamped and it would lead to the creation of accreditation eco-system for Higher Education.

All these recommendations are welcome. However, the devil lies in the details.

The final component of the regulatory architecture is the overall regulation of the Higher Education System. In this regard, the Draft NEP 2019 proposes setting up a new institution, titled National Higher Education Regulatory Authority (NHERA).

NHERA would be the sole regulator for entire Higher Education Sector including Professional Education. NHERA, as the sole regulator, would prepare a Model Act setting the relevant rules and procedures for establishing new Higher Education Institutions (HEIs).

This is probably going to be the toughest recommendation to implement. There were at least two earlier attempts—Independent Regulatory Authority in Higher Education (IRAHE) as recommended by the National Knowledge Commission and National Commission for Higher Education and Research (NCHER) as recommended by the Yashpal Committee. Both attempts did not fructify.

The main reason for their failure, perhaps, was their strong unitary features (as if Education is a subject in the Union List). There were also strong reservations from Professional Education bodies (such as Medical Council etc.) which preferred to work in silos.[31]

If properly implemented, NHERA could be expected to promote a holistic and integrated approach to Higher Education, provided that

31. As the then Member of Planning Commission in charge of Education, I extensively toured all over India as a part of an Expert Group to gather support for NCHER but did not succeed. Our efforts were severely criticised for centralising all the powers in a one Commission constituted by the Central Government with a complete disregard to the roles, responsibilities and privileges of the State Governments.

legitimate concerns of the State governments are addressed fairly.

That said, it may be noted that while the Draft NEP sets out a detailed new institutional framework, it does not provide a clear roadmap. As has been pointed out, '...the demands of development are urgent and require the highest intellect and competence and the ability to work across disciplines and agencies. The necessary institutional and individual skills are simply not there.'[32] The Draft NEP 'could have provided a roadmap to get there, of delicate decentralisation, innovative pedagogies and partnerships between Central and State institutions and regional agencies.' It is unfortunate that rather than recognising the State Universities (and colleges) as the mainstay of the Higher Education System in India, and making them 'primary agents of changes', the Draft NEP 'proposes to entangle them in a bureaucratic web of NTA, NAAC, NHERA and others'.[33]

VI. Teacher Education

1. Restoring Integrity and Credibility

The Draft NEP 2019 notes clearly: 'Heartbreakingly, teacher education has been beleaguered with mediocrity as well as rampant corruption due to commercialisation' (p.283) and adds: 'The integrity and credibility of the teacher education system has unfortunately taken a great hit and witnessed a severe decline due to the thousands of "Teacher Education Institutions" that are solely commercial operations where little if any teacher education is taking place' (p.284).

The Draft NEP 2019 categorically recommends 'closure of substandard and dysfunctional teacher education institutions' (P.15.1.1). According to the Kasturirangan Committee these harsh measures are necessary 'if teacher education is to improve and reach the levels of integrity and credibility required to restore the prestige of the teaching profession and thereby attain a successful school system' (p.284).

This recommendation is highly commendable. However, there is a serious question about the feasibility of its implementation. In many

32. Milind Sohoni and Oshin Dharap, 'New Education Policy will ensure our higher education system remains a client of global science', *The Indian Express,* 18 July 2019, https://indianexpress.com/article/opinion/columns/the-aspiration-trap-national-education-policy-5834797/

33. Ibid

cases, relevant licenses seem to have been acquired through political patronage or illegal means. Entrenched vested interests are unlikely to allow the implementation of the recommendation without putting up a strong resistance.

2. The 4-year Integrated B.Ed. Programme

The Draft NEP 2019 envisions that 'all teacher education will happen in multidisciplinary institutions—Teacher Education will be an integral part of the Higher Education System' (p.285).

According to the Draft NEP the 4-year integrated stage-specific B.Ed. programme will eventually be the minimum degree qualification for teachers and TET will be strengthened.

This recommendation is most welcome.

3. Fate of Para-teachers

According to the Draft NEP 2019, all para-teachers—*Shiksha karmis, Shiksha mitras* etc.—will be wound up by 2022. The reasoning behind this recommendation is appealing: 'we must ensure that teachers are invested in, and can build strong long-term relationships with their communities' (p.123). Nevertheless, thought may be given to the idea of using these para-teachers for hand-holding support to out-of-school children (OoSC) or as pre-School Assistants and the like.

4. Short-term Measures

The Draft NEP 2019 assures that 'all HEIs will be adequately resourced and staffed with high quality teams of faculty and members in other roles, including leadership roles' (p.213). The Draft NEP however, does not go much beyond suggesting transitional measures, such as sharing faculty with other institutions in the vicinity, which are essentially short term in nature. Nevertheless, two ideas stand out and merit endorsement: first, inviting rolling faculty of eminent and superannuated scientists/ professors/experts from industry and from overseas and secondly, providing expensive professional development opportunities for faculty in Higher Education.

VII. Equitable and Inclusive Education

While the Draft NEP 2019 makes all the right noises about equity and inclusiveness in education for the URGs, it does not come up with any concrete and time-bound action programme. If anything, there are critical areas where the Draft NEP 2019 actually (and surreptitiously) goes against the interests of the URGs which are categorised into with sociocultural identities (such as SC, ST, OBCs, Muslims, migrant communities), or gender identities (including women and transgender individuals) or those with special needs (such as learning disabilities), and adverse socio-economic conditions (such as the urban poor).

The Draft NEP 2019 has hardly any worthwhile new prescription for equity and inclusion, except, as mentioned before, some 'lofty intentions'. At best, one can identify three *specific* areas of action proposed for URGs in the Draft NEP 2019:

- Special Education Zones to be set up in disadvantaged areas,
- Financial support through creation of a Special National Fund,
- Alternative pathways for recruitment of high-quality teachers from URGs.

Under these three specific areas, the Draft NEP 2019 proposes as under:

- Increase the access to bring URGs into school and focus on educationally lagging regions by creating 'Special Education Zones'. These zones will have special focus of the government in policy implementation with additional funding from the Centre and States. The Central Government will support extra investment and per-child expenditure in the ratio of 2:1 for each rupee spent by the State in these zones. This extra investment will be spent on multiple aspects required for improving educational outcomes in these regions.
- The Draft NEP has called for the creation of a Special National Fund specifically for providing scholarships and developing resources and facilities for students from URGs. Students will be able to apply for financial support in a simplified manner—from a single national agency—and will be able to register complaints if they are denied due support or services. This is to encourage representation from URGs in all levels of education while providing opportunities to overcome initial barriers in education.
- The Draft NEP 2019 has also favoured addressing the issue of

> underrepresentation of teachers from URGs. The Draft NEP in this regard, suggests adopting alternate pathways for the recruitment of high-quality teachers from URGs. These pathways will include a 'recruitment followed by training' model (instead of the typical 'training followed by recruitment' model) for teachers from URGs.

The Draft NEP 2019 does not seem to have adequately dealt with equity issues—regional, social, and gender, either in School Education or in Tertiary Education. Establishment of Special Education Zones in educationally lagging regions is not a good idea at all. The UGC has already identified 370 districts with very low GER for setting up model colleges. The scheme is a part of Rashtriya Uchchatar Shiksha Abhiyan (RUSA) which covers only about 130 colleges so far; most of them still reeling under teething troubles. Another case to the point is Dravidian University, which was set up in a remote place in Andhra Pradesh because plenty of land was available and for development of the district. More than two decades have gone by and the University has grown, but it has not posted any credible performance despite support from all the Southern States.

On the other hand, the districts of Bengaluru and Jaipur have 970 and 616 colleges, respectively. Why? It is because these districts have a conducive educational environment with infrastructure, well-developed air, rail and road transport system and communication network.

The proposed Special Educational Zones in order to address the equity issues may not have educational environment at all. Look how Amarkantak Tribal University in Madhya Pradesh remains cut off from other institutions and is lacking educational environment just like the Dravidian University.

India has about 75 to 80 important industrial, trade and business centres, which are well connected in terms of transport and communication systems. These are spread all over the country and offer scope for new institutions. If not in the centre, there are nearby satellite towns around for setting up new institutions or a cluster. For example, Mohali cluster of institutions caters to Punjab, Haryana, HP and J&K. The States of MP, Chhattisgarh, Jharkhand, and Odisha need several such clusters, for Higher and Technical Education. Special Education Zones should be set up in the vicinity of industrial/business towns to prosper and certainly *not* within low GER districts. Area development should not be the criteria for educational investments.

There are several issues which are not addressed in the Draft NEP 2019. These issues, which are critical for creating Equitable and Inclusive Education in the country, include:

- The Draft NEP 2019 advocates large School Complexes on the grounds of the optimal utilisation of resource. While this argument is reasonable, there arises an important concern about the accessibility. For example, well-equipped libraries and laboratories would be mainly located in the urban centres, making accessibility to children from rural areas unreasonably difficult.
- First generation learners will find the proposed standardised tests in schools difficult since they do not have educational environment at home. As mentioned earlier, they will get to know the results and while the school may not fail them, it cannot prevent them from dropping out.
- The Draft NEP 'proposes a roll-back of existing mechanisms of enforcement of private school making parents 'de facto' regulators of private school. Parents, and particularly poor and neo-literate parents, cannot hold the onus of ensuring that much more powerful and resourced schools comply with quality, safety and equity norms'.[34]
- While the Draft NEP 2019 emphasises the need to bring 'unrepresented groups' into school, 'it misses a critical opportunity of addressing inequalities within the education system. Solutions to close the gap of access to quality education between India's rich and poor children are not mentioned. It proposes to remove the expectations that all schools meet the common minimum infrastructure and facility standards'.[35]
- In Higher Education, across most key fields of study, SC/ST enrolment is remarkably low throughout the country, while female enrolment in premier institutions is even more worrisome. Reducing gender disparities in Higher Education is a very hard task and solution lies in School Education. A stark omission in NEP is a complete miss to the sanitary and medical needs of the girl children which is often a major factor for their dropping out of school as well as reduced confidence levels. It is really a shame that the share of female students is lowest

34. Taneja, 'New education policy misses a critical chance to address inequalities in system', Livemint, 12 June 2019.

35. Ibid.

in the Institutions of National Importance in Higher Education.

- A major concern regarding inclusivity remains the accessibility of children with disabilities. Major facilities are likely to be centred in proposed large School Complexes. The Draft NEP does not talk about reasonable accommodation for persons with disabilities (PwD), the failure of which makes it discriminatory. In this regard, reasonable accommodation refers to the necessary and appropriate modifications and adjustments to the environment so as to enable PwDs to enjoy and exercise their rights equally with others. The Draft NEP fails to promote inclusiveness of Transgender community, whereas the LGBTQ+ is not even mentioned in the Draft NEP.
- For all the equity issues, the Draft NEP simply depends on existing schemes and reiterates their concerted and targeted implementation including ECCE. The Draft NEP lists the causes of inequity but offer nothing towards affordability of School and Higher and Technical Education. The Draft NEP ignores the private expenditure on education. Scholarships, at best, cover only tuition fees and a minimal cushion for other charges. Scholarships are hardly indexed for inflation. Affordability is a core issue in equity and should be dealt with on priority.
- Affordability is supposed to be one of the strong foundational pillars of Tertiary Education Policy. With the increase in access, mostly through private institutions colleges and Universities, there is a new generation of learners from disadvantaged social groups. The scholarships are often seen as a social welfare measure. It may be noted, however, that in reality the funding has never been adequate and the worst part of it is that it hardly ever reaches the students before the commencement of the academic year. A vicious cycle is pushing poor government school children, who struggle to manage through NEET, to private institutions with a very high fee structure. These children all along have studied only in government schools on account of poor affordability. They are not in a position to spend Rs 50,000–60,000 at coaching institutes to clear competitive entrance examinations. Whereas the children belonging to affluent society with best educated home environment, including guidance and their schooling in public schools all along, score high and get into government institutions for Professional Education and pay less than what they were spending on School Education. On the other hand, those dependent on government institutions

are being fleeced by both, the private institutions and the banks. The NEP 2019 has not seriously addressed any issue of affordability and only makes a passing remark of 50 per cent scholarships. There is private expenditure on education which is many-fold higher in private institutions as compared to government institutions. This never gets covered under any scholarship regime for the poor students.

- As to the inclusivity of tribals, the Draft NEP has discussed and correctly identified that the prescribed curriculum needs to be contextualised in order to make it more relatable to tribal students and yet, it fails to address how the rest of the students in the system should relate to the tribal students. Arguably, 'missing out on this important piece of putting in the effort to harmonise the opportunities and acceptability of the underrepresented with the represented is unacceptable, given the lack of trust that already exists in our country'.[36]

What is truly appalling is that the Draft NEP has recommended repealing of Clause 12(1)(c) of the RTE Act which reserves 25 per cent seats in private schools for the disadvantaged children. The NEP claims that this clause has not worked effectively, calling for 'autonomy and innovation' to encourage best practices. Calling this measure to be in 'better alignment with the principles of this policy' is disturbing because it goes against the spirit of the Constitution of India by getting rid of reservations for the disadvantaged. Surprisingly, while sweeping reform ideas such as school vouchers are being experimented across the world, the Draft NEP 2019 does not even mention it. (It is surprising because the BJP Government under Prime Minister Narendra Modi has boldly deployed direct benefit transfers (DBTs) and effectively so in several areas such as former subsidies, Ujjwala LPG gas subsidy, etc.) It has been documented that the use of DBTs has 'led to the removal of 80 million fake beneficiaries from the records, with savings of Rs 1.1 lakh crore (Rs 1,100 billion)'. The same risk does exist while providing public money to private schools as reimbursement for educationally disadvantaged children under the RTE Act.[37] There is, thus, a strong case for giving public subsidy for educating disadvantaged children as a school voucher

36. Chimni, 'An Alarming Attempt To Redefine India', *Business World,* 31 July 2019.

37. Kingdon, 'Draft National Education Policy amounts to rearranging deck chairs on the Titanic', *The Times of India,* 24 June 2019.

(which is a form of DBT) instead of giving that money to private schools via leaky government structures. An added advantage of this mechanism is that it gives the parent the freedom to choose a school. The additional purchasing power, in turn, empowers them to hold schools accountable. Further, there are several areas that have not been identified by the Draft NEP 2019 but actually require attention in the larger interest of Equitable and Inclusive Education in the country. These are:[38]

- The Central and State Governments, and District Administration should ensure that the budget allocated and amount spent on education of SCs, STs and OBCs is at least in proportion to their population in the respective districts. While granting scholarships, the public educational institutions, government-supported accredited institutions, private institutions, and all HEIs (private and public) should meet all requisite expenses of SC/ST students to enable them to concentrate on their studies. HEGC and other such bodies concerned should ensure implementation of this provision.
- Institutions should support SC/ST students with: admission without payment of any fees; adequate amount of scholarships with 50 per cent of it disbursed in advance; special allowance to buy laptop; hostel accommodation; and personal loans at priority sector lending rates so as to maintain dependent family members till completion of their studies.
- Permissions to set up new HEIs by any mode (i.e., by the Parliament or a State Legislature or with an 'HEI Charter' from NHERA) should be given, subject to the condition of following the extant reservation policy in admissions of students, appointments of faculties and non-teaching staff, doctoral and postdoctoral programmes, fellowships, scholarships, projects, hostel rooms, and committees appointed.
- The basic parameters in SQAAF and LSS should include compliance of reservation policy in recruitment of teaching staff of each stage and non-teaching staff.
- District Education Council (DEC) should include at least one representative each from SC, ST, OBC parents; at least one representative each from SC, ST, OBC teachers from each stage and at least one representative each of SC, ST, OBC Principals.

38. Based on a Memorandum submitted to MHRD by Bhartiya Anusuchit Jati Jamati Sangh. I am grateful to Sandesh Wagh for sharing a copy with me.

VIII. Financing Education

It is stated that the Draft NEP 2019 has been built on the foundational pillars of Access, Equity, Quality, Affordability and Accountability. Not surprisingly, the thrust of the Draft NEP seems to be on Higher, Technical and Professional Education together with higher incremental outlay proposed for the next 10 years.

The Draft NEP 2019 makes far-reaching changes with focus on across the board quality improvement from ECCE to Higher, Technical and Professional Education. A striking feature of the Draft NEP is the mega regulatory framework which involves not only streamlining the system and procedures but also setting up entirely new institutional arrangements on a permanent basis. That means a very substantial additional expenditure. The massive educational policy reforms call for equally massive financial support for translation of the Draft NEP 2019 into reality.

That in spite of the criticality of financing, for reasons not known, the Draft NEP 2019 relegates discussion of the financing issues to an Appendix.

The Draft NEP 2019 does explicitly recognise the necessity of substantially raising public expenditure on education. In fact, it recommends 'significant increase in public investment in education' (p.403). The Draft NEP reiterates the ever elusive goal of allocating 6 per cent of GDP to education (as in the NPE 1968 which was subsequently reaffirmed in 1986 as well as in 1992 versions of Education Policy).

The Draft NEP 2019 recommends raising public expenditure on education as a proportion of total expenditure (by the Centre and States) from 10 per cent as of now, to 20 per cent in 10 years.

As has been pointed out[39], the recommendation in terms of public expenditure is 'based on weak database and/or a limited view that (Kasturirangan) Committee took'.

Apparently, the Draft NEP 2019 considered expenditure on education by MHRD alone and, therefore, presumed the baseline scenario or the present level to be at 2.7 per cent of GDP or 10 per cent of total government expenditure in 2017-18 (p.402 and 406). **This is incorrect.** If expenditure on education incurred by all Ministries is taken into account, instead of MHRD alone, the public expenditure on education

39. Tilak, 'Perennial Problems and Promising but Perplexing Solutions'.

in the year 2015-16 (budget estimates) worked out to be 4.07 per cent of GDP or 15.6 per cent of all expenditure.[40] It, therefore, turns out that the Draft NEP's recommendation of raising total public expenditure on education from 10 per cent to 20 per cent is exceedingly modest because the prevailing level already averages at around 16 per cent. Raising the total public expenditure on education from 16 per cent to 20 per cent cannot be said to be an ambitious goal. A much larger goal would be warranted in view of the comprehensive reforms that are contemplated by the Draft NEP 2019.

What is truly surprising is that the Draft NEP 2019 does not offer a detailed plan of raising public expenditure on education. It simply pins hope on improved tax–GDP ratio for enhanced funding.

The Draft NEP 2019 maintains throughout the document that education will be a non-profit activity, while as a matter of fact, the Medical Education has already embraced the Indian Companies Act, 1956 without any fetters, not only for the new institutions, but also for enabling the existing ones to be converted into a company. Can any private company run without profit? While there is a need to recognise the legitimate role of the private providers of education in the country, the Draft NEP should have anchored the principles of affordability, healthy competition and internationalisation of education.

The UGC provides funds through Special Assistance Programme (SAP) around Rs 150-200 million for research, including infrastructure support. It also supports Major and Minor research projects (Rs 300-400 million). The projects grants vary from Rs 1.2 million (Major) and Rs 0.1 million (Minor). There has been no systematic transparent procedure for these research grants.

Importantly, there is no monetary incentive for researchers and no assistance is provided for research persons in minor projects. UGC norms require a complete overhaul and research projects need to be funded meaningfully. The process has to transcend beyond departmental hierarchy in the University set-up so that project work is provided to the really talented faculty and not by virtue of seniority. The researcher could have an incentive payment; say 20 per cent in the project cost besides other grants for travel, etc.

The UGC has 100 odd schemes that have never been subjected to

40. Ibid.

zero-based budgeting exercise due to block grants. There are quite a few schemes that should come to NRF and there are many small schemes with UGC that should be weeded out.

There is no need to create a Research National Foundation merely to distribute fellowship funding as a grant which in any case UGC and other agencies were doing in the past. What is catalytically more important is to bring researchers and funding agencies together on project mode. How is it possible for NRF to monitor research proposals from 40,800 institutions? NRF needs State/Regional units. It should promote and support research culture in all the Higher Education Institutions in accessing research funding not just from MHRD but also lay hands on other Ministries and private establishments purely based on projects. It should have Facilitation Units in Universities and colleges (Research Bureaus) to process and upload research projects for the Foundation to scout for third parties for acceptance of the proposals. All third party evaluation of Plan programmes of the Central and State Governments should be done through University research faculty.

NRF should lend support and facilitate competitive bidding for projects. Universities need to generate more funds other than student fees and government grants through legitimate means, i.e., funded research work and short-term courses to augment resources. Faculty should have a share of funds generated on projects and also absolute freedom to work on specialisation without being bound by hierarchy. All world-class institutions have such an ecosystem.

The Draft NEP 2019 has played very safe on some of the vexed issues with the University administration, viz. contribution by the students and the faculty. It has not addressed the issue of generating internal extra budgetary resources that could cushion the funding gap and expand freeships. Quality education is not a costless process and budgetary resources always leave a deficit crippling newer activities and poor maintenance of infrastructure facilities. Fee structure has to be revised and indexed for inflation. Fee contribution, including examinations and those for various services, also need to be indexed and this contribution should at least meet some significant part of the maintenance cost of the campus. The faculty should be asked to run innovative certificate courses during vacation. The University should unshackle hierarchy for this to succeed and those faculty members that have knowledge and skills and organising abilities to run short-term courses should be engaged and rewarded, with a definite proportion of funds going to the University. Some Central institutions are already doing it.

The Draft NEP 2019, instead of promoting disguised trusts and pseudo non-profit entities, could allow private participation for profit and they could be taxed. Their area of operation could be regulated to meet the goals of bridging regional inequity and these institutions could be subjected to government's reasonable supervision.

In February 2009, the then UPA Government allowed companies registered under Companies Act, 1956 to open medical colleges though with a caveat that 'permission shall be withdrawn if the colleges resort to commercialisation'. In January 2017, the MCI eligibility clause was further amended to enable all companies registered under the Act of 1956 to open colleges and further enabled even the existing medical colleges to be converted into a company under the Companies Act, 1956. If this is the policy stance of the government, where does the NEP 2019 statement that schools are not for profit stand? Arguably, market is preferable to sheltered shady *shanties* running Medical, Engineering and Teacher Training institutions in the country.

Part Four

7

Draft National Education Policy, 2019: Way Forward

In the Preamble to the Draft National Education Policy, Kasturirangan rightly says, 'The success of the Policy is wholly dependent on the quality of its implementation' (p. 34). Quoting Dr B.R. Ambedkar from one of his phenomenal speeches in the Constituent Assembly, where he had said: '...however good a Constitution may be, it is sure to turn bad because those who are called to work it, happen to be a bad lot. However bad a Constitution may be, it may turn out to be good if those who are called to work it, happen to be a good lot. The working of a Constitution does not depend wholly upon the nature of the Constitution'.[1]

A valid point. Kasturirangan hastens to add: 'Although the NEP is not to be compared with the Constitution, its impact on the lives of over 50% of the citizens of this country who are below the age of 25 years will be phenomenal, and it, therefore needs to be implemented with the utmost

1. For a collection of all major speeches by Dr Ambedkar, see Narendra Jadhav, *Ambedkar Speaks,* vol. I, II and III, (New Delhi: Konark Publishers, 2013).

care and commitment' (p. 35). Again, a very valid point, indeed.

Going forward, however, it is important to note that one is not dealing with a binary situation here — i.e., good or bad. The Draft NEP is a mixed bag. As mentioned earlier (i.e., Chapter 6), the Draft NEP has some recommendations which 'are pathbreaking, many deserve applause and quite a few require rethinking'.[2]

As detailed in Chapter 6, many proposals of the Draft NEP are welcome, but several of their recommendations are simply unacceptable while there are others which require amendments.

The Draft NEP does offer a 'Way Forward' but not in the main text. It has been relegated to Addendum A2 along with Addendum A1 about Financing and several appendices. The Draft NEP's Approach to Roadmap for Implementation has been couched in the form of a matrix of 'Key Actions led by various bodies' rather than in terms of a timeline for policy actions.

Placed below is a timeline for policy actions by various bodies, suitably amended in the light of the detailed critique offered in the previous chapter (Chapter 6). For the sake of clarity, the Policy Action Programme also shows which recommendations of the Draft NEP 2019 are deleted or amended.

TIMELINE FOR POLICY ACTION PROGRAMME

YEAR 2020

a. Actions by Ministry of Human Resource Development (MHRD)

- The RSA should be established. All relevant initiatives for its formation to be facilitated by MHRD.
- The RSA Appointment Committee (RSAAC), consisting of the Prime Minister, the Chief Justice of India, the Speaker of the Lok Sabha, the Leader of the Opposition in Parliament and the Union Minister for Education, should be constituted to enable the appointments to the RSA and to other key related roles.
- The MHRD should be redesignated as the Ministry of Education (MoE).

2. J.B.G. Tilak, 'Perennial Problems and Promising but Perplexing Solutions'.

b. Actions by Rashtriya Shiksha Aayog (RSA) and Ministry of Education (MoE)

- The RSA and its bodies should be constituted and relevant appointments be made by the RSAAC. These appointments should include the Executive Council, the Standing Committees on Coordination and the Advisory Council, besides appointment of the Executive Director of the RSA. The transition must include formalising the roles and responsibilities of MoE, RSA, and its bodies.
- The entire Higher Education regulatory system should be transformed into a single regulatory body. The National Higher Education Regulatory Authority (NHERA) should be set up as the single regulatory body for the entire Higher Education sector. The UGC and other existing regulatory bodies should be transformed into the Higher Education Grants Council (HEGC) and Professional Standard Setting Bodies (PSSBs), respectively. The General Education Council (GEC) should be constituted as an academic leadership institution.
- *The recommendation of the Draft NEP 2019 to combine three years of ECCE/pre-School (ages 3–6) with Grades I and II of Primary School should be discarded.*
- *The Draft NEP recommendation of changing the pedagogical structure to 5+3+3+4 should be discarded.* Instead, the pedagogical structure should be ECCE/pre-Education (3–6 years) + Primary (6–11 years, Classes I–V) + Upper Primary (11–14 years, Classes VI–VIII) + Secondary (14–16 years, Classes IX and X) + Higher Secondary (16–18 years, Classes XI and XII).
- A detailed plan should be prepared and initiated so that every child in the age range of 3–6 has access to free, safe, high quality and developmentally appropriate care and education by 2025.
- MHRD (or MoE) business rules should be restored so that the oversight of ECCE/pre-Education, once again, becomes its responsibility, while Ministry of Women and Child Development (MWCD) and Ministry of Health and Family Welfare (MHFW) will continue to be responsible for their mandates.
- The Right to Education (RTE) Act should be amended so that free and compulsory education is available from pre-School to Class XII, covering the age groups from 3 to 18 years, instead of 6 to 14 years as at present.
- *The Draft NEP recommendation of repeal of the clause 12(1)(c)*

of the RTE Act earmarking 25 per cent seats in private schools for disadvantaged children should be discarded.

- *The Draft NEP recommendation of making the RTE Act 'substantially less restrictive' should be discarded.*
- The National Research Foundation (NRF) should be established with the intent to strengthen research capacities and catalyse vibrant research primarily focusing on the Higher Education System.
- An autonomous National Educational Technology Forum (NETF) should be set up to facilitate review of initiatives related to the use of technology in education along with sharing of best practices.
- The potential of technology for improving governance and management should be facilitated by setting up the National Repository of Educational Data (NRED).

c. Actions by Rashtriya Shiksha Aayog (RSA) and State Departments of Education

- Once RSA and its bodies are constituted, interface mechanisms should be established between the States and the RSA. A Rajya Shiksha Aayog (RjSA)/State Education Commission (SEC) may be constituted in each State, chaired by the Chief Minister with the Minister of Education (nominated by the Chair) as the Vice-Chair. These bodies may have structure, constitution, and norms similar to those of the RSA, and perform similar functions within the State.

d. Actions by State Governments and State Departments of Education

- Individual State governments along with State Departments of Education should develop comprehensive plans to resource all schools adequately, and group schools into School Complexes according to the population distribution, connectivity, and other local considerations. While the size and specific composition of the School Complexes may vary, the grouping should ensure convenience of access/support for safe access for students and families, administrative ease and a support system for teachers and Principals. The resourcing plan should ensure adequate teachers, physical infrastructure, learning resources and support facilities.

This plan should also include a strategy for consolidating schools that have very small student numbers (<20). Such consolidation should be done only if it does not impact access to the school.

e. Actions by Ministry of Education (MoE) and State Departments of Education

- Initiatives should be taken so as to protect the rights of the child. This endeavour should include generating awareness through online programmes for students, teachers and parents, and formalising processes for enforcement in schools.
- Programmes should be initiated to focus on functional literacy and numeracy, and follow up through Basic Education, Skill Development and Continuing Education programmes. Programmes should particularly target women and individuals from socially and economically disadvantaged groups.
- The new institutional architecture for Higher Education should comprise three Types of institutions: Type 1 institutions focusing equally on research and teaching; Type 2 focusing primarily on teaching but conducting significant research as well; and Type 3 focusing only on teaching. Plans should be developed for this transformation into three Types of HEIs based on a careful evaluation of current status.

f. Actions by State Departments of Education

- The State School Regulatory Authority (SSRA), an independent State-wide body with quasi-judicial status, should be set up as the sole regulator for the entire School Education (including Early Childhood Care and Education [ECCE]), with responsibility also for oversight of the system and implementation of accreditation. Both public and private schools should be treated in the same manner to encourage private philanthropic efforts and to ensure the public-good nature of education. Operations of the public schooling system of the whole State should be handled by the Directorate of School Education.

g. Actions by National Council of Educational Research and Training (NCERT)

- A National Curricular Framework (NCF) for all school stages, from ECCE to Grade XII, should be developed in accordance with the stated pedagogical structure (which is ECCE (3 years) +5+3+2+2). The framework should have an integrated and flexible approach, keeping the focus on essential learning and critical thinking, flexibility, multilingualism, languages and literature, communication, quantitative reasoning, creativity, physical wellness, vocational exposure, ethical and moral reasoning, digital literacy, and knowledge of India and current affairs. The mandate of NCERT should be expanded to include the role of ECCE.

h. Actions by Relevant Appointing Body/Committee

- Appointment of people in leadership roles in all bodies and institutions—RSA, NHERA, NCERT, NIEPA, SCERT, BITE, DIET, school leaders, etc.—should be through rigorous and transparent processes, and shared in the public domain for scrutiny. Only persons with a strong academic and personal record of the highest integrity should be placed in leadership positions so that they can perform their responsibilities with commitment and transparency.

YEAR 2021

a. Actions by National Council of Educational Research and Training (NCERT)

- A new assessment paradigm should be put in place that focuses on the assessment of core concepts and skills along with higher order capacities. Formative assessment will be carried out in a variety of modes in order to optimise learning. Guidelines should be provided for assessment for learning and development in each area of the National Curricular Framework in accordance with this new paradigm.

b. Actions by State Council of Educational Research and Training (SCERT) or equivalent organisations in each State

- Once National Curricular Framework (NCF) is completed, SCERTs (or equivalent organisations) should develop State Curricular Frameworks aligned with the NCF.

YEAR 2022

a. Actions by State Governments and State Departments of Education

- Teacher recruitment and deployment should be carried out on the basis of detailed planning and assessment of requirements at the school and School Complex levels to ensure that each school within the complex has the desired number of teachers across subjects. Due focus should be on teachers' professional development, service conditions and performance management. While resources may be shared across schools in a complex, it should be ensured that each individual school has adequate resources to deliver the desired outcome.

b. Actions by Ministry of Education (MoE) and State Departments of Education

- Delivery of ECCE at the institutional level should be planned for all States via a four-pronged approach contingent on local needs, and feasibility of geography and infrastructure. A comprehensive plan for each State for implementation of suitable infrastructure and delivery of Early Childhood Education Curriculum should be developed by 2022 and fully implemented by 2028.
- School curriculum and pedagogy should be restructured in the following stages, with internal coherence and integrity, appropriate to the relevant age groups:
  - 3 years of pre-Primary/ ECCE Stage: (3–6 years),
  - 5 years of the Primary Stage: Grades I–V (6–11 years),
  - 3 years of the Middle (or Upper Primary) Stage: Grades VI–VIII (11–14 years), and,

- 4 years of the High (or Secondary) Stage: Grades IX– XII (14–18 years).
- The Secondary Stage should comprise four years of study from Grades IX–XII, where each year is divided into two semesters, for a total of eight semesters.

- Foundational Literacy and Numeracy should be addressed urgently and with unconventional measures as will be necessary. Large-scale mobilisation and engagement of the community should be leveraged for this purpose. The Remedial Instructional Aides Programme (RIAP) and the National Tutors Programme (NTP) should be launched to suitably support school teachers. School teachers should be trained to lead the RIAP and NTP, and should also undergo specific capacity development to ensure Foundational Literacy and Numeracy amongst all students. All public school teachers are to be covered.

YEAR 2023

a. Actions by State Governments and State Departments of Education

- The curricular reforms mentioned above should also be accompanied by the creation of enabling environments and the provision of relevant learning resources across all schools to deliver on the new curricular, pedagogical and assessment paradigms.

b. Actions by Ministry of Education (MoE) and State Departments of Education

- All academic and non-academic posts in HEIs should be filled in permanent (tenure) track. Processes for professional development of faculty should be institutionalised both at the level of the HEI and at the National level. MoE and State Departments of Education should coordinate with NHERA to fulfil this responsibility.

c. Actions by State Departments of Education

- Processes for teacher recruitment and management should be changed and improved. School Complexes should be formed.

d. Actions by State School Regulatory Authority (SSRA)

- SQAAS for the State, developed in collaboration with NIEPA, should be used by the SSRA for its regulatory practice and should be the basis for the requirements and criterion for License to Start a School (LSS).

e. Actions by Directorate of School Education (DSE)

- Decentralisation of governance should be enabled through the constitution of District Education Councils/Zila Shiksha Parishad (headed by the Collector/District Magistrate) and through participation of teachers, school leadership and the community in the governance mechanisms of the school/School Complex through the School Management Committee/School Complex Management Committee.
- All school leaders should be appointed on the basis of their capacity of leadership and suitability for the roles, not on the basis of seniority. Continuous Professional Development support should be made available to school leaders.

f. Actions by State Council of Educational Research and Training (SCERT) or equivalent organisations in each State

- Textbooks and materials should be developed in a variety of languages for all curricular areas in accordance with the State Curricular Frameworks and assessment paradigms indicated above.

g. Actions by NCERT and SCERT or equivalent organisations in each State

- The Continuous Professional Development system for teachers should be redesigned across all States. CRCs, BRCs, DIETs and SCERTs should be rejuvenated by appointing adequate number of high-quality people, improving infrastructure and empowerment; it should be ensured that they do not get caught up in administrative tasks. NCERT should support SCERTs in fulfilling this responsibility.

h. Actions by Central and State Boards of Assessment

- Certificate examinations of Central and State Boards should be redesigned in keeping with the curricular and assessment reforms as mentioned above. In particular, the comprehensive Grade X and XII Board Examinations should be eliminated and replaced with modular assessments for each subject that can be taken anytime between Grade IX and Grade XII.
  - ❖ The certification requirements for the end of the Middle Stage (Upper-Primary) and for Grades X and IX should be redesigned. In particular, certificate examinations for Grades X and XII should reflect the semester and modular examination-based scheme.
  - ❖ While certification of competencies of students at the school-leaving stage should be handled by the Boards of Assessment, the Boards should have no role in determining the curricula (including textbooks).

i. Actions by Ministry of Education (MoE) and National Testing Agency

- The autonomous NTA should conduct aptitude tests and tests in various subjects, which can be taken on multiple occasions during the year.

j. Actions by National Higher Education Regulatory Authority (NHERA)

- Poorly performing teacher education institutions, not adhering to basic norms, should be shut down.

k. Actions by Higher Education Grants Council (HEGC)

- A fair and transparent system for determining public funding based on criteria aligned with accreditation norms should be put in place.

l. Actions by General Education Council (GEC)

- A National Higher Education Qualifications Framework (NHEQF) outlining the learning outcomes associated with degree/diploma/ certification should be developed as the guiding document for curricula across all disciplines and fields that do not have their individual Professional Standard Setting Bodies. In case of Vocational streams, correspondence between the National Skills Qualifications Framework should be established to the NHEQF to enable equivalences and mobility.

m. Actions by National Higher Education Regulatory Authority (NHERA) and General Education Council (GEC)

- Norms, standards and guidelines for systemic development and regulation of ODL should be prepared by NHERA, and a framework for quality of ODL to be recommendetory for all HEIs should be developed by the GEC.

n. Actions by Higher Education Institutions

- All Undergraduate programmes, including Professional and Vocational, should offer liberal education programmes with rigorous specialisation through a multidisciplinary approach. These programmes should have multiple exit options; all undergraduate programmes should be redesigned with these principles.
- Professional and Vocational areas of studies (e.g., Engineering, Medicine, Law and Teacher Education) should be completely integrated into Higher Education and follow the same liberal education approach. This responsibility should be facilitated by the regulatory system, the GEC and Professional Standard Setting Bodies (PSSBs).

YEAR 2025

a. Actions by Rashtriya Shiksha Aayog (RSA) and Ministry of Education (MoE)

- Indian Institutes of Liberal Arts (IILAs) or Multidisciplinary Education and Research Universities (MERUs) should be set up as models of the liberal education approach, with specific focus on integration of Vocational and Professional education into mainstream Higher Education.

- At least one high-quality HEI offering multidisciplinary education, including liberal arts programmes, should be set up in each district.

b. Actions by Ministry of Education (MoE) and State Departments of Education

- Initiatives to include educationally disadvantaged and underrepresented groups at all stages of education should include Special Education Zones (SEdZs) with targeted funding, *not within the educationally disadvantaged regions across the country. Area development should not be the criteria for educational investments.* SEdZs should be set up in the vicinity of industrial/business towns to prosper. This should be applicable to both School and Higher Education. Funds at the National level should be created for providing scholarships to students at both School and Higher Education level. These funds could also be used for research on improving inclusion. Targeted support and programmes to address specific URGs as per their particular needs should be provided.

c. Actions by NCERT and SCERT or equivalent organisations in each State

- Teachers and institutional leaders should be oriented towards effective use of technology in pedagogy, other curricular matters and management of education.

YEAR 2030

a. Actions by Ministry of Education (MoE) and State Departments of Education

- High-quality resources, including translations between various Indian languages, and between Indian and foreign languages should be made available through online repositories for a range of educational materials. Original texts should be commissioned and developed in all Indian languages, beginning with the Schedule 8 languages but not limited to them.

- The Teacher Education System should be overhauled completely. Teacher preparation for all School Stages should be offered only in multidisciplinary universities through a four-year programme, with the curricula and processes being revamped to address current issues with teacher preparation. Institutions currently offering two-year programme should either transition to this mode or be phased out; no new two-year programmes should be given recognition. MoE and State Departments of Education should coordinate with NHERA and NCTE as PSSBs to fulfil this responsibility.

b. Actions by National Higher Education Regulatory Authority (NHERA)

- All HEIs should have complete administrative, academic and financial autonomy, with empowered and independent Boards of Governors, after having been accredited. The system of Affiliating Universities should be stopped. NHERA should work with NAAC to fulfil this responsibility.

c. Actions by Higher Education Institutions (HEIs)

- Innovative, vibrant, rigorous and responsive curricula should guide the design of stimulating learning experiences and assessment for development, based on NHEQF. An effective and enriching learning environment should be in place across all HEIs. HEIs should be supported by GEC and the respective PSSBs in fulfilling this responsibility.
- In order to ensure equitable access to all desirous of Higher Education, curriculum and pedagogy of ODL programmes should be strengthened so that their quality is better or equivalent to the best-in-class programmes. HEIs should be facilitated by NHERA in fulfilling this responsibility.
- Student support should be provided in HEIs not only to succeed academically; students should also be provided care, to support their well-being and holistic development.

d. Actions by Union Government and all State Governments

- An incremental increase in public investment should be made progressively till it reaches around 20 per cent of total public expenditure.

YEAR 2032

a. Actions by National Assessment and Accreditation Council (NAAC)

- NAAC should create a fully developed accreditation ecosystem, comprising around 100-150 Accreditation Institutes, within which all HEIs are accredited on an ongoing basis.

YEAR 2035

a. Actions by Rashtriya Shiksha Aayog (RSA) and Ministry of Education (MoE)

- A significant number of high-quality HEIs of all three Types should be distributed equitably across the country, with *special consideration for the* disadvantaged districts, to achieve a GER target of 50 per cent by 2035. Access to quality Higher Education should be made possible through the Nalanda and Takshashila Missions.

A Postscript

The National Education Policy, 2020

Finally, after a gap of 34 years, a new National Education Policy (NEP), 2020 was announced on 29 July 2020.

The National Education Policy, 2020 has been received very well throughout the country and abroad. In fact, Prime Minister Narendra Modi has said that the National Education Policy will lay the foundation of a New India of the 21st century. The Prime Minister also said, among other things, that 'our education system focussed on "what to think" so far. New Policy emphasises on "How to think".... The NEP 2020 was approved (by the Union Cabinet) after extensive discussions over 3-4 years and deliberations over lakhs of suggestions.'[1]

The National Education Policy, 2020 is the culmination of a long-drawn process and it is primarily built on the Herculean effort made in the form of the Draft New Education Policy, 2019 (which was not really a 'Policy' but essentially a Report of the Committee headed by Dr Kasturirangan). In contrast to the bulky Report by the Kasturirangan Committee, the National Education Policy, 2020 is a slick, sharp and concise document of only 60-odd pages.

This book will not be complete until one draws a comparison of the content between the two above-mentioned documents – i.e. the Draft NEP 2019 and the NEP 2020, and offer a critical appraisal of the additions, deletions and modifications therein.

As mentioned in Chapters 6 and 7, the Kasturirangan Report was the

1. 'PM Narendra Modi says New Education Policy will shape the future of this century,' *Livemint*, 7 August 2020, https://www.livemint.com/news/india/narendra-modi-live-nep-2020-is-foundation-of-new-india-of-21st-century-11596777124250.html (accessed 7 August 2020).

result of a monumental exercise suggesting several metamorphic changes in the Indian Education System aimed at a 'future-ready' generation of large and growing numbers of learners in India.

Most of the path-breaking and transformative reforms of the Indian Education System proposed in the Draft NEP 2019, have seemingly been approved by the new National Education Policy, 2020. To the extent that such reforms have been drawn from the Kasturirangan Committee Report, both commendations and as well as criticisms (as discussed in detail in Chapter 6), apply.

At this stage, three questions arise:

i. What are the entirely new proposals in the NEP 2020, vis-à-vis the Draft NEP 2019 (i.e. Kasturirangan Report)?
ii. What important proposals in the Draft NEP 2019 have been deleted or modified in the NEP 2020?
iii. What is still missing in the new NEP 2020?

These three questions are addressed ad seriatim as under:

(a) New Proposals in NEP 2020

(i) Mother Tongue as Medium of Instruction

The new NEP 2020 document states: 'Wherever possible, the medium of instruction until at least Grade V, but preferably till Grade VIII and beyond, will be the home language/mother tongue/local language/ regional language. Thereafter, the home/local language shall continue to be taught as a language wherever possible. This will be followed by both public and private schools' (NEP 2020, p. 13).

This focus on students' mother tongue as the medium of instruction is most welcome. Since the proposal applies to all schools, both private and Government schools, it would certainly reduce the chasm and elitism prevailing in schools and act as a harmonizer.

Continuation of the three-language formula is also welcome, especially with the specific assurance that no language would be imposed on anyone. This formula would continue in promoting national integration.

(ii) National Assessment Centre

The new NEP 2020 proposes setting up of a National Assessment Centre with a view to making the assessment and evaluation in School Education more holistic.

The National Assessment Centre has been aptly titled as PARAKH (Performance Assessment, Review, and Analysis of Knowledge for Holistic Development). PARAKH would act as a standard setting body under the MHRD that fulfils the basic objectives of setting norms, standards and guidelines for student assessment and evaluations for all recognized School Boards of India.... (NEP 2020, p.19).

This reform is an exceedingly desirable addition to the Education Policy.

(iii) Multi-disciplinary HEIs with Multiple Exit Options and Academic Bank of Credit (ABC)

According to the NEP 2020 document, 'by 2030, there shall be at least one large multi-disciplinary Higher Education Institution (HEI) i.e. a University or a College, in or near every district' (NEP 2020, p.35). Importantly, an Undergraduate degree could be either of 3 or 4 year duration with multiple exit options – i.e. students leaving after one year will get a Certificate, those leaving after two years will get a Diploma while all others completing 3-4 years in a discipline or field, including Vocational and Professional areas, will get a Bachelor's Degree.

What is even more important is that the artificial distinction between Arts, Science and Commerce would be gone, once and for all. Students can select subjects of their choice across the streams and earn credits. The academic credits earned would be digitally stored in an Academic Bank of Credit (ABC). This would facilitate earning credits from different HEIs, which can be transferred across educational institutions towards the desired Degree.

This reform, much needed and long-awaited, would ensure a great degree of flexibility with individually and socially desirable outcomes.

(b) Proposals from Draft NEP 2019: Deleted or Modified

(i) The RTE Act

The Draft NEP 2019 had recommended a comprehensive review of the Right to Education Act, especially the mandates and obligations in accordance with ground realities, local needs and constraints.

As argued in Chapter 6, the Right to Education is a Fundamental Right. Nevertheless, despite being in operation for 10 years, the RTE Act has not been implemented in full measure — certainly not in letter and spirit. The above-mentioned proposal in the Draft NEP 2019 would have certainly amounted to a further dilution of the Act. This could have been socially counter-productive.

The NEP 2020 does not indicate any such review of the RTE Act. If this means eschewing the idea of a review of the RTE Act towards its dilution, that would certainly be a welcome move.

(ii) National Education Commission

The Draft NEP 2019 had proposed the setting up of a National Education Commission at the National level and a corresponding one at the State level. In the new NEP 2020, while the all-important proposal for National Education Commission has been retained, the State level Education Commission is conspicuous by its absence. Apparently, the Department of School Education would be the apex body at the State level.

This change would be a hard sell with the State Governments, who may see this running counter to the spirit of cooperative and consultative federalism. For the States to play a meaningful role in fine-tuning the NEP and its efficient implementation, unlike the Draft NEP 2019, in NEP 2020, the Central Advisory Board of Education (CABE) is going to be strengthened. How far this would appease the States and dilute their resentment, remains to be seen.

(iii) Funding of Education

The Draft NEP 2019 had reaffirmed the ever-elusive goal of public expenditure on education reaching 6 per cent of GDP and had specifically promised doubling of public expenditure on education as a ratio of total government expenditure (Centre plus States) – from 10 to 20 per cent.

In the NEP 2020, the assurance of doubling the public expenditure on education as a ratio of total government expenditure does not find a place. Instead, the NEP 2020 appears to be content by merely reaffirming the commitment to allocation to education of 6 per cent of GDP.

This is certainly a retrograde step.

(c) What is Still Missing in the New Education Policy, 2020?

Even after the Draft NEP 2019 and the new NEP 2020, what is still missing? Quite a lot, actually.

(i) Out-of-School Children (OoSC)

As indicated in Chapter 6, as per Census (2011) estimates, there are around 80 million children in the age-group 6-18 years, who drop out of schools. The NEP 2020 indicates that as per NSSO data, in 2017-18, the number of out–of-school children in the age group 6-17 years were 32.2 million (NEP 2020, p.10). Either number is unacceptably high.

The NEP 2020 rightly emphasises that 'It will be a top priority to bring these children back into the educational fold as early as possible…' (p.10).

Neither the NEP 2020 nor the Draft NEP 2019, go beyond this cursory recommendation that all OoSC should be brought back to the educational fold. Without any strategic plan of action to achieve the all-important goal of universal access to education at all levels, there is a danger of the Policy turning out to be merely a set of noble intentions.

(ii) Transition to Education 4.0

The NEP 2020 talks about 'introduction of contemporary subjects such as Artificial Intelligence, Design Thinking, Holistic Health, Organic Living, Environmental Education, Global Citizenship Education, etc…' (NEP 2020, p.15). This is good, but not good enough.

The new NEP 2020 (as also the Draft NEP 2019)—supposedly visionary documents—hardly make any conscious efforts towards the much-needed transition to Education 4.0, corresponding to the ongoing Industrial Revolution 4.0. This involves the entire range of the New-Age Technology (which, besides Artificial Intelligence also includes Machine Learning, Data Analytics, Robotics, Blockchain Technology, Additive Manufacturing, Internet of Things, etc.). The New-Age Technology ought to find a place in the curricula right from High School Education.

(iii) Constitution in the School Curriculum

The new NEP 2020 in its well-drafted 'Vision' clearly states that 'our institutions must develop among the students a deep sense of respect towards the Fundamental Duties and Constitution values, bonding with one's country, and a conscious awareness of one's roles and responsibilities in a changing world' (NEP 2020, p.6).

Well said, but what is the plan of action to operationalise this laudable action point? It is not at all clear from the NEP 2020. One way of actually doing this would be to introduce Constitution and Civics in the High School curricula as a compulsory subject at the Higher Secondary level.

This would go a long way in creating socially conscientious proud Indians and truly global citizens.

A Summing up

The New Education Policy (NEP), 2020 is the first comprehensive Education Policy since 1986.

In sum, the New Education Policy, 2020 has great potential to be a critical turning point and a massive game-changer, in completely transforming the education ecosystem in India into a world-class one, and in the process, laying the foundation of New India of 21st century, provided that:

i. The omnibus framework presented in the Policy is fine-tuned further (hopefully, on the lines suggested here);
ii. A detailed time-bound programme of action is prepared;
iii. The Governments (Centre and States) make concerted efforts to raise the public expenditure on education as percentage of the country's GDP to 6 per cent as early as possible;
iv. The private sector responds positively to 'light but tight' regulations and makes honest self-disclosure of all aspects of their educational operations; and,
v. The Central Government and all States effectively collaborate, going beyond the political party lines, on the meticulous and effective implementation of the New Education Policy, 2020.

Our future depends upon it, literally.

Annexure A

An attempt was made to explain the inter-State variation of some identified variables (education outcomes) and to capture the impact of relative changes in specific independent variables on the relative changes in the dependent variable for the reference period (2004-05 to 2009-10), for which the Planning Commission's comparable poverty estimates were available.

In the multivariate regression analysis, two dependent variables were used: first MYS (State-wise) and second Net Enrolment Ratio (NER), both representing access to education. The explanatory variables used included head count ratio (HCR1) and its relative change in 2009-10 over that of 2004-05 (HCR2). There are several other proximate variables influencing the changes in the dependent variables, such as the per capita expenditure on education (PCEE), the coverage of children with free education (FREEEDN), coverage of children under Mid-Day Meals Scheme (MDMS) and changes in female literacy (FM Lit) etc. While the HCR1 of 2009-10 was tried in some equations as the independent variable, its variation in the form of changes in 2009-10 over that of 2004-05 (HCR2) was used as an alternative.

In the multivariate regression analysis, we first used State-wise MYS derived from NSS data as the dependent variable and variables such as HCR, per capita expenditure on education and female literacy as independent variables while estimating relevant coefficients by the Ordinary Least Squares (OLS) method.

$$Y = a + b1\,(HCR) + b2X2\,(PCEE) + b3X3\,(FM\ Lit) + e$$

Where,

Y: MYS

a: constant

b: coefficients

e: error term

X1: HCR1 or HCR2 (i.e., ΔHCR, 2009-10 over 2004-05)
X2: Per capita expenditure on education 2009-10 (PCEE)
X3: Female literacy in 2009-10 (FM Lit)

Table A1: Regression Results – MYS as a Dependent Variable

Dependent	Constant	HCR	Per capita Expenditure on Education	Female Literacy	R2	R -2
MYS (22 States)	-2.0885	0.0749 (3.522) *	0.00023 (2.3214)**	0.1218 (9.471) *	0.88	0.87

Note: Level of Significance – *1 per cent; **5 per cent
(Figures in parenthesis are t values)

Annexure B

The Selected Education Statistics (SES) does not provide data on NER. District Information System for Education (DISE) data on NER is somewhat incomplete as some States are left out. However, DISE provides details on underage/overage enrolments. We have derived NER using enrolment and age-specific population figures of Selected Education Statistics (SES) and underage/overage enrolment data from DISE for the same reference period.

In view of the limitations in using GERs, we have utilised NER especially for analyses relating to Elementary Education. The equation takes the functional form:

NER = f (HCR2, FREEEDN, PCEE and MDMS).

The estimates obtained through OLS method are given below in Table B1.

Table B1: Regression Results, Dependent Variable — NER

Constant	Explanatory Variables				R-Sqr	R-Bar Sqr
	HCR2	FREEEDN	PCEE	MDMS		
0.515	0.011 (2.947)*	0.00017 (1.589)	2.859 (1.611)	0.0058 (2.967)*	.57	.47
	HCR1		PCIEE	MDMS		
0.444	0.0054 (2.739)*		0.0001 (2.357)**	0.0033 (1.978)**	.54	.46

Note: Level of Significance: * 1%; **5%

(Figures in the parenthesis are students' t values.)

About 57 per cent of inter-State variation in NER at Elementary Education is explained by the independent variables. The per capita expenditure on education (PCEE) is a wider measure or indicator. However, PCEE's denominator being the whole population, specification could probably be narrowed. Accordingly, we utilised State-wise actual expenditure or Per Child Investment in Elementary Education (PCIEE) in government and aided schools and substituted PCEE with it. The new equation takes three independent variables and the results were more or less similar.

Bibliography

'Engineering student commits suicide'. *The Hindu,* Madurai Edition, 16 July 2016. https://www.thehindu.com/todays-paper/tp-national/tp-tamilnadu/Engineering-student-commits-suicide/article14491744.ece.

'Knowledge and Skills for Life: First Results from the PISA 2000', (OECD, 2001).

'UN: India to be world's most populous country by 2028'. *BBC News,* 14 June 2013. https://www.bbc.com/news/world-asia-22907307.

Agarwal, Pawan. *Indian Higher Education: Envisioning the Future.* New Delhi: SAGE Publications India Pvt Ltd, 2009.

Agrawal, Rashmi. *Educational Technology Management and Evaluation.* Delhi: Shipra Publications, 2009.

AICTE. *Technical Education in Independent India, 1947–1997: A Compendium to Commemorate the 50th Year of Anniversary of Independence.* New Delhi: AICTE, 1999.

Altbach, Philip G. *A Half-Century of Indian Higher Education,* edited by Pawan Agrawal. New Delhi: SAGE Publications India Pvt Ltd, 2012.

ASER. 'Annual Status of Education Report (Rural) 2012'. New Delhi: ASER Centre, 2013. http://img.asercentre.org/docs/Publications/ASER%20Reports/ASER_2012/fullaser2012report.pdf.

ASER. *Annual Status of Education Report 2017.* Delhi: ASER Centre, 2018.

Azim Premji Foundation and MHRD, Government of India. 'Equitable Education for Equitable Society: Proceedings of National Learning Conference 2007'. Bangalore: Azim Premji Foundation, 2007.

Barro, Robert J. and Jong-Wha Lee. 'A New Data Set of Educational Attainment in the World, 1950-2010'. Working Paper No. 15902. Cambridge, MA: National Bureau of Economic Research, (2010). Subsequently published in the Journal of Development Economics, vol. 104.

Basu, Durga Das. *The Constitution of India*, 11th edition. Delhi: LexisNexis India, 1985.

Batra, Sunil. 'Equity in Education in India: A Distant Dream or an Elusive Reality?' National Seminar on Universalising Elementary Education in India. New Delhi: IHD, 2006.

Bhattacharya, Amitabha. 'Fine-tuning the education policy'. *The Hindu,* 5 June 2019. https://www.thehindu.com/opinion/op-ed/a-brave-new-education-policy/article27473093.ece.

Bloom, David E., David Canning and Jaypee Sevilla. 'The Demographic Dividend: A New Perspective on the Economic Consequences of Population Change'. Monograph MR-1274. Santa Monica: RAND, 2003.

Bloom, David E., and David Canning. 'Global Demographic Change: Dimensions and Economic Significance'. *Population and Development Review,* vol. 34, 2008. www.jstor.org/stable/25434758.

Bloom, David E. 'Population Dynamics in India and Implications for Economic Growth'. Program on the Global Demography of Aging, Working Paper No. 65. Harvard University, 2011.

Braga, Michael, Daniele Checchi, and Elena Meschi. 'Institutional Reforms and Educational Attainment in Europe: A Long Run Perspective'. IZA Discussion Paper No. 6190, Institute of Labor Economics (IZA)

Germany (December 2011). Retrieved from http://ftp.iza.org/dp6190.pdf.

British Council. 'Understanding India: *The future of higher education and opportunities for international cooperation*', February 2014.

Census of India 2011. Cultural Tables, August 2015.

Census of India 2011. Social and Cultural Tables, c21, 2015.

Chenoy, Dilip. 'Skill Development in India: A Transformation in Making', in *India Infrastructure Report 2012*. New Delhi: Routledge, 2013. Retrieved from http://www.idfc.com/pdf/report/IIR-2012.pdf.

Chimni, Ramit Singh. 'The National Education Policy 2019: An Alarming Attempt To Redefine India'. *Business World*, 31 July 2019. http://www.businessworld.in/article/The-National-Education-Policy-2019-An-Alarming-Attempt-To-Redefine-India/31-07-2019-174188/.

De, Anuradha, Claire Noronha and Meera Samson. 'Private Schools for Less Privileged: Some Insights from a Case Study'. *Economic and Political Weekly (EPW)*, vol. 37, issue no. 52 (28 December 2002).

Debroy, Bibek. 'Vocational Education and India's Skills Deficit'. Working Paper No. 103. Singapore: Institute of South Asian Studies, National University of Singapore (2009).

Department of Education, Employment and Workplace Relations (DEEWR), Australia. 'Transforming Australia's Higher Education System'. Canberra: DEEWR, 2009.

Desai, Sonalde B. et al. 'Human Development in India: Challenge for a Society in Transition'. New Delhi: OUP, 2010.

Dhankar, Rohit. 'A case of confused thinking: on draft National Education Policy'. *The Hindu*, 13 July 2019. https://www.thehindu.com/opinion/lead/a-case-of-confused-thinking/article28415519.ece.

District Information System for Education (DISE), 2011-12.

Dossani, Rafiq. 'The Cost of Higher Education: The Big Picture', RAND *Center for Asia Pacific Policy* (12 July 2013). https://www.rand.org/blog/2013/07/the-cost-of-higher-education-the-big-picture.html.

Dreze, Jean and Geeta Gandhi Kingdon. 'School Participation in Rural India'. *Review of Development Economics,* vol. 5, issue 1, pp. 1-24 (2001). http://dx.doi.org/10.1111/1467-9361.00103.

Euromonitor International reports.

FICCI and Ernst & Young. 'Reaping India's Promised Demographic Dividend – industry in driving seat'. New Delhi: Ernst and Young (2014).

FICCI and Ernst & Young. 'Higher Education in India: Twelfth Five Year Plan (2012–17) and beyond'. FICCI Higher Education Summit 2012, New Delhi: FICCI, 2012. https://learnos.files.wordpress.com/2012/11/ey-ficc_higher_education_report_nov12.pdf.

Filmer D. Quoted in 'Education and Poverty in Rural China' by Philip.H. Brown and Albert Park. *Economics of Education Review,* 21 (2002).

Ghosh, Suresh Chandra. *The History of Education in Modern India: 1757–2012,* 4th edition. New Delhi: Orient Blackswan, 2013.

Goyal, Aparajita and Jean Dreze. 'Future of Mid-Day Meals'. *Economic and Political Weekly (EPW),* vol. 38, issue no. 44 (1 November 2003).

ILO. 'Estimates and Projections of the Economically Active Population: 1990–2020'. October 2011.

Jadhav, Narendra. *Ambedkar Speaks*, vol. I, II and III. New Delhi: Konark Publishers, 2013.

Jadhav, Narendra. *New-Age Technology and Industrial Revolution 4.0: Global Public Policy Issues in Economy, Democracy, National Security and World Peace.* New Delhi: Konark Publishers, 2019.

James, K.S. 'India's Demographic Change: Opportunities and Challenges'. *Science,* vol. 333, issue no. 6042 (29 July 2011).

Kaul, Venita. 'A commendable reform in the draft National Policy on Education.' *The Hindu,* 25 June 2019. https://www.thehindu.com/opinion/op-ed/a-sound-foundation/article28127434.ece.

Kaushal, Ravi. 'A Not So "National" Education Policy'. *Newsclick,* 2 November 2019. https://www.newsclick.in/not-so-national-education-policy.

Kim, Sean. 'How to Deconstruct Any Skill You Want to Learn Faster'. *Lifehack.* https://www.lifehack.org/324939/how-deconstruct-any-skill-you-want-learn-faster.

Kingdon, Geeta. 'Poor remedies to learning crisis: Draft National Education Policy amounts to rearranging deck chairs on the Titanic'. *The Times of India,* 24 June 2019. https://timesofindia.indiatimes.com/blogs/toi-edit-page/poor-remedies-to-learning-crisis-draft-national-education-policy-amounts-to-rearranging-deck-chairs-on-the-titanic/.

Kothari, D.S. 'Report of the Education Commission, 1964-66: Education and National Development'. Ministry of Education, Government of India. https://ia800206.us.archive.org/26/items/ReportOfTheEducationCommission1964-66D.S.KothariReport/48.Jp-ReportOfTheEducationCommission1964-66d.s.kothari.pdf

Kumar, Krishna. 'Educational Experience of Scheduled Castes and Tribes'. *EPW,* vol. 18, issue no. 36-37 (3 September 1983): pp. 328–47.

Labour Bureau, Ministry of Labour and Employment, Government of India. 'Education, Skill Development and Labour Force 2013-14', Fourth Annual Employment & Unemployment Survey Report (2013-14), vol. III (November 2014). https://labour.gov.in/sites/default/files/Report%20Vol%203%20final.pdf.

Mascarenhas, Patricia. *'The Great Indian Tuition and Coaching Industry'. Mumbai: Daily News & Analysis (DNA),* 1 April 2014. https://www.dnaindia.com/academy/report-the-great-indian-tuition-and-coaching-industry-1973985.

McKinsey Global Institute Report. 'India's urban awakening: Building inclusive cities, sustaining economic growth' (April 2010). https://www.mckinsey.com/~/media/mckinsey/featured%20insights/Urbanization/Urban%20awakening%20in%20India/MGI_Indias_urban_awakening_full_report.ashx

Mehrotra, Santhosh. *Realising the Demographic Dividend: Policies to Achieve Inclusive Growth in India.* New Delhi: Cambridge University Press, 2015.

MHRD, 'Draft National Education Policy 2019, Preamble', July 2019, pp. 23–24.

MHRD, Government of India. 'Sarva Shiksha Abhiyan: Seventeenth Joint Review Mission', Aide Memoire, 2013. http://14.139.60.153/bitstream/123456789/1638/1/SARVA%20SHIKSHA%20ABHIYAN%20SEVENTEENTH%20JOINT%20REVIEW%20MISSION_14th%20to%2028th%20JANUARY%202013_D-14296.pdf.

MHRD, Government of India. 'Annual Report 2013-14': p.153. https://mhrd.gov.in/sites/upload_files/mhrd/files/document-reports/AR2013-14.pdf.

MHRD, Government of India. 'Fourth Year Right of Children to Free and Compulsory Education Act Report,' 2015.

MHRD, Government of India. 'Implementation of RTE Act, IVth Year Report'. 2014.

MHRD, Government of India. 'Some Inputs for Draft National Education Policy 2016': pp. 14–15. https://mhrd.gov.in/sites/upload_files/mhrd/files/nep/Inputs_Draft_NEP_2016.pdf.

MHRD, Memorandum by Bhartiya Anusuchit Jati Jamati Sangh.

MHRD, Government of India. 'National Sample Survey of Estimation of Out-of-School Children in the Age 6-13 in India'. Social and Rural Research Institute – Indian Market Research Bureau (SRI-IMRB) and EdCIL India Ltd, 2014.

Minister HRD. 'Formulating the New Education Policy'. MyGov Blog, 29 November 2015.

Ministry of Health & Family Welfare, Government of India. 'Annual Report 2013-14'(2014).

Ministry of Health and Family Welfare, Government of India. 'National Family Health Survey 2015-16 (NFHS-4): India, Key Indicators'. Mumbai: IIPS, December 2017.

Ministry of Rural Development, Government of India. 'Socio-Economic and Caste Census 2011, Summary Tables (2015)'.

Ministry of Social Justice and Empowerment, Government of India. 'Annual Report, 2013-14', http://socialjustice.nic.in/writereaddata/UploadFile/2013-14eng.pdf.

Ministry of Statistics & Programme Implementation, Government of India. 'Education in India 2007-08 – Participation and Expenditure': NSS 64th Round, Report No. 532 (May 2010). http://www.mospi.nic.in/sites/default/files/publication_reports/532_final.pdf.

Ministry of Statistics & Programme Implementation, Government of India. 'Employment and Unemployment Situation among Social Groups in India'. NSS Report No. 563 (2014): p. 10.

Ministry of Statistics & Programme Implementation, Government of India. 'Employment and Unemployment Survey 2004-05'. NSS 61st Round (September 2006).

Ministry of Statistics & Programme Implementation, Government of

India. 'Employment and Unemployment Situation in India: 2009-10'. NSS Report No. 537 (66/10/1), November 2011.

Most Populous Nations by 2030, Demographics of India, UN.

Nanda, Prashant K. 'Draft new education policy is robust, but has its limitations'. *Livemint,* 12 June 2019. https://www.livemint.com/education/news/draft-new-education-policy-is-robust-but-has-its-limitations-1560282687888.html.

Narsimhan S., R. Balasubramaniyam, and M. Venkataraman. *Higher Education & Economic Development (HEED),* vol. I & II, Department of Economics and Business Economics, Dwaraka Doss Goverdhan Doss Vaishnav College, Chennai.

National Commission for Enterprises in the Unorganised Sector (NCEUS), Government of India Report.

National Knowledge Commission, Government of India. 'Compilation of Recommendations on Education', 2008. http://www.nipccd-earchive.wcd.nic.in/sites/default/files/PDF/NKC_Education.pdf.

National Knowledge Commission, Government of India. 'Report to the Nation 2006-09', March 2009. https://www.aicte-india.org/downloads/nkc.pdf.

NCERT & EdCIL (India) Ltd. 'Teaching of English at Primary Level in Government Schools: Synthesis Report' 2012. http://www.ncert.nic.in/departments/nie/del/publication/pdf/English_Primary_level.pdf.

Nicoll, Carol. 'How can Higher Education maintain and improve quality?', Tertiary Education Quality and Standards Agency, Australia, IMHE General Conference, Attaining and Sustaining Mass Higher Education, Paris (September 2012).

NUEPA. 'Secondary Education in India, Flash Statistics: 2013-14,' (July 2014). http://dise.in/Downloads/Publications/Documents/

SecondaryFlash%20Statistics-2013-14.pdf.

Organisation for Economic Co-operation and Development (OECD). 'Education Indicators in Focus', May 2012. http://www.oecd.org/education/50495363.pdf.

Parliament of India, Rajya Sabha. '305th Report: Demands for Grants 2018-19 (Demand No. 57) of the Department of School Education & Literacy,' March 2018. http://164.100.47.5/committee_web/ReportFile/16/98/305_2018_6_17.pdf.

Planning Commission, Government of India. 'Mid-Term Appraisal of the Tenth Five-Year Plan' (2005).

Planning Commission, Programme Evaluation Organisation (PEO). 'Study on SSA, 2010'.

Planning Commission. 'Twelfth Five Year Plan (2012–17)', vol. III, New Delhi: Sage Publications India Pvt Ltd, 2013. https://mhrd.gov.in/sites/upload_files/mhrd/files/document-reports/XIIFYP_SocialSector.pdf.

PMO. 'Sachar Committee Report on the Social, Economic and Educational Status of the Muslim Community of India', 2006. http://www.minorityaffairs.gov.in/sites/default/files/sachar_comm.pdf.

Powar, K. B. *Understanding Internationalisation of Higher Education.* Pune: DPU Publications, 2013.

PTI. 'HC directs bank to accept farm land as collateral for edu loan,' *Business Standard,* 26 June 2017. https://www.business-standard.com/article/pti-stories/hc-directs-bank-to-accept-farm-land-as-collateral-for-edu-loan-117062601034_1.html.

PTI. 'PM Narendra Modi likely to unveil new National Skills Policy on July 15'. *The Economic Times,* 8 July 2015. https://economictimes.indiatimes.com/news/politics-and-nation/pm-narendra-modi-likely-to-unveil-new-national-skills-policy-on-july-15/

articleshow/47991947.cms.

PTI. 'New Education Policy will establish India as knowledge superpower, get global recognition: Ram Nath Kovind'. *Outlook*, 30 October 2019. https://www.outlookindia.com/newsscroll/new-education-policy-will-establish-india-as-knowledge-superpower-get-global-recognition-kovind/1651720.

Radhakrishnan, S. 'The Report of the University Education Commission (December 1948- August 1949)'. Ministry of Education, Government of India.

Rai, Vinay, and Narendra Kumar. *Right to Education: The Way Forward*. Delhi: Perfect Publications Private Limited and ASSOCHAM, 2010.

Ramachandran, Padma, and Vasantha Ramkumar. *Education in India*. New Delhi: National Book Trust, 2005.

Rao, Parimala V. (ed.). *New Perspectives in the History of Indian Education*. New Delhi: Orient Blackswan, 2014.

Ravi, Chaitanya, Juhi Sidharth and Shivakumar Jolad. 'National Education Policy: How liberal education can be Indianised to produce pragmatic technocrats.' *Business Today*, 9 October 2019. https://www.businesstoday.in/opinion/columns/national-education-policy-how-liberal-education-can-be-indianised-to-produce-pragmatic-technocrats/story/383660.html.

Ross, John. 'Understanding the Demographic Dividends'. *POLICY Project (2004)*. http://www.policyproject.com/pubs/generalreport/Demo_Div.pdf.

Schensul, Daniel, Kathrin Weny, and Rachel Snow. 'Foundation for the Future'. UNFPA, May 2016.

Schreuder, Deryck M. (ed.). *Universities for a New World*. The Association of Commonwealth Universities. New Delhi: Sage Publication, 2013.

Sen, Amartya. 'The Importance of Basic Education'. Speech given in Commonwealth Education Conference, Edinburg, UK (28 October 2003).

Shukla, Samir. 'The world needs a new education policy that teaches interconnectedness'. Science Nomad, *The Times of India,* 3 August 2019. https://timesofindia.indiatimes.com/blogs/science-nomad/the-world-needs-a-new-education-policy-that-teaches-interconnectedness/.

Sohoni, Milind and Oshin Dharap. 'New Education Policy will ensure our higher education system remains a client of global science'. *The Indian Express,* 18 July 2019. https://indianexpress.com/article/opinion/columns/the-aspiration-trap-national-education-policy-5834797/.

Subramani, A. 'Previous years' students may bag over 1,000 MBBS seats'. *The Times of India,* 23 June 2015. https://timesofindia.indiatimes.com/home/education/news/Previous-years-students-may-bag-over-1000-MBBS-seats/articleshow/47777392.cms?.

Taneja, Anjela. 'New education policy misses a critical chance to address inequalities in system'. *Livemint*, 12 June 2019. https://www.livemint.com/opinion/online-views/new-education-policy-misses-a-critical-chance-to-address-inequalities-in-system-1560282262183.html.

Thakur, Ashok and S.S. Mantha. 'Skill India is ailing'. *The Indian Express,* 17 November 2018. https://indianexpress.com/article/opinion/columns/skill-india-is-ailing-world-youth-skill-day-2022-narendra-modi-5450627.

The McKinsey Global Institute Report (2007). Cited in 'The Emerging Middle Class in Developing Countries'. OECD Development Centre, Working Paper No. 285 (January 2010).

The Parthenon Group. 'Private Universities in India: An investment in National Development'. Indian Education Congress (2012).

Tilak, Jandhyala B.G. (ed.). *Higher Education in India: In Search of Equality, Quality and Quantity.* New Delhi: Orient Blackswan, 2013.

Tilak, Jandhyala B.G. 'Perennial Problems and Promising but Perplexing Solutions': A Commentary on the Report of the Committee on National Education Policy 2019'.

Tooley, James. *The Beautiful Tree: A Personal Journey Into How the World's Poorest People are Educating Themselves.* Washington, DC: Cato Institute, 2009.

UN Decade of Education for Sustainable Development (DESD 2005–2014). 'Review of Contexts and Structures for Education for Sustainable Development for a Sustainable World 2009': Paris: UNESCO, 2009: p. 7. https://unesdoc.unesco.org/ark:/48223/pf0000184944.

UN. 'The Right to Education with Equity: Access and Quality Education for All in India', Global Education First Initiative, UN-INDIA, 2015.

UN. 'World Population Prospects: The 2010 Revision', New York: UN Population Division, Department of Economic and Social Affairs, 2011. available at http://esa.un.org/undp/wpp/index.htm.

UN. 'World Population Prospects, the 2012 Revision'. New York: UN Population Division, Department of Economic and Social Affairs, 2013.

UNDP. 'Human Development Report 2014 – Sustaining Human Progress: Reducing Vulnerabilities and Building Resilience'. http://hdr.undp.org/sites/default/files/hdr14-report-en-1.pdf.

UNESCO. 'Education 2030: Equity and Quality with a Lifelong Learning Perspective'. Education for All Global Monitoring Report (EFA-GMR) Policy Paper 20, May 2015.

UNESCO. 'Education for All 2000-2015: Achievements and Challenges, EFA Global Monitoring Report'. Paris: UNESCO, 2015.

UNESCO. 'Education for All Global Monitoring Report (EFA-GMR) 2015'.

UNESCO. 'EFA-GMR 2015', Statistical Tables.

UNESCO. EFA-GMR, 2007.

UNESCO. 'Strong Foundations: Early Childhood Care and Education—EFA Global Monitoring Report 2007'. http://lst-iiep.iiep-unesco.org/cgi-bin/wwwi32.exe/[in=epidoc1.in]/?t2000=023596/(100).

UNFPA, 'Demographic Dividend', 2016.

van der Berg, Servaas. 'Poverty and Education'. Education Policy Series 10. The International Academy of Education, The International Institute for Educational Planning and UNESCO (2008).

Vital Statistics Division, Office of the Registrar General. 'Sample Registration System (SRS) Survey 2013'.

World Bank (2010), http://data.world bank.org/indicators/SI.POV.2 day on 05/11/2013.

World Bank. 'India Country Strategy (CAS) 2009–12'. April 2010. https://www.worldbank.org/en/news/feature/2010/04/06/india-country-strategy.

Yadav, S.B. 'An Empirical Study of Socio-Economic Status of Meo Muslims in Mewat Region'. *International Journal of Advances in Social Sciences,* 2018.

Yamunan, Sruthisagar. *'The "bad" side of education loans'. The Hindu,* Chennai Edition, 22 June 2016. https://www.thehindu.com/todays-paper/tp-national/tp-tamilnadu/The-%e2%80%98bad%e2%80%99-side-of-education-loans/article14394716.ece.

Index